Manners of Interpretation

SUNY Series, The Margins of Literature

Mihai I. Spariosu, Editor

Manners of Interpretation

The Ends of Argument in Literary Studies

Miguel Tamen

State University of New York Press

Published by
State University of New York Press, Albany

Printed in the United States of America

For information, address State University of New York Press, State University Plaza, Albany, N.Y. 12246

Production by M. R. Mulholland
Marketing by Lynne A. Lekakis

Library of Congress Cataloging-in-Publication Data

Tamen, Miguel.
Manners of interpretation : the ends of argument in literary studies / Miguel Tamen.
p. cm. — (SUNY series, the margins of literature)
Includes bibliographical references and index.
ISBN 0-7914-1503-1 (acid free). — ISBN 0-7914-1504-X (pbk. : acid free)
1. Criticism. 2. Hermeneutics. I. Title. II. Series.
PN81. T316 1993
801'. 95--dc20 92-2412
CIP

10 9 8 7 6 5 4 3 2 1

'Nein", sagte der Geistliche, 'man muß nicht alles für wahr halten, man muß es nur für notwendig halten.' 'Trübselige Meinung', sagte K. 'Die Luge wird zur Weltordnung gemacht.'

['No', said the priest, 'one mustn't take everything as true, one must only take it as necessary.' 'Melancholy opinion', said K. 'It turns lying into a cosmic principle.']

Franz Kafka, *Der Prozeß*

Contents

Postscript

> I apprehend that *Prefaces*, wherever they may be placed in a book, are for the most part, with respect to works themselves, *Postscripts*; that is to say, *written after* the completion of the undertaking, whatever it may be.
>
> *Heraldic Anomalies or Rank Confusion in Our Orders of Precedence*, London, 1823

I

This book deals with some aspects of the relation between literary theory and hermeneutics. Although it was invented by other fields, such as theology, law, history, and eventually philosophy proper, in the last thirty-odd years the question of interpretation has become a prominent concern of the nebulous regions of literary criticism and literary theory, to the point that, in some quarters, its destiny became linked with the destiny of literary theory itself and the source of an abundant literature.

However, what follows is not a history, a discussion, an application, let alone a textbook of or an introduction to hermeneutics Rather, I am more interested in the question of how a field (the field of literary studies), acquired certain concerns (the concerns of hermeneutics) and in the epistemological consequences of some of such concerns. My point may appear somewhat puzzling to those used to thinking in terms of an opposition between hermeneutic and epistemological procedures. Nevertheless, I shall try to argue that it was precisely hermeneutics that brought to literary studies the nonreturnable gift of verification. Moreover, and given the prominence of the hermeneutic concern in contemporary literary studies, there appears to be a certain necessity to all hermeneutic concerns and disturbances. So, there are two other things this book is not; namely, a consolation written in the name of an alternative for hermeneutics (Boethius's predicaments should have made us weary, if not wary, of such solutions) and an apology for all absence of consolation.

It is my hope that the title of the book is sufficiently clear and, as most clear things, deserving of an explanation. The subtitle (ends of argument in literary studies) was meant as an explanation, but it seems to me to be patently afflicted itself by the ambiguity the word 'ends' has in English. Be that as it may, the ambiguity is somewhat helpful because it will be a question, in the text, although circuitously perhaps, of both purposes and ends of argument. Indeed, I call "manners of interpretation" the figures of argument that purport to limit argument itself by means of an often unspecified appeal to either its ends or its purposes. The articulation between the title and the subtitle suggests then a relation between certain modalities of argumentation (the ends of argument in literary studies) and what I call *manners of interpretation.*

Such would be the question of the limits of interpretation. The question of the limits of interpretation, however, that, like all questions in this form, began as a transcendental question, has become mostly a question of common sense. Thomas Kavanagh recently has dubbed the latter king of sense *mathematical sense.* Referring to what he calls the *limits of theory,* Kavanagh specifies that "the word 'limit'...in its mathematical sense...designates a frontier beyond which a change occurs, a border beyond which one thing becomes another" (1989b, pp. 1-2).

I am not sure whether Kavanagh's use of the word *limit* has to do primarily with mathematics, though. As it turns out, the expression *limits of theory* marks, for him, the supremacy of what he calls a "grasp of the real" (p. 15), over certain activities affected by the "potential pathology of the master-disciple relationship" (ibid.). By pointing to an alienated theory, it denotes the very institutionalization of the wish for a *limited* field: the field of literary theory *ma non troppo,* as it should be taught in the academy, as a body of positive knowledge with indisputable results and a clear mission. Kavanagh's referring to situations where the "drive to theorize becomes something quite different from what it presents itself as being" (ibid., p. 1), can be understood then perhaps not so much in the well-known meaning of a dialectic between blindness and insight as in the older and more respectable meaning of the categorical opposition between authenticity and inauthenticity; that is, the meaning of truth and lies in a very moral sense. In fact, Kavanagh's use of the expression *limits of theory* represents the embodiment of an ethical choice in theory: pedagogy against pathology, teachability against scholarly solipsism.

The question of manners of interpretation has less to do with common sense (indeed, in Chapter 5, it is explicitly played against notions such as 'consensus' or 'agreement'), than with the old forgotten transcendental use of the topic. It is not that I subscribe to Arthur Danto's program of description of "the principles, whatever they are, that enable us to tell and follow stories, to construct and read poetry" (1989, p. 384) entirely. The question of the possibility of a discourse for such a description seems to me to be open to question itself, and in Chapter 5 again, I cast some doubts as to the feasibility of such an enterprise. I was led nevertheless to lend some necessity to the ways in which the purely pragmatic problem of a closure is connected to the very possibility of interpretation in the first place (although the invoking of necessity is perhaps just another expedient, a manner of my own interpretation, in this respect). Thus taken, anyway, the expression *manners of interpretation* denotes the sum of the figures of the *end*—rather than the *purpose*—of interpretation, a repertoire of prospective mishaps where, so to speak, the end supersedes the choice. These terminating acts point to a notion of 'end' that coincides with the pragmatic bracketing of the necessity of the purpose. Rather than a choice, they imply the kind of events that displace choice, and thus purpose, indeed, all events through which the determinacy of hermeneutic purposes is upset: in this sense, the prudent armistices and uninvoked obviousnesses through which so many interpretive controversies discreetly end are no less of a disappointment for ethics than the sudden death of the interpreter.

II

Chapters 3 and 4 (and the greater part of Chapter 5 as well) are relatively easy to describe, in that they deal with the changes and the metamorphoses of several families of ways of ending an interpretation.

In Chapter 3, the appeal to the author is understood as an appeal to an ultimately irrefutable construct, while, at the same time, the metamorphoses in such an appeal show that irrefutable constructs change, even if the necessity of irrefutability does not. The chapter follows roughly a temporal line, from Johnson to the so-called New Pragmatism (with a few glances towards the Middle Ages and Montaigne, as well as Hegel). There, I imagine some genealogies that are quite obvious, even to the unsympathetic reader (Johnson, Boswell on Johnson, Macaulay on Boswell on Johnson; Wimsatt and Beardsley, Hirsch on Wimsatt and Beardsley, Juhl on Hirsch on Wimsatt and

Beardsley and Knapp and Michaels on them all) and some relations that are not so obvious or so fully developed (such as the relation between Sainte-Beuve and Freud).

Chapter 4 tells a comparable story, and the heterogeneity of the explanations is perhaps overshadowed by a unifying allegory: the presence of China in literary studies (from Kircher, through Leibniz, Fenollosa, and Pound, to Jakobson), as a metaphor for a language often understood as the best part of language (hence the title of the chapter). The appeal to the text again is understood as a last resort: there is no appeal outside of the text, as the saying could very well go. 'It's in the text' is in this sense a way to end a controversy. Furthermore, I follow two other questions raised by the model of textual determination. The first is that of the relations between the best part of language, the *characteristic* part of language, as one could phrase it with Leibniz, and the *other* part of language. I trace it down through the notion of combinatory, from Leibniz to Jakobson (of course, many other authors could have been included here, among them Friedrich Schlegel, Schelling, and Coleridge). The second question has to do with the patterns of object-formation and controversy-ending that such relations presuppose. There, I try to see Paul de Man's notion of a "return to philology" from both sides of the "Was ist Metaphysik?" controversy, that is, in both its Heideggerian and in its Carnapian implications, as well as link it to de Man's reading of Kant's theories of the sublime.

Chapter 5, again, runs parallel (at least in part) to Chapters 3 and 4 in that it follows some versions of a contemporary way of theorizing agreement: the appeal to narrative. Several such versions, always pragmatic, even if not always issuing from a Pragmatism (the case of Jameson's is in point here), are understood in Chapter 5 as indicating both a significant swerve in the notion of verification and the persistence of the problem of verification. I try to show that, even in the more casually pragmatist versions of narrativity (e.g., where 'We have only stories' becomes 'It's only a story'), there is a moment when narrative has to be seen as the duplication of something else (as representation, for short) and so the postulation of a principle of verification of some sort.

The latter part of Chapter 5 leads to my own understanding of Chapters 3 to 5 and to what I take to be the distinct pathos of the bond between the acts of agreeing on something and the acts of appealing to such grounds to end an interpretation, the pathos of verification and mimesis, the pathos of all theories of the decisive nature of the hermeneutic representations (in short, the pathos of interpretation). In fact, verificational appeals to the order of authors, texts, and narratives are eminently pathetic in the simple enough sense that there seems to be a recognizable tone (somewhat heroic perhaps) to the way in which they envision the end of controversy as the achievement of a *particular* representation. Now I try to imagine the end of controversy without that tone, suggesting that such is the problem of triviality or silliness (as I call it). I imagine controversies that end or do not start due to a burden of verification that is ultimately unmentionable, very silly indeed, due to accidents such as sudden deaths, or changes of mind, or unthinkable circumstances. For those readers who are thinking by now of the *use* of my own concerns, I suggest that the question is deeply tied to the question of the very teachability of literature: one does teach the unmentionable, at least at an undergraduate level. It is as if we all had to learn the unthinkable, that from which no discussion can ever issue.

Whereas in the first chapter I deal with the question of manners of interpretation under the already somewhat traditional topic of the theoretical interferences in the technique of interpretation (which takes me back to Aristotle's *Poetics* and *Nicomachean Ethics*, as well as to Augustine and, of course, Gadamer), Chapter 2 complicates my whole argument considerably, because it describes the construction of possibilities of a rhetorically acceptable transition between theory and technique, as formulated, as a problem, in the earlier days of modern philology and hermeneutics. The problem was decisively episodic and originated the ultimate separation of philology and hermeneutics and indeed the constitution of what one calls now, perhaps with some pomp and certainly with much circumstance, the reading subject. Friedrich Schlegel's zoological description of the *homo legens* refers to the existence of two stomachs and thus postulates a double digestion: technical digestion (whose gastroenterology he called philology proper) and theoretical digestion (whose discipline Schleiermacher called, much to our confusion, technical interpretation). The decisive role of Schleiermacher in this process lies in his being the last writer to believe in the possibility of a felicitous double digestion. Before him, Kant had already reduced the question of contemplation to the question of the interest in *deciding* a priority of the technical (or, in his terms, of practical reason) over perceptual apprehension, whereas the exegetic hermeneutic traditions tended to trust onesidedly the virtues of the perception of similarities. Hermeneutics, as it developed after Schleiermacher, always tended to emphasize the predominance of the second kind of approach or, in Schlegel's terms, the idea that the previous contemplation of the digestible is determinant in the process of digestion.

I take nineteenth and twentieth century hermeneutics to be doctrines of the conceptual thinking of objects of the intuition rather than versions of the constitution of such a thinking. This latter point means simply that no doctrine of interpretation as such has ever gone beyond the conceptual thinking of the objects of intuition (and that is what being a doctrine of the *understanding* means), or that a doctrine of interpretation is what cannot doubt or cannot see as historically engendered a certain destiny of "texts": being interpreted. Central questions of the hermeneutic tradition (such as the epistemological question of the validity in interpretation) derive exclusively from this decisive feature, and it seems to me to be ultimately futile to try to dissolve the problem of validity in the framework of a hermeneutics (such as by saying that the question of validity is the question of a *feeling* or of an epiphany of validity: an invasion of the truth, so to speak).

III

The composition of this book is a sometimes blatant but invariably embarrassing illustration of some of its theses. In fact, several questions directly or indirectly presupposed by the very nature of my maneuvers were literally sacrificed to intelligibility, if not to brevity. In this and in the next section, however, I shall follow (with no illusions as to my own naivete) two such questions and point therefore to an altogether different project.

The first question has to do with the very notion of 'theory'. The idea that there is "a domain as yet unnamed but often called 'theory' for short" (Culler, 1982, p. 8) entertained, in the early 1980s, a curious relation with the pathos of homelessness. In his influential *On Deconstruction*, Jonathan Culler argues that

> what distinguishes the members of this genre [theory] is their ability to function not as demonstrations within the parameters of a discipline but as redescriptions that change disciplinary boundaries. The works we allude to as "theory" are those that have had the power to make strange the familiar and to make

> readers conceive of their own thinking, behavior, and institutions in new ways. (Ibid., p. 9)

In this above passage, Culler's first expression "'theory' for short" becomes paraphrasable by words such as "power". But this power (or that theory) is the power of a repetition. Just as "redescriptions" are opposed to Culler to "demonstrations," so the "strange" is the theoretical repetition of the "familiar" and a new conception is seen as a theoretical reenactment of an old one (the model is open perhaps to Marx's shrewd remarks on the modification of genre that invariably accompanies repetition). In short, the pathos of the homelessness consists in keeping on one's horizon the image of a home ("demonstration," "thinking," "behaviour," and "institutions") and imagining (theoretically) that homelessness itself is a matter of choice. In this sense, the word 'theory' is, in Culler, a name for the field where the ethical supremacy of the "new" is institutionally asserted, or a name for the activity where the contemplation of regenerated values is located.

Nonetheless, Culler's homeless description of "Theory" could prove, after all, that, to paraphrase Richard Rorty, theory too is a kind of writing or, at least, that theoreticians are a kind of critics. The 1980s have seen perpetual glosses on the theme that the "exalted status" of demonstration (Paul de Man's expression, invented before the glosses) "was a myth" (de Man's expression, again). But even if one is personally sympathetic toward the glosses or at least toward their perpetuity, one cannot help wondering about the way in which such glosses are predicated on a jargon of authenticity, that is, on the vocabulary of a new demystifying seriousness for theory, literary theory, criticism, whatever.

Culler's description of 'theory' falls under Steven Knapp and Walter Benn Michaels's celebrated metadescription of the descriptions of 'theory'. "By 'theory'," they wrote, also in 1982, "we mean a special project in literary criticism: the attempt to govern interpretations of particular texts by appealing to an account of interpretation in general" (1982, p. 11). And indeed, the power of redescription Culler argues for entails the power of the *re* of 'redescription'; that is, the sense that one has theory when one has interpretations determined by that principle of reenactment. Ironically enough, however, Knapp and Michaels's metadescription falls under Culler's definition of food for theory; that is, "works [that] exceed the disciplinary framework within which they would normally be evaluated" (1982, p. 9). In other words, the problem is that some attempts to govern interpretations feed on some attempts to govern the government of interpretations. Ethically minded omnivoraciousness, one could say, is less selective than its epistemological counterpart.

In that same year of 1982 Paul de Man used the word 'theory' as an abbreviation for 'literary theory', rather than as an abbreviation for 'nonexistent name':

> The advent of theory, the break that is now so often deplored and that sets it aside from literary history and from literary criticism, occurs with the introduction of linguistic terminology in the metalanguage about literature. By linguistic terminology is meant a terminology that designates reference prior to designating the referent and takes into account, in the consideration of the world, the referential function of language or, to be somewhat more specific, that considers reference as a function of language and not necessarily as an intuition. (1982a, p. 8)

"The advent of theory" is described as a "break." However, this kind of break does not presuppose its own ethical superiority, at least immediately. It is characterized as a change of vocabulary. The effects of such a change are complex. They consist, among other things, in showing the interference of *linguisticity* in the organization of the sense of a repetition. In other words, they immobilize the metaphor of "redescription" by assuming that the vocabulary introduced entails some doubt as to the possibility of a commensurability of redescriptions (or the possibility of a seamless contiguity between *re* and *description*). This means that, in the vocabulary Paul de Man attributes to literary theory, the connection between the intended object of a redescription (or, in other words, "literature"), the act of intending such an object, *and* a metalanguage cannot be held as necessary. Such is the possibility that what is *given* for literary theory, and because "reference [is]...not necessarily [seen] as an intuition," is itself a by-product (or a side effect) of the "referential function of language." As Paul de Man also puts it, "literature is a fiction not because it somehow refuses to acknowledge the 'reality', but because it is not *a priori* certain that language functions according to principles which are those, or which are *like* those, of the phenomenal world. It is therefore not *a priori* certain that literature is a reliable source of information about anything but its own language" (ibid., p. 11). The passage makes a case against the possibility of grounding a hierarchical connection between metalanguage and language. Indeed, some of de Man's other allusions to the problem (e.g., 1979, pp. 8-9) suppose a semiotic model of interpretation where it cannot be proven that there are instances of nonmetalinguistic working (that is, instances where a sign does not refer to other signs) because interpretation ("a reading, not a decodage," ibid., p. 9) can never be stopped.

However, in de Man's last clause, that possibility is reintroduced by the assumption of a principle of epistemological reliability in the restricted case of "literature": literature can reliably refer to its own language; that is, can take itself as its own intuition. Moreover, the change in vocabulary of literary theory carried by the introduction of linguistic terminology seems to vouch for such a dispensation. In one of the passages quoted previously, de Man uses the expression "the break that is now so often deplored" as a paraphrase of the "linguistic turn" in literary theory and adds, shortly afterward:

> More than any other mode of inquiry, including economics, the linguistics of literariness is a powerful and indispensable tool in the unmasking of ideological aberrations, as well as a determining factor in accounting for their occurence. Those who reproach literary theory for being oblivious to social and historical (that is to say ideological) reality are merely stating their fear at having their own ideological mystifications exposed by the tool they are trying to discredit. (1982a, p. 11)

The passage is striking perhaps in its being an apology for a "linguistics of literariness," but also in its being an apology for a *power* and thus, predictably enough, adopting the full rhetoric of unconcealment whose main by-product (even if it demoted to the category of a side effect) cannot help but being built as a demystifying subject. The predicament points to a decisive question that transcends the homely question of the survival of literary theory and concerns, rather, the *consequences* of metalinguistic activities.

In de Man's own terms, perhaps, the first question seems to shed light on the second, because the notion of literary theory as a "linguistics of literariness" is conditioned prima facie by the possibility of its not reproducing the opposition between mystified and unmystified language (that, as we saw, even a justification through the institutional consequences of adopting the vantage point of a metalinguistic dispensation for literary language would entail). The inevitability of such a reproduction, on the other hand, would mean that there is a dismal direct proportionality between the degree of resistance literary theory encounters and the perpetuation of the precise oppositions that its "linguistics of literariness" appears to exclude; namely, an opposition between an alienated understanding and some sort of literality, and ultimately the present impossibility of conceiving agency beyond a hierarchy of discourses. The stakes appear to be fairly high now, as the predicament described previously would indicate the perverse way in which the political consequences of institutionalized disciplines are tied to their being organized as a strict hierarchy of discourses. And the model in which demystification and effectiveness are connected (which seems to point to a conception of action that cannot think the *destiny* of the patterns of what it defines as "myth") is of course the very model that gave birth to the figure of the critic.

IV

I suspect, finally, that there is a sense in which the famous crisis of literary theory (so famous that one can indeed suspect with some legitimacy that there was no literary theory before the crisis of literary theory), the decline and fall of literary theory, is inscribed in rules of argumentation; that is, in a specific institutional working of rationality. What I mean by *crisis*, though, is not so much what is traditionally lived *in* arguments as the endemic threat of a return (with its correlative apocalyptic supposition that such a return duplicates an originary state), as the intermittent conceptions of the ultimate nonexistence of an ontological difference between turn and return, that the very role of the protagonist of literary theory (the critic proper) seems to deny, but that, nevertheless, some of the theory's instances tend to assert.

The sense in which manners of interpretation are manners *of* interpretation has to do perhaps with the overall importance of a similar function of rationality in both instances (manners of interpretation and interpretation), which one can see perhaps as a function of management. Furthermore, my description of manners of interpretation implies a doctrine of the functions of interpretation and thus points to a version of the place of interpretation in the general symbolic economy of its own universe, *grosso modo* the economy of the symbolic systems whose point of literality is the purposiveness of the intuition.

The five chapters that follow do not provide an outline of such a version, nor is it their aim to elaborate directly a (much needed) critique of interpretation. The genre ("critique of interpretation") is now embarrasingly established. However, most of the current instances of such a critique are disappointing. In fact, they cannot help taking a thematic shape. And that means that what is taken as their object is primarily the contents of certain or all of the available major hermeneutic discourses; that is, they entangle themselves in the predicaments that go with the legitimation of their special dispensation, resorting to the same kind of last arguments I analyze here and falling into the ethical and bottomless pit of the justification of the authority of an explanation.

There is then an important respect in which such a critique would never be an objectifying thematization proper. Indeed, the horizon of a technical inquiry on the economy of critical discourse, such as the one I tried to undertake, even if it has its fair share of theoretical mishaps, because it does not have to assume the naturalness of a destiny of intuition, seems to lead more easily into the formulation of a critique of that discourse. The kind of destruction and reassembling activities entertained by philology has only to suppose the inescapable priority of the language in which a repertoire of thematizations takes place: in this sense, philology is always a critique of thematics before becoming a critique of hermeneutics. A possibility for the latter enterprise, and a nonthematic one at that, could very well depart from the relationship between language and the alleged necessity of the connection between concept and intuition that determines interpretation, as the product of a hermeneutics of the understanding. Here, too, sense is a matter of *sensibility*, that is, a matter of assuming the destiny of intuition as inscribed in the history of the concept, in sum, a matter of forgetting the very historicity of sensibility: not what in a Hegelian mood one might call historicity of the concept but rather, more modestly, the historicity of 'concept'.

Again this is not the occasion for suggesting that I have a solution for the problem. Instead, and to close, allow me a stylistic observation on the end of my last paragraph: there, I contrast "concept" with "'concept.'" Even if the distinction between use and mention, assumed by the use of quotation marks, is open to some questioning (that is irrelevant to pursue at this point), I believe that the post-Fregean gesture of quoting, not unlike the notorious philological quotations, has curious effects: it is the double and ambiguous sign of an attentiveness to a vocabulary one does not take for granted. Between "concept" and "'concept'" there is not just the difference between the absolution of a mention in the notion of use and the absolution of a use in the notion of mention; rather, something takes place in the second case: seeing the first case as historically engendered, as it were. In "'concept'", "concept", by being quoted, and as philologists know well, acquires an *age*, and so, by becoming perishable, it acquires a history: the quotation marks point invariably to the possibility of a time without the word they read—and yet they could not operate without that word. In these metalinguistic exercises, then, it is simultaneously acknowledged that there was always language and that there was not always "always." They reproduce the predicaments of the status of a metalanguage for literary theory that we saw in the last section as formulated by de Man. And, indeed, to revise ever so slightly de Man's sentence, a metalinguistic principle shows that it is not a priori certain either that literature is a reliable source of information about anything but its own language or that 'about' cannot be put in quotation marks.

Where quotation becomes the main procedure (in fields that know no limits but the limits of their own procedural infelicities) there is an important sense in which similarities are not a function of perception but rather what is instituted by quoting. In this sense, one does not have the romance of the journey of intuition to the homeliness of the concept or its pastoral counterpart (where intuition stops at the concept's backyard and mumbles something about *Unheimlichkeit*): rather, one realizes perhaps that the creation of similarities, the creation of a home, is a function of the same kind of linguistic devices that by opening the possibility of a past, prefigure yet another homeless age.

Acknowledgments

Throughout the writing of what is now this book, my work was sponsored by several institutions. I benefited from a Fulbright-Hays grant (made possible by the Comissão Cultural Luso-Americana and the Institute for International Education), a Fellowship from the Instituto Nacional de Investigação Científica, in Lisbon, and a graduate dissertation fellowship from the Graduate School of the University of Minnesota, in Minneapolis. The book is also indebted deeply to innumerable conversations: among many others, those with Maria de Lourdes Ferraz, Wlad Godzich, Michael Hancher, Ron Sousa, and Darren Witwer. Finally, in thanking my wife, Ana, I am fully aware of satisfying two different orders of conditions: the rhetorical condition of a book written in English and the rhetorical condition of this book. Even at the risk of losing some imperturbability I would like to emphasize the latter over the former.

1

The Theoretical Eye

I

I believe the sense in which I shall be using the expression manners of interpretation will have to remain unspecified for some time, but I also believe such is ultimately an irrelevant enigma. I shall illustrate rather the enigmatic nature of the latter irrelevancy with the help of a passage from the founding text of the canon of literary theory, namely Aristotle's *Poetics*.

Chapter XXII of the *Poetics* consists in a rather detailed criticism of some poets' lack of propriety in "several modes of expression". The prescriptions offered by Aristotle are technical prescriptions, just as the *Poetics* is, of course, a technical work. Conversely, as one can see for instance in the *Nicomachean Ethics* (e.g., 1140a, 6ff.), any *tekhnè* is, by definition, *poietikè*. A poetics would thus be doubly technical, if we like: it deals not only with a matter of technical production (such as shoemaking) but also with the very matter of producing production itself. And, like any other *tekhnè*, like any other craft, the fact that poetics is "a certain state involving reason concerned with production" (ibid.) implies its entire subordination to the prescriptions of reason, not just in the sense that a pair of shoes, like a tragedy, cannot afford the luxuries of nonfunctionality (aesthetics was invented much later) but especially in the sense that the rationality of shoemaking is reductible to a set of shoemaking prescriptions. Chapter XXII of the *Poetics*, which is relatively short, in fact, develops a whole arsenal of detailed rules, supported by at least nine different examples.

The discussion of such prescriptions is not the object of my concern. It is sufficient for the reader to be aware that they are essentially what one would call today stylistic prescriptions. Toward the end of the chapter, however, Aristotle writes: "But the greatest thing by far is to have a command of metaphor. This alone cannot be imparted by another; it is the mark of genius, for to make good metaphors implies an eye for resemblances" ["eu metapherein to to homoion theorein estin": literally "to metaphorize well is to look to the similar"] (*Poet.*, 1459a). The passage is crucial because it exemplifies the problematic notion of "what cannot be imparted by another" within a technique such as poetics. "What cannot be imparted by another" is not attributed to the following of rules but to an "eye for resemblances," to an ability of perceiving as identical (*homoion theorein*). The converse idea that a unique (in the sense of 'incomparable') product can derive from a set of technical prescriptions would be contradictory (for reasons not unlike the ones of Wittgenstein's "private language argument"): and the greatest part of the efforts of some of the heirs of Aristotle's problem, such as the Longinus of *On the Sublime*, can be seen as the efforts to reconcile the contradiction (namely, through the very interesting notion that "natural genius" itself is technically produced).

Be that as it may, a curious scheme follows from Aristotle's passage: even if poetics is meant as a *tekhnè*, the most important thing about its technicality (the rational rules of technical composition) is not due to technical knowledge but rather to "an eye": *theorein* being here the mode on which the bypassing of technical knowledge is grafted. And just as, so to speak, the rationality of the rules has to be invented (in the rhetorical sense later made famous by Cicero, Quintilian, and Hermogenes) so ultimately the center of a poetic technique is, for Aristotle, neither technical nor poetic but, properly speaking, theoretical. This latter point means that, for Aristotle, poetics is a technique that cannot keep itself fully technical; that is, a technique that has to paralyze itself as a technique. Moreover, the point where such a technique ends is far from being unimportant: it is rather a pivotal point for a theory of production; namely, the point where conditions of production are produced.

In the five chapters of this work, I propose to follow this particular structure, along some of the arguments and disputations that have marked literary studies (without necessarily being all restricted to the institutionalized fields of literary studies) since their emergence. But it is perhaps clear from my Aristotle excursus how such a structure tends to be the very figure of theory: the figure of the termination of argument in the name of an irrefragable last perception, the figure that makes argument necessary in the first place, and the figure of what thinks the paralysis of argument.

II

The distinction that Aristotle utilized in his *Nicomachean Ethics* between technical knowledge and practical knowledge has been used by Hans-Georg Gadamer as a way of dealing conceptually with the problem of methodological shortcomings in hermeneutics. It would be accurate to say, perhaps, that in his famous title *Truth and Method* the second term corresponds to the horizon of a purely technical knowledge, whereas the first term corresponds to a practical desire of overcoming such a horizon. Moreover, if, as Gadamer writes, "understanding is...a particular case of the application of something universal to a particular situation" (1960, p. 278), then it is fairly clear that the criteria of such an application lie on a *homoion theorein*, on the perception of an analogy between something accepted as a rule and something recognized to be the case.

As Gadamer remarks, "it is obvious that this is not the knowledge of science" (ibid., p. 280). And his use of Aristotle is above all the use of an alternative mode of knowledge, "not detached from a being that is becoming, but determined by it and determinative of it" (ibid., p. 278). Aristotle, in the beginning of Book VI of the *Nicomachean Ethics*, contrasts two different families of knowledge: "when thought is concerned with study, not with action or production, its good or bad state consists [simply] in being true or false. For truth is the function of whatever thinks; but the function of what thinks about action is truth agreeing with correct desire" (*Eth. Nic.*, 1139a). The distinctive trait that interests me here, though, is related to the modalities of the transmission of knowledge. Since "what is known scientifically is by necessity...every science seems to be teachable, and what is scientifically knowable is learnable" (ibid., 1139b). On the contrary, objects of knowledge that do not exist by necessity, that is, "what admits of being otherwise" (ibid., 1140a), must be known through different processes. Aristotle considers two different kinds of knowledge of such objects: the knowledge of things made and the knowledge of things done. The former are due to a *tekhnè*: through technical knowledge, something is brought into existence, even if produced objects cannot be said to be necessary, because they belong to the set of varying things. "In a way," Aristotle writes, "craft [*tekhnè*] and fortune [*tukhè*] are concerned with the same things" (ibid.). On the other hand, knowledge of things done, of action, is attained through deliberation. The practical wisdom that makes deliberation possible Aristotle calls *phronesis*. And, once it is understood that the reason for the difference between *to produce* and *to act* lies in the fact that "production has its end beyond it; but action does not, since its end is doing well itself" (ibid., 1140b), it is easy to realize that phronesis is the ability to build an analogue of scientific demonstration for the realm of things that are both not susceptible to demonstration and not susceptible to technical regulation: "it seems proper, then, to an intelligent person [*phronimon*] to be able to deliberate finely about what is good and beneficial for himself" (ibid., 1140a). The building of this analogy has, however, a deep consequence: to conduct an efficient deliberation one has to possess phronesis, whereas it is possible to conduct a scientific demonstration without necessarily being scientifically competent. One of the favorite similes of Aristotle's commentators is dance. Although it is possible to learn how to make a pair of shoes without actually making one, one does not learn how to dance without dancing, because the process of learning how to dance *is* the process of dancing (we shall see later the same reasoning in Augustine).

That is precisely why phronesis is not

> about universals only. It must also come to know particulars, since it is concerned with action and action is about particulars.
>
> Hence in other areas also some people who lack knowledge but have experience are better in action than others who have knowledge. For someone who knows that light meats are digestible and healthy, but not which sorts of meats are light, will not produce health; the one who knows that bird meats are healthy will be better at producing health. And since intelligence [phronesis] is concerned with action, it must possess both [the universal and the particular knowledge][1] or the [particular] more [than the universal]. Here too, however, [as in medicine] there is a ruling [science]. (ibid., 1141b)

Because it operates a mediation between the universal and the particular, the deliberative process, as Aristotle says, "may be in error about either the universal or the particular" (ibid., 1142a). It is, however, as if this double possibility of error were irrelevant to the purpose of deliberation, for " we can reach a good by a false inference, as well [as by correct deliberation], so that we reach the right thing to do, but by the wrong steps, when the middle term is false" (ibid., 1142b).

And last, but by no means least, comes a very important restriction to the learning of phronesis; that is, to the quality of being able to deliberate:

> whereas young people become accomplished in geometry and mathematics, and wise within these limits, intelligent young people [that is, young people possessing phronesis] do not seem to be found. The reason is that intelligence [phronesis] is concerned with particulars as well as universals, and particulars become known from experience, but a young person lack experience, since some length of time is needed to produce it. (ibid., 1142a)

One has now an extensive set of arguments that tend to render incompatible the notions of deliberation and method. They proceed in two main directions: deliberation can transgress the "syntactic" postulates of a method (either by being satisfactory *and* syntactically questionable or by being unsatisfactory *and* syntactically beyond reproach) and deliberation can transgress what one could call perhaps the democratic principle of method, because the possession of phronesis is independent from a phronetic position, so to speak. As a matter of fact, time is, as it were, the sanction for deliberation; it takes time to acquire phronesis, both in the sense that the process of deliberation is more devious than the process of demonstration and in the sense that the one who is entitled to deliberate tends to be characterized as *older* than the one who is entitled to demonstrate. In the first sense the geometrical model of proof as the syntactically shortest distance between two points is called into question (by suggesting that at least some proofs cannot be evaluated in terms of either economy or elegance). In the second sense the notion of an automatism of preconditions for proof is restricted (by suggesting that at least some proofs require as precondition an override of the automatism of preconditions, viz. one requirement that demands that the access to the situation of proof not be determined on the basis of requirements alone—and *age* is conceptually the name of such a dispensation). The substitution of an alleged syntax of deliberation is precisely what makes deliberation a difficult process; the very notion of difficulty denotes in fact here what cannot be comprehended by syntax—no one can tell in advance the *form* of a deliberation. But at the same time the difficulty of deliberation is, for Aristotle, a necessary one.

III

The idea of a method, for Gadamer, would correspond to the belief in an analogy-generating procedure. And, as in the case of Aristotle in the *Poetics*, such an idea is put aside, under the assumption that there are no universal conditions for the perception of identity.

Gadamer's use of Aristotle's *Nicomachean Ethics*, then, can be due only to Gadamer's very particular eye for resemblances. In fact, Aristotle's theory of moral knowledge is seen as the model for a hermeneutic theory. But what makes such an eye required and indeed indispensable is that, as Gadamer acknowledges, "Aristotle is not concerned with the hermeneutical problem and certainly not with its historical dimension, but with the right estimation of the role reason has to play in moral action" (1960, p. 278). Gadamer's argument, then, rests on the possibility of theoretical (in both sense of the word) consideration of three families of structural resemblances between his particular project and Aristotle's theory.

The first family derives from the contrast between technical knowledge and moral knowledge; that is, between the two main branches of nonepistemic knowledge:

> we learn a tekhnè and can also forget it. But we do not learn moral knowledge, nor can we forget it. We do not stand over against it, as if it were something we can acquire or not, in the way that we can choose to acquire or not an objective skill, a tekhnè. Rather, we are always already in the situation of having to act...and hence must already possess and be able to apply moral knowledge. (ibid., p. 283)

Gadamer's rhetorical demonstration of this first set of resemblances proceeds through the supposition of an intermediate case, the case of juridical knowledge. Even if "there are laws that are entirely a matter of mere agreement (e.g. traffic regulations)...there are also things that do not admit of regulation simply by human convention, because the nature of the thing constantly asserts itself" [*'die Natur der Sache' sich stets durchsetzt*] (ibid., p.285). We are then led to "a curious legal ambiguity" (ibid., p. 284):

> the person who is 'applying' law...in a specific instance...will have to refrain from applying the full rigor of the law. But if he does, it is not because he has no alternative, but because to do otherwise would not be right....The law is always imperfect, not

> because it is imperfect in itself, but because, in comparison with the ordered world of law, human reality is necessarily imperfect [*notwendig mangelhaft*] and hence does not allow of any simple application of the former. (ibid.)

Such an ambiguity was, of course, the object of Aristotle's remark that "what is decent [*epieikes*] is just, but is not what is legally just, but a rectification of it" (*Eth. Nic.*, 1137b). However, whereas Aristotle (although, not unlike Gadamer, acknowledging that "the source of the error is not the law or the legislator, but the nature of the object itself," ibid.) recommends that "the law choose the [universal rule] that is usually [correct], well aware of the error being made" (ibid.), Gadamer, as it were, rewrites the very notion of the law under the determination of the object, under the determination of the case. Consequently, the methodological prescriptions we are to find in the field of interpretation are, in his version of Aristotle, "not norms...nor...mere conventions, but really do correspond to the nature of the thing [*die Natur der Sache*]—only that the latter is always itself determined in each case by the use" (1960, p. 286).

This conclusion entails what Gadamer sees as a second family of structural resemblances; that is, "a fundamental modification of the conceptual relation between means and end" (ibid.). For "where there is a tekhnè, we must learn it and then we are able to find the right means" (ibid.), but "even if we conceive [moral] knowledge in ideal perfection, it is the perfection of this kind of deliberation within oneself (eubolia) and not knowledge in the manner of a tekhnè" (ibid.). The reason is of course that the results of a deliberation cannot be known in advance because the very process of deliberation lies on the consideration of an individual situation, a case, just like the question What to do? taken in itself does not mean anything: "the relation between means and ends here is not such that the knowledge of the right means can be made available in advance, and that because the knowledge of the right end is not the mere object of knowledge either" (ibid., pp. 286-287). What is being deliberately blurred here is the distinction, which applies to technical knowledge, between 'knowing how to do' and 'doing', because "moral knowledge must be a kind of experience" [*das sittliche Wissen enthält selbst eine Art der Erfahrung in sich*] (ibid., p. 288), precisely as knowledge of dancing must be a kind of dance and hermeneutic knowledge a kind of interpretation. Ironically enough, however, Gadamer's procedure, because it remains essentially a distinguo (*"eine Art der..."*), introduces the same relation between law and case his reading of Aristotle tries to dispel, which is to say that the relationship he assumes to exist between moral knowledge and experience is not, in his sense, an ethical relationship, but, rather, a technical one. In fact, Gadamer shares this same predicament with Aristotle, in that the only form Aristotle has in which to conceptually claim the irrelevance of technical preconditions for proof is through the introduction of yet another precondition ("be experienced"). If hermeneutic knowledge is to be a kind of interpretation, therefore, it can never help but be a case of interpretation—and, as a matter of fact, the notion of the hermeneutic circle is going to become decisive in Gadamer's theory, not so much in an ontological sense as in the sense in which it will become the figure through which the possibility of a law of interpretation is played down.

The third family of structural resemblances between Aristotle's theory of moral knowledge and Gadamer's theory of hermeneutics is seen by the latter as the dominance of what the former calls *sunesis*, that is, the dominance of the concern with the other throughout the process of moral reflection. The somewhat paradoxical nature of sunesis comes from the fact that it describes the inclusion of such a concern as the most radical feature of the evaluation of one's own unique situation; it is, if we like, the specific difference between a paratechnology of survival, in which an analogue of phronesis would be the ethical designation for strategy, and something like the demands of practical reason. Within Gadamer's theory, the counterpart of sunesis is rather to be found in his treatment of the notion of dialogue. But his rendition of Aristotle's term (employed to distinguish *deinotes*, cleverness, from phronesis), translated—and, of course, not just by him—as *Verständnis*, makes especially noticeable the double sense in which Gadamer's theory is a theory of the 'understanding of'. As I shall try to suggest later, such is the invariable trait of appurtenance to an ethical tradition in hermeneutics. In the case of Gadamer, nevertheless, it happens not so much because of his constant reference to Aristotle's *Nicomachean Ethics* (and perhaps even in spite of it, as it is possible to say that Aristotle hesitates constantly between an ethics and a self acknowledging "unjust technique") as because of his theory's being set on a rhetoric of comparison (which is here allegorized by translation) that invariably moves within the alternation of case and law. This latter alternation is the very movement of a relation toward the individual dominated by the requisites of an 'understanding of'. It is maybe in this sense that it can be said that all perception of the identical, all *homoion theorein*, tends to be ethically grounded or, rather, that ethics tends to be the ground for all theories of fiction as such (a point that Wayne Booth made—albeit *a contrario*—thirty years ago). At least from the time of the Kant of *The Conflict of the Faculties* on down (but with roots as remote as Augustine), such is the tradition of refusing any automatic subsumption of individual cases, by giving precedence to the pragmatic considerations of practical reason vis-à-vis the methodological principles of a constituted discipline (only to grant the possibility of such a subsumption later, once the law is conceived as excluding all possibility of syntactic derivation of consequences, as in the cases of the divine and the moral laws). In Chapter 2 we shall see how such a tradition is opposed to the tendentially technical tradition of philology one finds intermittently in authors like Friedrich Schlegel and Schleiermacher.

Like those who exercise their natural gifts "without being led in any way by moral being and hence without inhibitions and without orientation towards moral ends" (ibid., p. 289), the clever (*deinos*) interpreter who "dealing with a traditional text seeks to apply it to himself" (ibid.) is a misunderstanding interpreter, which is to say, an interpreter who refuses to acknowledge the *other* that the law simultaneously creates and exemplifies; in this sense, what such an interpreter does not understand is *Verständnis* itself. The gallery of *unverständige*, and often *unverständliche*, interpreters could very well extend from Carroll's Humpty Dumpty, an excellent patron saint for philology, to John Stuart Mill, the purely aesthetic (in the sense of "willing to be sensuously affected") reader of the *Autobiography*. Curiously enough, Oscar Wilde would be here a considerably accomplished Gadamerian reader—with some lapses in several different directions; namely, his letters.

But another decisive implication of Gadamer's appeal to Aristotle is linked to his configuration of the concept of the otherness of the law. In fact, through Aristotle's *Ethics* Gadamer introduces in *Truth and Method* a decisive comparison that usually goes unnoticed: the metaphor of the other as a person and, consequently, the notion of interpretation as dialogue. However, the possibility of seeing the other as identical (which is to say, the possibility of seeing cases as *comparable*) is carried out by a sunetic faculty; such a faculty is the faculty, again, of judging according to a perceived identity beneath the disparate sphere of individual cases: the faculty of, as Aristotle says in the *Poetics*, *metapherein*. In a good sense, then, a metaphor cannot help but be *just*, in that it invariably tends to convey the *critical* moment of the understanding of the other, translated in the perception of the other as a "case of the same." Perhaps the "prosopopeization" of the law is the latest episode in the adventures of the concept of "case of the same" (the one in which it takes the shape of "one of us"). Such an episode can be traced back to Kant and the discredit of the arguments for the divine right or the divine origin of the law. Be that as it may, it seems possible to say (and I shall adduce some arguments toward the end of this chapter) that for Saint Augustine (and even perhaps for Spinoza) the other of interpretation was not a person.

IV

That the most important thing is to have an eye for resemblances means that there are no sufficient rules for engendering comparisons. Gadamer's hermeneutics, understandably enough, offers a straightforward rejection of the idea that the process of interpretation can be subject to methodological prescriptions, and the point is usually duly emphasized by commentators. For his theory of dialogue, such a point entails the impossibility of a conception of conversational rules: "To conduct a conversation," writes Gadamer, "means to allow oneself to be conducted by the object to which the partners in the conversation are directed" (ibid., p. 330). However, the very considerations that allow for the dismissal of the technical aspects of interpretation introduce, as we have seen earlier, a principle of phronesis that overrides any syntactic determinants.

There arises, thus, the question of the status of the constraints entailed by such a principle. In this respect, the "rules" of action dealt with by phronesis (like the "rules" of critical judgement dealt with by sunesis), when compared to the constraints of both tekhnè and epistemè, would appear to be of a less syntactic nature. Less syntactic nature means here (and the expression is not excessively felicitous) the conception of a nature that tends to imply the rejection of a principle of automatic subsumption. For this realm, the universal is not purely axiomatic because it does not provide a strict ground for inference (which explains why Gadamer's use of the term dialectics refers to Plato, rather than Aristotle) as it is merely regulatory. The "universal" of conversation tends, thus, to be literally inconsequential (non sequitur being here the rhetorical mode of a refusal of automatic subsumption), but, on the other hand, consequential enough for statements such as "Love thy neighbor" being used as if produced by it.

Although not too explicitly, in *Truth and Method*, Gadamer develops the topic of these "conversational ideas" (as opposed perhaps to "conversational rules"). But such ideas are, first and foremost, envisaged as *precautions*, as negative rules. They are not so much an etiquette of interpretation as they are its manners. That is, they are the prudent fulfillment of practical potentialities as opposed to a method for action. During his discussion of the concept of *Bildung*, Gadamer retains from Helmholtz's talk "Über das Verhältnis der Naturwissenschaften zur Gesamtheit der Wissenschaften" a term that is central in this respect: the term *tact* [Takt]. "By 'tact'," he writes, "we understand a particular sensitivity and sensitiveness [Empfindlichkeit und Empfindungsfähigkeit] to situations, and how to behave in them, for which we cannot find any knowledge from general principles" (ibid., p. 16). Tact as an element of *Bildung* (or as a *Bildung* formation prerequisite) does not mean an inferential ability that would allow for the production of practical maxims, but rather the very ideal of pure practice that acknowledges somewhat the unique configuration of practical problems and hence the permanent inconsequentiality of moral prescriptions regarding action. Within an Aristotelian framework, both being tactful and learning how to become tactful can mean performing only actions that deploy "a particular sensitivity and sensitiveness" to situations: "Hence an essential part of tact is inexplicitness and inexpressibility. One can say something tactfully; but that will always mean that one passes over something tactfully and leaves it unsaid, and it is tactless to express what one can only pass over" [und taktlos ist, das auszusprechen, was man nur übergehen kann] (ibid., pp. 16-17). This particular aspect illustrates further the distinction between tact and a "positive" etiquette (because for the realm of tact to say is not to say) and shows why the notions of method and tact are incompatible. The idea is of course that tact is not the ability to perform certain acts embodied in some sort of positivity, but rather the ability to perform certain acts that consist in *not* performing certain other acts as, for instance, not becoming *tactilis*. There is, then, a sense in which Gadamer's notion of a tactful action is irreducible to a rhetoric of omission, in which each omission would gain a positional value, so to speak, within a rule-ordered system; the limitational aspect of tact is due not to the fact that there is a strategic knowledge of the value of limitation, but, on the contrary, to the fact that such a knowledge is never fully specifiable.

It is therefore very understandable that Gadamer sees tact as a quality of distance, in a way clearly related to the core of Aristotle's notion of phronesis: "tact helps one to preserve distance, it avoids the offensive, the intrusive, the violation of the intimate sphere of the person" (ibid., p. 17). Even if here we are more than ever under the spell of the founding comparison between hermeneutics and human relations, it would be absurd not to acknowledge the enormous power of such a spell. Within Gadamer's own theory that power is built through a process of amplification; "the tact that functions in the human species is not simply a feeling and unconscious, but is at the same time a mode of knowing and a mode of being" (ibid.). But independent from the ontologizing and epistemologizing of tact (very similar to what one finds in authors like Polanyi) it is perhaps noteworthy that the argument for tact is built by Gadamer as an argument for human rights (namely and perhaps significantly, for the right of privacy), grafted on and perhaps shaped as an ethical argument. There is, therefore, an important respect in which the hermeneutical ontology Gadamer proposes is a hermeneutic ethics, contaminated by the theme of procedural limits in a way that makes it all too evidently and awkwardly a companion to the more technical tradition of Schleiermacher and Dilthey. In some of the following chapters I shall be insisting on an essential proximity of all hermeneutic traditions, vis-à-vis, for example, philological traditions.

The question of knowledge through tact in the human sciences could be seen as an equivalent to the question of the possibility of nonregulated in the sense of nonteachable true insights in interpretation. However, because the latter base themselves on an ongoing reserve toward the communicability of perceptions of sameness, Gadamer's hermeneutics is also the precise opposite of the so-called subjectivism and the indifference of principle that subjectivism tends to profess. In fact, it does not deal with either the possibility or the legitimacy of the production of mutually incompatible statements as it deals with the legitimacy of avoiding certain statements that in some cases could even be syntactically compatible. At this juncture, Gadamer's theory is equally opposed to aesthetics *and* philology. The latter point shall be discussed later in Chapter 2. But the former point can be easily made from Gadamer's notion of tact. The introduction of a principle of distance that, beyond the pleasure principle, would regulate *in absentia et per absentiam* the process of interpretation carries not just the denial of the exemplary role of every methodological instance but, and most important, the denial of a kind of truth built through an accumulation of singular perceptions (which is to say that the concept of experience is understood not aesthetically but historically). And when theories of modes of knowledge become antiaesthetic, they tend to become theories of the limits of knowledge (but this is after all just another aspect of the Kantian lesson).

V

Gadamer's idea that the structural role of method in hermeneutics is played by an analogue of phronesis finds its most radical formulation in Saint Augustine's theory of interpretation of the Scriptures, contained in his treatise *De doctrina christiana.* It is perhaps trivial to remark that the consequences of Augustine's theory's being modeled on the reading of the Bible are overwhelming, but for the time being I shall prefer triviality to cursoriness.

In fact, notions like authorial intention and reconstruction of intended meaning (to name just two traditional topics of the historiography of hermeneutics) lose their point if one assumes, as Augustine does, that the author of the Scriptures is the Holy Spirit; that is, the third person of the Trinity as opposed to the first person of knowledge. Therefore, one of the major issues of Augustine's hermeneutics has to do with the intrinsic complexity that the structure of authorship has in its framework, which leads him to elaborate a very sophisticated rhetoric of authority that, in fact, knows several procedures of proof and has to tackle the very problem of such a diversity:

> he who examines the divine eloquence, desiring to discover the intention of the author [*ut ad uoluntatem perueniatur auctoris*] through whom the Holy Spirit created the Scripture, whether he attains his end or finds another meaning in the words not contrary to the right faith, is free from blame if he has evidence [*testimonium habens*] from some other place in the divine books. For the author himself may have seen the same meaning in the words we seek to understand. And certainly the spirit of God, who worked through that author [*qui per eum haec operatus est*], undoubtedly foresaw [*praeuidit*] that this meaning would occur to the reader or listener. Rather, He provided that it might occur to him, since that meaning is dependent upon truth. For what could God have more generously and abundantly provided in the divine writings than that the same words might be understood in various ways [*ut eadem uerba pluribus intellegantur modis*] which other no less divine witness approve? (*Doc. Christ.*, III, xxvii)

The right understanding, then can never correspond to the positivity of a reconstruction, for there is no argument-finding procedure. What is elaborated, rather, is the ironization of all procedures, which amounts to some sort of methodological credo quia absurdum; not only can everything become an argument, but also the potential becoming argument of everything is a supplementary argument for the structure of authorship from which the former principle was derived in the first place. Whereas the possibility of envisaging interpretation as a matter of recovering an intention has to account, so to speak, for a moment of decayed intention, Augustine's author is by definition the very figure of the refusal of any decayed intention: there is nothing from which to reconstruct the word of the Holy Spirit because such a word is immune to destruction. The signs for such an archeology would be only *too* present: they cannot but be completely present. The studious contemplation of the signs of a hopeful recovery, that is, the whole procession of the emblems of erudition, is, then very remote to Saint Augustine's doctrine. The former is the traditional allegory of the pathos (and the bathos) of absence, whereas the latter tends to emphasize the former's inaptitude in dealing with both evidence and apathy: "Whoever . . . thinks that he understands the divine Scriptures or any part of them so that it does not build the double love of God and of our neighbour does not understand it at all" (ibid., I, xxxvi).

We are once more in the realm of the specific truth of action, from which, incidentally, would stem the notion of application that is central to both pre-Kantian hermeneutic theories and their reappraisal by Gadamer. But action is not a mere consequence of understanding, even an indispensable step in the process of edification: action is both the cause and the reason, in a Wittgensteinian sense, of understanding: "whoever finds a lesson there [in the Scriptures] useful to the building of charity, even though he has not said what the author may be shown to have intended in that place, has not been deceived nor is he lying in any way"(ibid.). Augustine's emphasis on what one could call, for lack of a better term, *practical truth*, then, can be shown to portray a movement that is similar to the one we noticed when we discussed tact: the ultimate end of interpretation (and its ultimate cause) being action, interpretation itself consists primarily in the *end* of interpretation. Those who become active do not need any further interpretation, and those who are already active do not need any reading at all: "a man supported by faith, hope and charity, with an unshaken hold upon them, does not need the Scriptures except for the instruction of others. And many live by these three things [*per haec tria*] in solitude without books" (ibid., I,xxxix). It is not difficult to understand the sense of Augustine's restriction "except for the instruction of others" [*nisi ad alios instruendos]:* instruction is *not* a matter of practical truth and requires in consequence a method, but it is also clear that if everyone were "fide et spe et caritate subnixus" there would be nothing to teach and literally nothing to say. Not to read means to know how to act well. Conversely, reading in spite of the promise of redemption it conveys, corresponds to the moment of indecision that precedes deliberation. Therefore, the subject of reading (to use perhaps a too-formal expression) is in a very important sense an unreconciled subject. Such a sense is perhaps twofold: unreconciled because it awaits redemption but also because it cannot yet incorporate action as a legitimate dimension of itself.

Augustine's ironization of method (like his notion of an end of interpretation) is closely related to a specific theory of the nature of hermeneutic problems. Referring to the "many and varied obscurities and ambiguities [that] deceive those who read casually," Augustine does not doubt "that this situation was provided by God to conquer pride by work and to combat disdain in our minds, to which those things which are easily discovered seem frequently to become worthless" (ibid., II, vi). In passages like the preceding one, in fact, it is again the status of nonpractical knowledge, such as the one emblematized by erudition, that is redirected. It is as if the pathos of science would *not* correspond to any scientific depth but, rather ironically, again, to the depths of an antiscientific argument; in this sense, even hermeneutic problems are practical problems, in that they are seen as connected primarily and exclusively to the apprenticeship of patterns of action. Hermeneutic discourse thus becomes the equivalent of a form of deliberation within oneself that precedes, but preferably accompanies, action. Augustine's precept concerning figurative language is particularly helpful here: "what is read should be subjected to diligent scrutiny until an interpretation contributing to the reign of charity is produced" [*uersetur diligenti consideratione quod legitur, donec ad regnum caritatis interpretatio perducatur*] (ibid., III, xv). Not only "pure heart . . . good conscience and . . . unfeigned faith" (1 Timothy 1:5., quoted by Augustine in *Doc. Christ.*, I, xl) are required to be part of the essential posture of those who need interpretation, but also what will later become a secularized philological attitude is required, consisting in one's being "meek through piety so we do not contradict Divine Scripture, either when it is understood . . . or when it is not understood" (ibid, II, vii). Augustine's formulation shares with some contemporary formulations of what J. Hillis Miller called an ethics of reading the notion that the ground of hermeneutic arguments is to be found in what is written and therefore that such a ground is not only independent but also a priori in relation to interpretation. But to the willingness in yielding to such paradoxes one finds in Miller (as, for instance, C. Norris remarked, e.g., 1988, p. 115), a trademark of the aestheticized ethics of high modernism, corresponds, in Augustine, a total distrust of singular perception. The point is crucial in order to distinguish Augustine's formulation from an ethics of reading, properly speaking: whereas in the latter the *homoion theorein* is primarily a perception of the other as identical (and thus the forgetfulness of perception itself), in Augustine all *homoion theorein* carries the awareness of its own tropological nature, that is, the awareness of the other's being identical only for the momentary sake of edification; the other, one could say, is never indifferent. The functional role of the proliferation and the variety of stimuli triggered by Miller's philological imperative is occupied in Augustine by a whole topic of restriction of the aesthetic. The basic attitude of the interpreter consists here in the exercising of an ability not to do (and not to enjoy) certain things; that is, the ability to see perception as yet another replacement, of not detaining oneself on what one could call the evidence and the singularity of perception. Prompted by the rejection of any psychological account of identity, such is the ability, which Miller is unable or unwilling to think, of seeing subjectivity as engendered: the ability to be terrified by perception (and terror here is the mode of enthusiasm, of the possession by God). "It is necessary," writes Saint Augustine,

> that we be turned by the fear of God toward a recognition of His will [*ad cognoscendam ejus uoluntatem*: towards (the part of) His will that is to be known], so that he commands that we avoid. Of necessity this fear will lead us to thought of our mortality and of our future death and will affix all our proud motions, as if they were fleshy members fastened with nails, to the wood of the cross [*Timor autem iste cogitationem de nostra mortalitate et de futura morte necesse et incutiat et quasi clauatis carnibus omnes superbiae motus ligno crucis affigat*]. (. (Doc. Christ., II, vii)

We are definitely beyond the pleasure principle. That it is so, in Augustine's text, is signaled by the bluntness of the final allegory (*quasi clauatis carnibus . . . ligno crucis*). The allegory works in a double way in that it is built on the paradox of the passion of Christ: to think of our mortality is to think of Christ's resurrection. But once the interpreter is "clauatis carnibus ligno crucis" the interpreter becomes simultaneously redeemed and redeemer. The identification between redeemed and redeemer, interpreter and author, however, is framed, as it were, by the precautionary measures of syntax: the adverbial prefix *quasi* maintains the ultimate impossibility of such an identification; indeed, there is a sense in which the author can never be a metaphor for the interpreter because the act of transporting oneself beyond is hopelessly one-sided: the interpreter only can wish to become like God; but God can never wish to become an interpreter. Augustine's allegory exemplifies the irrelevance of all singular perceptions in that it is precisely the place where two opposite singular perceptions (seeing the other as oneself, seeing the other as what can never be seen as oneself) are maintained.

Curiously enough, the dismissal of a pleasure principle carries the partial dismissal of the sciences of disputation, that is rhetoric and dialectics, because "the love of controversy [*libido rixandi*] is to be avoided, as well as a certain puerile ostentation in deceiving an adversary" (ibid., II, xxxi). The ability to draw correct inferences can be learned and may be useful; but the laws of propositional connection are one thing and their use is something else; for "correct inferences may be made concerning false as well as true propositions" (ibid.). What cannot be learned is "the truth of propositions": such is, in fact, "a matter to be discovered in the sacred books of the Church" (ibid.). Augustine shows, nevertheless, a constant distrust of inferential procedures that reminds us of Aristotle's concerning the realm of practical truth: "he who knows that there is a resurrection of the dead is better than another who knows that it follows from the proposition that there is no resurrection of the dead that `then Christ is not risen'" (ibid., II, xxxiv.). And this is, of course, the ultimate sense of Gadamer's use of Plato's seventh *Letter* (namely, of 343 c-d), against the possibility of an identification between refutability and falsity.

Dialectics, however, is not Augustine's sole target. The essential ambiguity that Aristotle already noticed in the core of all techniques of proof, namely in rhetoric, is emphasized by him when he remarks that "an expression of charity conciliates an audience . . . [it] is easy to understand a brief and open account of events. . . [and] the variety of discourse keeps the auditors attentive and without fatigue" (ibid., II, xxxvi). But he also adds that "it frequently happens that men more easily learn the things themselves on action of which these principles are learned than the very knotty and spiny precepts of these disciplines" (ibid., II, xxxvii), thus making of their knowledge a very minor issue: "studious and intelligent youths who fear God and seek the blessed life might be helpfully admonished that they should not pursue those studies which are taught outside the Church of Christ as though they might lead to a blessed life" (ibid.,II, xxxix). The simile he uses to illustrate this thesis, in a rather proto-Wittgensteinian way, emphasizes once more what could be seen as the priority of pragmatics over syntax:

> it is as if one should wish to give rules for walking and admonishes that the rear foot is not to be raised until the first foot is put down, and then goes on to describe in detail how the hinges of the joints and knees are to be moved. He speaks truly, nor is it possible to walk in any other way. Yet men more easily do these things when they walk than pay attention to them while they are doing them or understand them when they are described. (ibid., II, xxxvii)

The role of rhetoric in Augustine's hermeneutics is, then, that of an antidote not only to rhetoric's essential ambiguity but also to rhetoric's ill uses; that is, and once more, a practical role. Practical role means here, among other things, the role of restraining the use of rhetoric through metarhetorical precepts and recognizing that such a use is inescapable:

> for since by means of the art of rhetoric both truth and falsehood are urged [*suadeantur*], who would dare to say that truth should stand in the person of its defenders unarmed against lying, so that they who wish to urge falsehoods may know how to make their listeners benevolent, or attentive, or docile in their presentation, while the defenders of truth are ignorant of that art? Should they speak briefly, clearly and plausibly while the defenders of truth speak so that they tire their listeners, make themselves difficult to understand and what they have to say dubious? Should they oppose the truth with fallacious arguments and assert falsehoods, while the defenders of truth have no ability wither to defend the truth or to oppose the false? Should they, urging the minds of their listeners into error, ardently exhort them, moving them by speech so that they terrify, sadden and exhilarate them, while the defenders of truth are

> sluggish, cold and somnolent? Who is so foolish as to think this to be wisdom [*Quis ita desipiat, ut hoc sapiat*]? (ibid.,IV, ii)

Augustine does not provide us with any kernel of rhetorical rules (cf. ibid., IV, i), for such rules can be learned outside the Church. Rather, he is concerned with what in a more technical language is usually referred to as the ethical and hypocritical components of rhetorical devices; that is, those components that are connected to the ethos of the speaker and the nature of the performance (cf. ibid., IV, xxvii). By doing this Augustine points inadvertently to the core of the tension that inhabits the systems of ancient rhetoric; that is, the asymmetrical relationship between the propositional and compositional features of discourses and their metasyntactic (and in a way metasemantic) features: to be righteous, to act rightly. But even if it is possible to see eloquence as some sort of antidote, subject to the specific demands of doctrine teaching, it should never be forgotten that, precisely as the wise do not need interpretation (for they already know what to do with it) so the general horizon of Augustine's *De doctrina christiana* is the disappearing of doctrine itself: the coming of the reign of pure and right practice means the end of theology, the end of a logos of (and on) God:

> since infants are not taught to speak except by learning the expressions of speakers, why can men not be made eloquent, not by teaching them rules of eloquence, but by having them read and hear the expressions of the eloquent and imitate them in so far as they are able to follow them? Have we not seen examples of this being done? For we know many men ignorant of the rules of eloquence who are more eloquent than many who have learned them; but we know of no one who is eloquent without having read or heard the disputations and sayings of the eloquent. For boys do not need the art of grammar which teaches correct speech if they have the opportunity to grow up and live among men who speak correctly. (ibid., IV, iii)

VI

In what is perhaps the central chapter of *Truth and Method*, Gadamer argues that "we have the task of redefining the hermeneutics of the human sciences in terms of legal and theological hermeneutics" (1960; p. 277). This aim entails two different theoretical maneuvers: the formulation of a concept that expresses the terms of the redefinition (or, in simpler words, the perceived similarity between the two families of hermeneutics) and the suggestion of the eventlike structure of hermeneutic experience. The first maneuver consists primarily in the rehabilitation of the concept of *subtilitas applicandi* and focuses both on the notions of *applicatio* and *subtilitas*. Referring to J. J. Rambach's *Institutiones hermeneuticae sacrae* (1723) and to the distinction between *subtilitas intelligendi* (understanding), *subtilitas explicandi* (interpretation), and *subtilitas applicandi* (application), Gadamer remarks that "it is notable that all three are called subtilitas, i.e. they are not considered so much methods that we have at our disposal as a talent that requires particular finesse of mind [*Feinheit des Geistes*]" (ibid., p. 274). The very notion of *subtilitas* is seen then both as an alternative to that of method and a practical virtue comparable to tact or phronesis. However, the nature of application prevents Gadamer's use of pietist hermeneutics from being a mere revival of a somewhat pre-Kantian theory of knowledge as, from his point of view, there is a natural heterology between the three classical *subtilitates* that turns application into an all-encompassing feature of interpretation: "understanding *always* involves something like the application of the text to be understood to the present situation of the interpreter" (ibid., my emphasis). And this means "that the text, whether law or gospel, if it is to be understood properly, that is, according to the claim it makes, must be understood at every moment, in every particular situation, in a new and different way" (ibid., p. 275).

As I remarked earlier, there are instances in which *application* is used by Gadamer in a less festive manner; namely, when application is seen as the ability *not to apply* something. There seems to be, therefore, a consistent and important tension in Gadamer's arguments: a tension between the "more" of the application (to apply is to produce more and renewed answers to an ever-changing question) and the "less" of the application (to apply is to be able to refrain from producing more and renewed answers). This double use of *application* is not necessarily aporetic when considered by itself. However, it signals the full burden of the redefinition of hermeneutics that Gadamer tries to undertake, because in the possibility of a double usage of *application* is entailed the conception of a subordination of what Gadamer calls the text to the realm of justice in general: the positional value of the "less" of the application in fact can be determined only within a metalinguistic code; in Gadamer's case, this is a code of practical virtues. Which is to say that there is a somber literality in the kind of law to be applied or tactfully suspended in the redefined hermeneutics of the human sciences; a principle that governs the very use of language.

The second theoretical maneuver mentioned previously stems from this point, because the radical historicity of interpretation subsumed under the dominance of a principle of application makes of each and every instance a case that can be evaluated only in the name of a legislative principle that by definition transcends any outcome of deliberation, as it belongs by definition to another realm. The notion of `event', therefore, apparently an effusive sign of the "more" of application, denotes again, for Gadamer, a theoretical exception taken to the principle of deliberation by the principle ex machina of pertinence:

> understanding is not so much a method by means of which the enquiring mind approaches some selected object and turns it into objective knowledge, as something of which a prior condition is its being situated within a process of tradition. Understanding itself proved to be an event [*Verstehen erwies sich selber als ein Geschehen*], and the task of hermeneutics, seen philosophically, consists in asking what kind of understanding, what kind of science it is, that is itself changed by historical change. (ibid., p. 276)

In this usually taken-for-granted denunciation of the charms of inference, however, Gadamer departs deeply from Aristotle, for whom, in the domain of ethics and to use J. L. Austin's expression, the foot of the letter remained the foot of the ladder, in that, as we have seen, a literal injustice was usually preferable to poetic justice. As Gadamer will also put it: "Seen from the point of view of the interpreter, `event' means that he does not, as a knower, seek his object, `discovering' by methodological means what was meant and what the situation really was" [*mit methodischen Mitteln 'herausbekommt', was eigentlich gemeint ist und wie es eigentlich war*] (ibid., p. 419). On the basis of this distinction lies an opposition between a methodologically regulated ideal of deliberation, for which deliberation, so to speak, is made systematic, and what Derrida once called the conception of the *non-iteration of an event* (1972; p. 192). But because one *does* have an opposition here—all conceptualization of the systemacity of an event can emanate only from a principle of fairness toward events, in which a future is therefore necessarily prefigured. For Gadamer, such is the function of the concept of 'tradition': "the actual event is made possible only because the word that has come down to us as tradition and to which we are to listen really encounters us and does so in such a way that it addresses us and is concerned with us" (1960, p. 419).

Things are further complicated, however, because, in Gadamer's own terms, "the word that has come to us as tradition" is already a sediment of past contingencies. That every interpretation has to confront the prefiguration of its own demise, not just in its own "moreness" or in the restricting aspects connected to tact, but also in the very structure of determinacy of application, points perhaps to the important sense in which Gadamer's conception of interpretation cannot but remain essentially the conception of a negative task. In fact, the structure of addressing described by Gadamer is not just the irresistible appeal of the logos of contemporary hermeneutics' more aestheticized versions. Such versions derive in part, perhaps, from Gadamer's own occasional emphasis on descriptions of postures of satisfied interpreters. For example, "when we understand a text, what is meaningful in it charms us just as the beautiful charms us [*so nimmt das Sinnvolle desselben genau so ein, wie das Schöne für sich einnimmt*]" (ibid., p. 446). But, on the other hand, the very structure of addressing includes situations of resistance to such an aestheticizable appeal. And even if Gadamer does not say too much about it, there is the intermittent argument that application is a remedy for practical insufficiencies, even as interpretation arises from what could be called the counterpart of a pathogenic symptom (and thus *contains*—but in both senses of the word—the circumstantial ambiguities that gave rise to the symptom in the first place).

As to a first meaning of *contains* (which I have been following through its relationship toward an ethics), Gadamer remarks, after Schleiermacher, that "interpretation is necessary where the meaning of the text cannot be immediately understood. It is necessary wherever one is not prepared to trust what a phenomenon immediately presents to us" (ibid., p.301). Consequently, application is a moment of transcendence of immediacy, which is to say, it is based on a principle that inevitably describes a state of beyond distrust, in this instance under the shape of a refusal of manifestation. Application, one would like to say, translates a version of things-as-they-are into another, and the criterion of translation once the practical realm of *justice* (indeed *justice* and *justesse*) has been recognized and accepted as decisive is a principle of things-as-they-ought-to-be. Of course, one is not very far here from what is meant by Paul Ricoeur's expression *"hermeneutics of suspicion*", even if there is a decisive difference: Gadamer is suggesting (and it is highly instructive to understand it against his theory of dialogue, for instance) that in the beginning any act of understanding *is* a form of suspicion; that is, that, in Aristotle's terms, deliberation arises as a negating gesture. One is reminded once more of Saint Augustine's idea that the wise know how to act and can live "in solitudine sine codicibus". It is then as if all giving of reasons (*explicare*) would contaminate all sketching of ends (*applicare*): the universality of application denotes such a contamination while at the same time it contains (still in this first sense) the groundlessness of its very movement of transcendence.

But there is a second sense, far remote from the ethical one, in which interpretation, in Gadamer's conception, can be said to contain what one would call its necessary ambivalence toward tradition: the sense in which interpretation produces a genealogy of tradition itself, a version of the perishableness of the factors of its own engendering, which becomes inevitably a version of the theme of the unreliability of its own terms, not so much because every tradition is a memento mori as because every tradition is both that *and* the sum of all available discourses. And, as Heidegger remarked, this is the necessary ambivalence of every structure of overcoming, determined in fact by the necessarily "transitional" nature of all interpretation (in a sense similar to that which makes application necessary in the first place): no interpretation can duplicate its conditions of possibility (albeit all interpretations, in some way, tend to imply a rhetoricization of such an impossibility). And, as Heidegger writes, "it is of the essence of such traditions that they are, within certain limits, compelled to speak the language of that which they help to overcome" (1943, pp. 380-381). Moreover, for Heidegger, interpretation seems to be precisely the name of the mode and the movement of such a coalescence of heterogeneity. Therefore, the description of the theme of the overcoming of metaphysics, in a later essay by Heidegger, is also the description of the necessarily ambiguous structure of all overcoming:

> Suppose one attempts to make a transition from the representation of beings as such to recalling the truth of Being: such an attempt, which starts from this representation, must still represent, in a certain sense, the truth of Being, too; and any such representation must of necessity be heterogeneous and ultimately, insofar as it is a representation, inadequate for that which is to

> be thought. This relation, which comes out of metaphysics and tries to enter into the involvement of the truth of Being in human nature, is called understanding. (1949, p. 216)

VII

I began this chapter with an enigma, followed by an excursus. The first, I wrote, was irrelevant. The second, I suppose, is ironic, not so much in my use of it as in its being an excursus without a *cursus* proper. However, whereas the former irrelevancy ideally will be forgotten, the latter irony is deeply connected to the nature of my problems. Be that as it may, the excursus suggested that it is impossible for a *tekhnè* to remain fully technical. In the course of the subsequent sections I have tried to characterize the form of the problem allegorized by the *Poetics'* excursus. And so I was led to remark (albeit rather intermittently) that, just as it is impossible for the conception of a *tekhnè* to remain fully technical, so disturbances of the same form tend to arise in nontechnical conceptions. The form of this particular problem has proved to be one of the dominant concerns of literary studies in the last two decades and is implied perhaps even in the works of earlier authors (such as Kenneth Burke). There is a sense, however, in which the form of the problem I have glossed up to this point is *not* the one identified by Paul de Man when he wrote that there is "a fundamental difference in the level of expliciteness" that prevents "[contradictory] statements from meeting on a common level of discourse" (1971, pp. 102-103). Such is the sense in which the form of the problem is, again in Paul de Man's words, that "the difficulty of reading...exists...as a constitutive obstacle to literary understanding" (1972, p. 282).

That such a difficulty is *constitutive* should be apparent from several functions that theories of understanding perform. Nevertheless, I shall discuss only implicitly (in Chapters 2 and 5) the disturbing possibility of this very notion of theory's having been derived from the set of conditions that defines the model of understanding in the first place. The best known of those functions is, perhaps, the way in which theories tend to deal with the termination of argument. And because such a termination is invariably "made necessary", the necessary termination of argument acquires perhaps the status of a figure of theory (there is a rigorous sense in which one can think of a repertoire of theoretical figures, of figures of interpretation). In the previous sections I have dealt at some length with problems and theories of the termination of argument in general and, of course, that shall be one of my main purposes in the chapters that follow. In fact, as I shall try to show mainly in Chapters 3 and 4, it is not only in theories that belong to Gadamer's family that law is the law of reading, even as it is not only in things hermeneutic that law is the law of understanding. The difference between some of those theories and Gadamer's tradition, however (and that is why the latter lends itself so admirably to the purposes of an introductory chapter), is that Gadamer's tradition (in which I would loosely include Aristotle and Augustine) is the most venerable (albeit by no means the only) example of a second function of theory: the structural thinking of the paralysis of theory itself. There is a complicated sense in which my own efforts belong to such a family, and it is complicated because they do so more that I am willing to admit. For example, the notions of an appeal to the author (including such disputed accessories as the status of authorial intention, the notion of biography, and so on) and an appeal to the text (entailing the vexed questions of objectivity, philological respect, and so on) are nevertheless basically understood as being articulated themselves on what is assumed (but not theorized, generally) to be a moment of end of argument and a wish for the end of controversy—even if there is an embarrassing tension between the interminability of argument and the fixedness of its purposes. In that, they both presuppose theories of proof and theories and rules of argument: a full, albeit often very raw, doctrine of explanation. That literary criticism and literary studies in general were able to thrive in the last two centuries on such meager premises attests, I think, to the sense in which they too tend to move excursively as if that movement would be a matter of course.

To be sure, theories of interpretation tend to perform other functions, even if in a less conspicuous way. Among these, I can think of the function of the engendering of the argument. Such is the all-important role of what one could call the figure that makes argument necessary in the first place, not so much in the better known forms of the apology for discussion and debate as in the immanent justification of argument itself. For a long time this has been the allegedly Mallarméan problem of the birth of writing, which has brought us so many unforgettable depictions of critics and white sheets of paper. But, again, that I am describing a function and not a theme is shown by a completely different thematization of the same function. Allow me, then, another allegory, one that picks up the very problem of the excursus on the *Poetics*. In a polemical exchange with Ronald

Dworkin about the role of interpretation in law (and literature), Stanley Fish remarked that "similarity, in short, is not a property of texts (similarities do not announce themselves), but a property conferred by a relational argument in which the statement *A* is like *B* is a characterization (one open to challenge) of *both A* and *B*" (1982, pp. 557-558). In the preceding passage, Stanley Fish tried to formulate something we could call a tropological definition of the notion of 'precedent': a precedent is a sort of *manner of argument*. When arguments create or presuppose (*establish* is a current term used in the first case, whereas *fact* is probably the favorite term for the second) an interchangeability of units, that is, the possibility of replacement of a unit by another, the terminus of the replacement is said to be its precedent.

However, even if there is a sense in which similarities have to be argued, as Fish says (the sense in which *homoin theorein* is an explanation, but also the sense in which it is an *arguable* explanation), their being the product of argument itself introduces another sense in which similarities are *precisely* what cannot be argued: once the argument is accepted that (for certain purposes) "*A* is like *B*," the act of acceptance excludes the arguability (at least for the time being) of that replacement or, in other words, "establishes a fact" and its *subsequent* arguability. There remains, however, the question of what had to be established already for a fact to be established. As Fish again remarks, "to see a present-day case as similar to a chain of earlier ones is to reconceive that chain by finding it in an applicability that has not always been apparent" (ibid., p. 558). Fish's allegation is that juridical and interpretive arguments are engendered by "reconceptions" and that, as he adds a little later, such reconceptions are propelled by a will to "render manageable the issues raised by the present" (ibid.). The important thing for our problem here, however, is not so much the truth or falsity of Fish's allegation as it is the function such an allegation accomplishes within Fish's own theory; and such is the function of reconciling the impossibility of arguing beyond an acceptance with the necessity of arguing toward such an impossibility, that is, the function of redescribing the birth of argument.

Recourse to juridical distinctions in past and current theories of understanding has usually carried the covert prescriptive claim that interpretations ought to do justice to the complexities of hermeneutic problems. The situation is not unlike the way in which the application of the law always tended to reflect the problems of mediation between the given complexity of a case and the theoretical simplicity of the rule. Gadamer and Fish are two examples of such a concern. On the other hand, the recent interest that Critical Legal Studies has taken in issues traditionally linked to theories of interpretation has had the somewhat circuitous uncanniness that often goes with most fields, which consists in a keen interest for the production of a field's own image as reflected by the other fields. When dealing with Gadamer's theory earlier, I remarked that the exemplary nature of the legal hermeneutics for his theory lay on what one could call a *prosopopeization of normativity*; that is, in the ascription of human qualities to the laws and constraints of interpretation. And I believe the same could be said of Fish's theory. It is particularly difficult to think against such a prosopopeization, and I am not in the least interested in such a heroic task.

However, another sense is created by the sudden familiarity that developed between the two fields, which I think is independent of any commitment to the general truth of prosopopeia: the sense in which an interpretation appears to be a form of *use* of a law; that is, the sense in which every reading has to negotiate its own constraints. My use of the word *negotiation*, however, tries to avoid partly the pleasures of prosopopeia: instead of a well-known description of the architectonics of the subject that a *substantive* conception of the limits determines (I hit against, therefore I am), I concentrate on a rather dismal function of time-management, of the negotiation of the historic contingencies of an utterance that determines what each and every reading shall make of its law. Negotiation as I see it is perhaps here the opposite of a belief in the sublimity of metalanguage, as metalanguage itself is the belief in a science of the naturalness of a state of forces and the legality of the law or, to use an expression of Heidegger, a belief in the "will to will" of meaning. In my version, therefore, consummate negotiation becomes the freezing of a state of forces, somewhat of a fossil (to use a distinction from J.L. Austin, it is as if perlocution would strive to be locution). Locution, that is, literal meaning, seems thus to be the end there, not the beginning.

That an interpretation has constraints has become a trifling matter and usually an excuse for the acceptance of such constraints. But the thinking of the paralysis of interpretation need not necessarily be modeled on the image of the valiant Kantian reader's hitting against the opaqueness of the limits. Rather, there seems to be a whole rhetoric of the use of the limits of interpretation. When Gadamer speaks of tact, when Augustine speaks of fear, or when Stanley Fish speaks of rendering issues "manageable", they are in fact, without any irritable reaching after fact and reason, employing notions that in their respective doctrines are used to avoid the very conception of hitting against the limits of an interpretation. Such notions I call manners of interpretation.

2

The Constitution of the Reading Subject

I

Despite some evidence to the contrary, critics and readers have not always been human. In the *Lyceum* fragments, Friedrich Schlegel writes: "A critic is a reader who ruminates. Thus, he should have more than one stomach [*mehr als einen Magen haben*]" (1797b, Section 27). The situation is familiar to all readers of Nietzsche (who shared the same view and used a similar description of it). In this chapter, however, I shall not concentrate on the principle of rumination but rather on digestive transits. Critical theories from Schlegel on seem to be singularly indebted to a suggestion he expresses periphrastically in the preceding quote: "*mehr als ein*," more than one. In fact, the supposition that reading is a transit carries as a consequence the belief that it presupposes at least *two* domains. The problem, however, is that the straightforwardness of my last sentence carries as a consequence the belief that such is not the case. The undertaking of a chapter on interpretive transits seems in this respect to reawaken an awkward question that shall be intermittently evoked throughout my arguments: the question of whether a theory of reading is not primarily the restatement of rights of exemption, to be claimed by such a theory in relation to reading.

II

In Schlegel's collection of fragments *Zur Philologie*, the cause of reading occupies a strong, albeit not prominent, place. If the physiological description of the quote I began with is not particularly orthodox, the etiological explanations here are far removed from the current version of interest that prevails among opinions about culture: instead of the complete rhetoric of enrichment that modeled its predicates, perhaps, on the virtues of the *Bildungsroman* we find a somewhat less heroic stance: "One reads only out of boredom [*Langerweile*] or out of philology" (1797a, Section 83). And if behind the first situation, which Schlegel does not analyze, one can easily see lurking all kinds of explanatory devices that in some way or another can be brought back to the notion of compensation, the philological impulse to read (the theme of *Zur Philologie*, if there is one) cannot be so easily subsumed under one of the more current instances of causality. As a matter of fact, the satisfaction of a philological drive ("Lesen heisst den philologischen Trieb befriedigen," ibid., II, Section 82) seems to be more the case of an unnecessary digestion, in the ordinary sense of unnecessary. In Novalis's 1798 *Monolog*, one can see a perhaps more vivid instance of such a unnecessity, applied to the notions of speaking and writing:

> Speaking and writing is a crazy state of affairs really [*eigentlich...eine närrische Sache*]; true conversation is just a game with words. It is amazing, the absurd error people make of imagining they are speaking for the sake of things; no one knows the essential thing about language, that it is concerned only with itself [*dass sie sich bloss um sich selbst bekümmert*]. That is why it is such a marvellous and fruitful mystery—for if someone merely speaks for the sake of speaking [*dass wenn einer bloss spricht, um zu sprechen*], he utters the most splendid, original truths. But if he wants to talk about something definite, the whims of language make him say the most ridiculous false stuff. Hence the hatred that so many serious people have for language. (1798b, p. 93)

Schlegel's theory of philology can be understood only if one bears in mind the particular status that the cause for something like a philological drive has for him: philology is seen as the *cause* of reading.

At this point, we meet a problem whose form was very clearly inherited from Kant, in the sense that it presents an explanation that requires some sort of transcendental deduction. Moreover, Schlegel's occasional description of the philological work and his distinction between desirable and undesirable possibilities of philology denote the outline of a project that would lead eventually to such a deduction: "The *Literate* [*Litterator*] has to do with *Authors*, as the Antiquary with antiquities and the Philologist and Critic with *things classical* [*Klassicis*]; he works for the public as the Philologist and Critic work for the one who has knowledge [Kenner] and the Antiquary for the amateur [*Liebhaber*]" (1797a, II, Section 157). As a matter of fact, whereas the realm of the antiquary is the realm of those who can judge only because they love and the realm of the literate is the mere common public, the philologist deals with knowledge and, indeed, in the embryonic classification of tasks Schlegel portrays, he produces knowledge: he does not address the eminently immediate concerns of the public (that is, he does not conform his decisions to a public verdict, so to speak) nor does he produce reasons for the affection of the *Liebhaber* (his work in that case being decided upon a principle of taste). Indeed, one could see in the preceding quotation a particularly pervasive rereading of the partition between science, exegesis, and aesthetics, which locates philology within the realm of science. In passages like these, then, Schlegel's project appears a purely epistemological one that shapes itself as an inquiry on the possibility of cognitively valid philological judgments excluding all consideration of audience (and hence all empirical pressure) and all consideration of effect (that is, of the domain of aesthetic judgment). To use Jauss's terminology (perhaps through what in a Joycean mood one would call a commodious vice of recirculation), Schlegel's project would seem to be comparable here to a desire for a theory of literature independent not only from *Rezeption* (let alone from the empirical study of reception) but also from *Wirkung*. Or, in other terms, if the transcendental justification of philology is to be possible, for Schlegel such a justification is necessarily a matter of knowledge, as if no causes were conceivable outside that realm.

The point that follows (and that I shall follow intermittently from now on, trying to show how it inscribes a major disturbance in what is known as the subsequent evolution of hermeneutic thought) was made by Kant himself. In texts such as *Der Streit der Fakultäten*, the conflict Kant refers to, although being primarily allegorized as a dispute between the different colleges of a university, can also be seen precisely as a conflict between the pretensions of reason, which the "lower faculty" (that is, philosophy) embodies, and the necessarily nonrational approach of activities such as theology, law, and medicine. Later we shall see that the exegetic procedures the first two employ point to a hermeneutics independent from reason. But first it is perhaps important to see why, for Kant, such activities are unjustifiable: "the biblical theologian (as a member of a higher faculty) draws his teachings not from reason but from the *Bible*; the professor of law gets his, nor from natural law, but from the *law of the land*; and the professor of medicine does not draw his *method of therapy as practiced on the public* from the physiology of the human body but from *medical regulations*" (1798, p. 35). The common ground among the three higher faculties derives then from their being dependent on what Gadamer (interested of course in an altogether different hermeneutics) would call a principle of application. Such activities are related to the purveyance of interpretations or therapies, but they are so primarily in the more general sense of their having necessarily to presuppose a higher authority or, as Kant puts it, "teachings that proceed from an act of choice on the part of an authority (that do not issue directly from reason)" (ibid., p. 33). And the status of writing, in his own terms, is precisely that of allowing for the conveying of a relation of power, from which reason is independent:

> All three higher faculties base the teachings which the government entrusts to them on *writings*, as is necessary for a people governed by learning, since otherwise there would be no fixed and universally accessible norm for their guidance. [*Alle drei obere Fakultäten gründen die ihnen von der Regierung anvertraute Lehren auf Schrift, welches im Zustande eines durch Gelehrsamkeit geleiteten Volks auch nicht anders sein kann, weil ohne diese es keine beständige, fur jedermann zugängliche Norm, darnach es sich richten könnte, geben würde.*] (Ibid.)

Reason appears, then, to have here the shape of a critique of power. And because the latter is a matter of writings, the former becomes necessarily a (very literal) matter of textual criticism and, indeed, the supposition of a moment where it would be possible to deal with a text from the outside of hermeneutics. The conflict of the faculties is thus (as we shall see later in detail) *never* a conflict of different opinions but rather a conflict between interpretation and a denial of interpretation made in the name of practical reason:

> scriptural erudition in Christianity is subject to many difficulties in the art of exegesis, and the higher faculty (of biblical theologians) is bound to come into conflict with the lower faculty over it and its principle. For the higher faculty, being concerned primarily for theoretical biblical knowledge, suspects the lower faculty of philosophizing away [*wegzuphilosophieren*] all the teachings that must be considered real revelation and so taken literally, and of ascribing to them whatever sense suits it. On the

> other hand, the lower faculty, looking more to the practical—that is, more to religion than to dogma—accuses the higher of so concentrating on the means, dogma, that it completely loses sight of the final end, inner religion, which must be moral and based on reason. And so, when the conflict arises about the sense of a scriptural text, philosophy—that is, the lower faculty, which has truth as its end—claims the prerogative of deciding its meaning. (Ibid., p. 65)

But the denial of exegesis in the name of practical reason also does away with the protagonizings of power in texts; that is, with the mediating terms that are used by biblical exegesis in its task of theoretical justification, such as authorial intention and, indeed, literal meaning. Contrary to hermeneutics that, as Paul de Man said, "is always intentional, to the extent that it is a description of technical devices which exist independently of the meaning at which they aim, and are not determined by the intentional gesture in any sense" (1985, p. 94), the empire of practical reason, one would like to say, presupposes necessarily a scheme of allegoresis. And in such a presupposition is washed down the function of a meaning-granting moment. The interpreter who (pragmatically) decides in favor of a principle of textual indoctrination over textual authenticity is, in Kant's words, "free, in his exegesis, to ascribe to the text (philosophically) the meaning it admits of for morally practical purposes (the pupil's edification); for faith in a merely historical proposition is, in itself, dead" (1798, p. 121).

The possibility of a theory of reading derived exclusively from reason (and thus the formation of a class of rational readers distinct from amateurs), in Kant's sense, coincides then with the justification of what he call *doctrinale Auslegung* (ibid., p. 122), as distinct from an *autentische Auslegung* such as the one carried by sacred hermeneutics. The process of justification involved two distinct moments: in the first moment it is shown that sacred hermeneutics can never be theoretical because it is derived from the contingencies of the transmission of power and even concepts such as 'intention' are nothing but individual moments of ascription of power. In the second moment, however, it is shown that a hermeneutics can never have a practical interest as long as its principles do not derive from reason:

> Hence, *doctrinal* interpretation—which does not seek to know (empirically) what meaning the sacred author may have con-

> nected to his words but rather what teaching reason can ascribe (a priori), for the sake of morality, to a biblical text it is presented with—is the only way of handling the Gospels to instruct the people in true, inner and universal religion, which must be distinguished from particular church dogma, as a matter of historical belief. (Ibid., p. 123)

In this way Kant finally demonstrates that the only possible theory of interpretation is a theory of the denial not only of the authority of the text, but indeed of authority *in* interpretation. Such a denial is ascribed, of course, on the behalf of reason, to philosophical discourse.

The main reason the form of the problem Schlegel inherited is important here is that it is not going to be the *only* form of the solution, at all. As a matter of fact, Schlegel can conceive of no antinomy, in Kant's sense, in the relation between the form of reading and the shape of its cause (and hence of no conflict between authentic and doctrinal interpretation), because from the very beginning reading is conceived precisely as a transit, that is, as the *formalization of a shape*. Schlegel is quite aware of the fact that the problem seems to be rather that of the promiscuity of possibility and actuality, of one's not being able to distinguish the manifestation of reading from its conditions of possibility.

In this light it becomes more understandable why a problem that emerged as a problem in Kantian terms is going to be the object of the solution that Schlegel characterizes as the "deduction of the *cyclical* method" (1797a, II, Section 65). But choosing such a solution carries additional consequences: the abandonment of the question of the possibility of reading that, from now on, is going to be taken for granted, and the exclusive focus on the phenomenality of the reading. In this alternative solution, then, the form of philology is considered to be nothing more than the form of reading: "But what is then really reading? Obviously something *philological*" (1797a, II, Section 74).

As a direct consequence of this, one of Schlegel's main theoretical problems is going to be precisely the problem of formulating the concept of a causal relation that nevertheless would presuppose a relation of mutual implication between its terms; that is, the phenomenal process of reading *and* the (philological) form of its very possibility.

The problem, as I suggested earlier, is going to be solved with the help of an adjective—the adjective *cyklisch*: "All critical reading, all reading with respect to classicity...is *cyclical*" [*Alles kritische Lesen, alles Lesen mit Rücksicht auf Klassizität...ist cyklisch*] (ibid., II, Section 73).

Cyclicality is seen by Schlegel as "a totalization upwards [*wie eine Totalisazion von unten herauf*]" (ibid., II, Section 84). And this very movement translates within Schlegel's theory not just the way of reading, but also its end, or rather the intricate fashion in which the way of reading *is* its end. It is not just a matter of being holistic: as Novalis wrote (but Schlegel could have written it), "A whole which is made up of miserable parts is a miserable whole itself—or rather, it is not a whole at all" (1798a, p. 94). The very *direction* of totalization is implied in Schlegel's version of cyclicality. In the terms of our first digestive metaphor, there is never confusion between the syntactical incidents of transit and the fact that there is a transit. And as a matter of fact, Fichte's version of it is dismissed as being "ein Herabsteigen" (Schlegel, 1797a, II, Section 84), that is, a transit in the wrong sense or with the wrong intention.

For Schlegel, the main distinction between right transits and wrong transits seems to lie in the ability of the former to maintain a "more than miserable" relation in its parts. And in a number of his writings this kind of relation is portrayed as being one of similarity, based on the supposition that the desirable and absent whole is the term of an operation of figuration.

In his *Gespräch über die Poesie*, or rather in the "Rede über die Mythologie," included there, one of the main important questions seems to be the question of the guessing and subsequently of the creation of a whole from available parts. The examples of existent mythologies provided in the text extend from ancient versions of the world to then current explanations (such as Physics). However, whereas in Schlegel's sense Physics, as the typical mythology of the Reason, does exist, there is not *yet* any available instance of a mythology either of Understanding or of Judgment. Indeed, the whole text can be read as some sort of messianic urging for the creation of a mythology that can render the writing of poetry possible *in dürftiger Zeit*: it should be understood within the context of a program of restoration of poetry. On the other hand, the fluctuations of Schlegel's formulation of the problem of philological method correspond here to fluctuations in the realm of such a mythology; namely, between reason and understanding. It can be said, however, that every time the solution seems to be on the side of a comprehension of the world (as, and so we shall see later, in the case of his essay "Über die Unverständlichkeit"), Schlegel asserts the primacy of understanding over reason.

The talk begins with a straightforward avowal: "We have no mythology. But, I add, we are close to obtaining one or, rather, it is time that we earnestly work together to create one" [*Wir haben keine Mythologie. Aber setze ich hinzu, wir sind nahe daran eine zu erhalten, oder vielmehr es wird Zeit, dass wir ernsthaft dazu mitwirken sollen, eine hervorzubringen*] (1800a, p. 81). Ludoviko, the character that delivers the talk, exposes a program that is indeed a program of an engendering (and *hervorzubringen* suggests perhaps that such an engendering is comparable to an act of utterance, as if all mythology would reproduce the biblical gesture of creation by the word). However, in other passages of the talk, the programmatic exposition appears to be connected to his being endowed with what one would call a preliminary sense of guessing: Ludoviko can foresee the coming of the whole, not really because he is a seer but simply because he is a reader. Referring to what he terms *der gross Witz der romantischen Poesie* he adds: "Indeed, this artfully ordered confusion, this charming [*reizende*] symmetry of contradictions, this wonderfully perennial alternation of enthusiasm and irony which lives even in the smallest parts of the whole [*in den kleinsten Gliedern des Ganzen*], seem to me to be an indirect mythology themselves [*scheinen mir schon selbst eine indirekte Mythologie zu sein*]" (ibid., p. 86). As a matter of fact, in this passage Ludoviko assimilates the messianic stance which I allude to the analysis of the signs of something both desirable and not yet present: not yet a mythology but rather the metonymy of a mythology; an indirect mythology. The ability to recognize a mythology is in this sense no more and no less than reading: the acknowledgment of the *possibility* of a text. On the other hand (but maybe it is still the same hand), there is the reference to the alternation of enthusiasm and irony as something "which lives even in the smallest parts of the whole." Such a qualification allows for the motivation of the use of the adjective *indirekte*, for only by postulating a structural homology between the part and the whole can the part be subsumed under the shape of the whole and then considered to be a mediated, indirect sign of the whole. Reading, for Ludoviko, then, because it derives from the ability to recognize parts qua parts, is the perfect instance of a process of semiotic mediation, in the sense of Schlegel's use of the adjective in *Zur Philologie*: "Die Interpretationskunst kann sich nur an *semiotischen* Werken in wollem Lichte zeigen" (1797, I, Section 139). And cyclicality, in this sense, would simply be the property of reading that accounts for its semiotic character.

The preceding passage of the *Gespräch* illustrates not only the semiotic aspects of reading but its alternating movement as well: in this respect it seems, moreover, to be structured around a series of figures of alternation that are built on a double polarity. In some instances, such a polarity is represented oxymoronically, such as in *künstlich geordnete Verwirrung* and *reizende Symmetrie von Widersprüchen*. But in a third case (*ewige Wechsel von Enthusiasmus und Ironie*) we find a reversible never-ending alternation. It is, perhaps, important to realize the consequences of this kind of figuration not only for Schlegel's notion of mythology, but also for the underlying concept of being able to recognize an absent mythology when you read one.

It would be over-hasty to believe that Schlegel's notion of a mythology represents any sort of theoretical rehabilitation of a primeval chaos. Indeed, "the new mythology...must be forged from the deepest depths of the spirit; it must be the most artful of all works of art [*das künstlichste aller Kunstwerke sein*], for it must encompass all the others" (1800a, p. 82). The term Chaos, rather, is always used as the sign of the possibility of a parallel language, that is, a synonym of an "effect of order": "indeed, the highest order is yet only that of chaos" (ibid.).

However, contrary to other mythologies of reason, Schlegel's poetical mythology points to the very possibility of a discourse independent of the laws of propositional connection: "For it is the beginning of all poetry, to cancel [*aufzuheben*] the progression and laws of rationally thinking reason [*vernünftig denkenden Vernunft*], and to transplant us once again into the beautiful confusion of imagination [*schöne Verwirrung der Fantasie*], into the original chaos of human nature..." (ibid., p. 86). What changes, then, between different families of mythologies, is a relation toward chaos. The notion of a mythology for poetry in Schlegel could be thought as corresponding to a structure of discourses that would not cancel the movement of chaos while retaining the drive toward a system of complete descriptions. Such a double movement is very typical of the expressions I quoted previously: it is a question of the possibility of an "artfully ordered confusion" (ibid.), of a "charming [*reizende*, also irritating, provoking] symmetry of contradictions" (ibid.). In the first case methodized chaos is emphasized, to paraphrase Pope. But in the second case the method is the object of a "chaotization", the limits of which (defining an aporetics) being made unstable and arousing a sort of a chain reaction: the symmetry of contradictions (fearful symmetry indeed) *provokes*. It is easy to see that in a universe where contradictions can move, no antinomies of reason are possible (and hence no dialectics in Kant's sense is possible).

In the third example of mythology given in the passage ("wonderfully perennial alternation of enthusiasm and irony," ibid.), the emphasis through alternation is the object of an important qualification: the journey of contradiction becomes, so to speak, perpetual (*ewige Wechsel*). Moreover, it indicates perhaps that the nature of the alternation between enthusiasm and irony is one of modalities of presence of the subject, the former being an instance of absolute self-presence (to the point that, as if by some process of inflation, the subject would occupy all possible room) and the latter being an example of a no less absolute self-estrangement, of what, in "Über die Unverständlichkeit," Schlegel called a "nicht wieder aus der Ironie herauskommen können," a one's not being able to "disentangle oneself from irony anymore" (1800b, p. 37).

And it is significant, perhaps, that in this latter essay we find restated the importance of chaos as one of the basic ingredients of the world, again never the *sole* ingredient but always oxymoronically connected to the order of discourse: "And isn't this entire, unending world constructed by the understanding out of incomprehensibility or chaos?" [*Und ist sie selbst, diese unendliche Welt, nicht durch den Verstand aus der Unverständlichkeit oder der Chaos gebildet*?] (ibid., p.38). Irony, as the figuration of *Unverständlichkeit*, becomes not really a counterunderstanding but a counderstanding and, indeed, the dark side of Kantian *Verstand*. And although the realm of understanding can be said to coincide with some sort of categorizing enthusiasm of the subject (which as a matter of fact would be a wonderful description of some aspects of the Kantian project), the realm of *Unverständlichkeit* can be assimilated to the reverse of being *entheos*, that is, possessed by a god, especially when "irony runs wild and can't be controlled any longer" (ibid., p. 37). But then again it cannot be said that Schlegel goes out on the limb of irony, for what is considered wonderful is always the perpetual motion and *not* the specific contents of its polarities, that is, not is thematizations: we are facing a "*wonderfully perennial alternation* of enthusiasm and irony [*wunderbare ewige Wechsel* von Enthusiasmus und Ironie]" (1800a, p. 86, my emphasis). Even the last part of the catalogue of ironies in "Über die Unverständlichkeit," dedicated to what Schlegel calls the irony of irony, and where one would expect a predominance of the thematizing aspect, is typically built around attributes of movement and instability:

> the most fundamental irony of irony probably is that even it becomes tiresome if we are always being confronted with it. *But what we want this irony to mean in the first place is something that happens in more ways than one.* For example, if *one speaks of irony without using it,* as I have just done; if one speaks of irony ironically *without in the process being aware of having fallen into a far more noticeable irony; if one can't disentangle oneself from irony anymore,* as seems to be happening in this essay on incomprehensibility. (1800, p. 37, my emphasis)

Schlegel's methodological problem of philology is going, then, to be the problem of finding the equivalent of a method to deal with moving objects and, as he remarks in *Zur Philologie,* "The contents and the affinities between the cyclical method and philology lie in the word *enkuklopaidia*" (1797a, II, Section 59).

A method that would derive from such premises, an "encyclopaedic method" (ibid., II, Section 200), would have to solve two major problems. The first is Schlegel's problem and is a rhetorical one: what discourse would be available to micrological remarks constantly striving for the whole? Schlegel's answer is clear: not a fragmentary one, but rather a rhapsodic one (ibid., II, Section 202). Rhapsody becomes the major genre for circularity in that it emphasizes a connection between disparate elements (the connection that derives from their similar intentionality) that the fragment can render only problematic. But the allusion to rhapsody is perhaps also an allusion to Plato's only (and much derided) interpreter. Ion is precisely the character whose only ability is that of delivering what Socrates considers to be non-sense in a connected way: a rhapsodist.

The second problem will be inherited by Schleiermacher after 1805, at least, but Schlegel seems to foresee its major features: "In an *Encyclopaedia*...the method shouldn't be exclusively analytic or synthetic" (ibid., II, Section 200). That is, the features of the seeing of something as a sign of a whole do not fit into Kant's already traditional distinction between the analytic and the synthetic. Those features, nevertheless, do not preclude in any way an aiming at the whole: "The tendency to the systematic lies already in the concept of the rhapsodical" (ibid., II, Section 203).

A possible story, stemming from here, could very well describe another chapter of what Georges Poulet once called the metamorphoses of the circle considering indeed Hegel's ambivalent attitude toward the significance of its predicates, that lead him into considering both that "the circle is still just a curved line of little interest"

(1842, p. 139) and that "the circle is the simplest, firmly enclosed, intelligibly determinate, and most regular line" (ibid., p. 668). But, independent from such fluctuations, the adoption of a circular model by Schlegel has to do precisely with what Hegel (in a precisely opposite way) called the question of the very determination of the shape. The circle, as a matter of fact, for Schlegel, is the form that allegorizes the endless determinability (and hence the endless task) of philology: "The end of philology does not quite lend itself to be determined. It is determinable within the endless" [*Der Zweck der Philologie lässt sich gar nicht bestimmen. Er ist ins Unendliche bestimmbar*] (1797a, I, Section 135).

The endless end of philology (and one of the reasons of my translating *Zweck* as "end" instead of the more widely accepted Kantian "purpose" has to do with this) reflects the historical condition of philology, rather than its lack of pragmatic value. The reason why, for Schlegel, a self-identical philology, which would make its ends and its purposes coincide, is unthinkable has to do exclusively with historical reasons: "The perfect, absolute philology would cease to be philology. *It would annihilate itself* [*Sie annihilirt sich selbst*]. The principles of philology are totally borrowed [*entlehnt*], *historical*" (ibid, I, Section 158). But once again, and despite his obliviousness to the Kantian question of the conflict of faculties, Schlegel seems to envisage the becoming of philology as the becoming of a philology of reason (that is, philosophy) as opposed to a hermeneutic philology of the understanding, even though the origin of its principles (that is, their very morality) is supposed to be contained in history (and in this sense not given by reason). But the reasons why for Schlegel there can be no perfect philology are indeed analogous to the reasons why, for Kant,

> [The] conflict [of the faculties] can never end, and it is the philosophical faculty that must always be prepared to keep it going. For there must always be statutory precepts of the government regarding teachings to be set forth in public....But because all the government's statutes proceed from men, or they are at least sanctioned by them, there is always the danger that they may be erroneous or unsuitable....Consequently, the philosophy's faculty can never lay aside its arms in face of the danger that threatens the truth entrusted to its protection, because the higher faculties will never give up their desire to rule. (1798, p. 55)

In both cases, the critical discourse seems to be characterized by an impossibility to detain itself, to project an end for its task. and such an impossibility goes once more against the "merely terrestrial and natural vocation of understanding" [*bloss irdische oder Naturbestimmung des Verstandes*] (ibid., p. 129)

However, whereas Kant's contingency (historicity, one would like to say) of human decisions is the main presupposition for the necessity of an activity emancipated from them (and, consequently, from hermeneutics), the historical substratum of Schlegel's concept of philology, by being responsible for its intrinsic heteronomic status, is the reason for the methodological and terminological impurity of philology itself. In a way, whereas for Kant the fluctuations of history make necessary the point of view of reason, for Schlegel, the exclusive emphasis on such fluctuations prevents a priori the adoption of privileges of extraterritoriality (although what actually takes place is quite different, as we shall see later briefly). And thus the desire to deal with moving objects implies the abandonment of the question of the possibility of the objects' motion and becomes indeed the condition of the impossibility of autonomous disciplines, where methodological distinctions distinctions such as 'empirical', 'transcendental', 'analytic', and 'synthetic' simply do not apply or apply only in a blurred way.

Philology thus appears to be, in the core of its epistemological concerns, and from the moment of its constitution as a single discipline, a project of unification of the disciplines and interests that its very historical substratum requires, permanently divided between the pressures of its inner epistemological impurity (that lead it to constitute itself as a summa of heterogeneous areas of investigation) and the pressure of the self-identity of its epistemological status.

However, Schlegel's description of this precise state of instability is made possible only by his adoption of a general term for instability's general rule, which is, as it might be expected, fully Kantian: "philological, historical, philosophical criticism [*Kritik*]. The same can also be said of both *grammar* and *hermeneutics*" (1797a, I, Section 154). Schlegel's description brings us once more, then, to Kant's departmental organization of the faculty of philosophy, where philology is, indeed, included. In this respect philology would partake of the philosophical ability to "lay claim to any teaching, in order to test its truth" (1798, p. 45). But this latter claim is a claim of reason. In a good sense, then, philology can remain a general endless critical activity only as long as it sees itself as a demystification of power, and thus as an antihermeneutics. For Schlegel's project this means that the refusal to adopt a principle of extraterritoriality and therefore of restricting to the actual historical movement of objects engenders, as it were, a perverse side effect, reason itself. In Kant's terms:

> the businessmen of the three higher faculties [*Geschäftsleute der drei oberen Fakultäten*] will always be...miracle-workers [*Wundermänner*], unless the philosophy faculty is allowed to counteract them publicly—not in order to overthrow their teachings but only to deny the magic power [*magischen Kraft*] that the public superstitiously attributes to these teachings and the rites connected with them—as if, by passively surrendering themselves to such skillful guides [*kunstreiche Führer*], the people would be excused from any activity of their own and led, in ease and comfort, to achieve the ends they desire. (Ibid., p. 51)

Not only in the sociological, but also in the conceptual, sense was philology from the beginning, to use Novalis's expression, a *Kind der Armut*, a "child of poverty" (1798a, p. 95), the offspring of a lower faculty. However, as opposed to what Heidegger once called (1947, p. 119) "die Armut [eines]...vorläufigen Wesens, " the poverty of a preliminary essence, the possibility of its becoming hermeneutics is indistinguishable from its development. And that *is* the possibility of its becoming theology, law, and even medicine; that is, an activity that recognizes the undisputable authority of prior writings. The disinterested rational friendship for the logos cannot be fully separated here from an applicational hermeneutic infatuation with language.

III

"One who has lost his philosophical innocence," wrote Schleiermacher around 1809, "must for the most common cases rely on philological science" (2a, p. 77). And indeed, and from its very inception, Schleiermacher's project is remarkably deprived of innocence. Losing one's philological innocence, as in most illustrations of the concept from Rousseau on, consists in outgrowing a primitive state of language awareness. Such a primitive state corresponds to the possibility of an immediate perception of language through language: "Grasping the character of a language by means of the reflection of the totality of thinking in that language [*aus der Auflösung des ganzen Denkens in die Sprach*] is possible only in cases of primitive peoples living close to nature. Others can do it only by comparing several languages" (ibid.). Before this chapter ends I shall have the opportunity to return very often to the peculiar shape of philological science for Schleiermacher and, of course, to his idea of hermeneutic method. But, first, I would like to consider the somewhat less popular problem of the deduction of a method, in this case Schleiermacher's method (forgetting for the time being the evolution of Schleiermacher's hermeneutic thought, emphasized first by Heinz Kimmerle).

The immediate perception of language is a phenomenon that, for Schleiermacher, characterizes a state of philological innocence. Without getting into etymological debate, one could say that such an innocence is always read as a lack of knowledge. Primitive peoples simply do not know what language is, either because the order of knowledge corresponds to the abandonment of all consolations of immediacy (and then, in Schleiermacher's terms, innocence cannot even be philological) or simply because the immediate perception of language suggests the existence of a reliable metavocabulary. Schleiermacher's project stems precisely from this point, or as Kimmerle once put it, he "was driven to the consequence of eliminating immediate understanding, because he wanted to solve the problem of understanding as such" (1962, p. 112). Debatable as the formulation might be, the solution to the problem of "understanding as such" consists for Schleiermacher in a tortuous gloss on the belief that in the beginning there was already something there and, of course, that that something was, if not *the*, at least *a*, word: "Language is the only presupposition in hermeneutics [*Alles vorauszusezende in der Hermeneutik ist nur Sprache*], and everything that is to be found, including the other objective and subjective presuppositions, must be discovered in language [*muss aus der Sprache gefunden werden*]" (1, Section 55). The last presupposition (*aus*) is particularly important here, because it explicitly denies to philology any exteriority vis-à-vis language. Then again, if language is to be "the only presupposition" of the kind of science Schleiermacher is interested in, there is a homology of substance between the principle of philology and the aim of philology. Discovery, for philology, in this sense, and given the preceding homology, is always rediscovery (like construction will always be reconstruction), or at least the result of a methodological immersion in *the very stuff the process of discovery is made of*. The problem is, once again, a problem of vocabulary, and curiously enough, to return again to Schleiermacher anthropological allegory, the loss of philological innocence or the removal from nature signifies, in this respect, the loss of a vantage point, that is, the theoretical acknowledgment of the impossibility of making language the object of a *differently located* language.

Such a question is closely tied to a problem most commentators of Schleiermacher ignore; namely, his critique of the proposition that scientific language is essentially literal:

> There also arises a pretension that scientific expressions should be "exact" [*eine Pretension auf eigentliche Ausdrükke für die Wissenschaft*], but this pretention can never be fulfilled. There are always terms that are commonly called "figurative" [*bildlich*], and even when that does not seem to be so, it is only because the terms are no longer grasped genetically. This is an "ossification" [*Absterben*] and therefore a ruination [*Verderb*] of language, and the only possible remedy for it rests with what science is able to see by constantly renewing itself from the very center of its intuition and with the rejuvenated and living terminology created by this renewal. —If philosophy is the center of all science and if philosophy itself is based on intuitions of a higher order, then one can see the hegemony of the concept is only a point of transition for language [*die Herrschaft des Begriffs nur ein Durchgangspunkt für die Sprache ist*]. The notion that the true perfection of language is reached when it becomes figurative [*Die Ansicht dass das tropisch werden die wahre Vollkommenheit der Sprache ist*] goes together with the notion that the concept is the highest element in science. (2a, pp. 73-74)

In this amazing passage, literalness (that is, the idea of, say, a reliable vocabulary for perception) is dismissed as a mere pretension of science. More than such a dismissal, what interests us here are the grounds for it: as a matter of fact, and in passages such as this one, history, figured under the species of genetic investigation, is the way of proving that there was no original vocabulary or rather that, because everything was always language, there was no traceable beginning. This points to the very particular status of history within Schleiermacher's theories (and indeed to the outline of its destiny: the fulfilling of the role of dismissed metavocabularies in the sense that the grounding of a general metaphorics is always a very *literal* project). But it is most important to remark here that the genetic explanation of language used in this strategy is diametrically opposed to etymology: genetic arguments concerning language are, for Schleiermacher, the privileged way of proving that what was thought to be an origin is really just a moment in a never-ending process of *translatio verborum*, just an "ossified" term.

The whole passage seems to be organized around an opposition between terms like *Absterben* and *Verderb*, on the one hand, and expressions like "wieder neue und lebendige Terminologien", on the other. And contrary to what may appear, only within the realm of the first set of terms is the opposition between exact and figurative accepted. The rejuvenating process of science consists in showing that such an opposition is unfounded: and it is not by chance that the process, although enacted with the help of a strategy where oppositions play a major role, instead of organizing opposite fields, would strive to bring together concept and figure (and hence science and poetry) without granting the primacy to any one of them. One of the more disturbing consequences of the passage is indeed the suggestion of a proportionality, as it were, between the status of concept for science ("only a point of transition for language") and the status of figure for poetry.

Moreover, the process is never described as an agonistic process of antinomical reasoning but rather, and once more, as a process of therapeutic reimmersion, of contact with a source. The renewal of science, for Schleiermacher, consists in replacing the notion that there is a nonperishable vocabulary with the notion that there is a nonperishable center. And history is not instrumental here in the sense that it helps to locate an indisputable origin, that is, words that can be used to talk exactly about words, but rather in the sense that it constitutes itself as *the* therapeutical narrative of epistemic rejuvenating.

The idea that exactness is a moment (and a rather late one, too) in the history of a vocabulary, can be connected to Schleiermacher's other thesis that there is no vantage point over language once the subject is removed from what he calls *nature,* leading into the assumption that words have in this sense no "primitive" state ("The first usage of a word is not to be equated with its meaning," 1, Section 125). The resulting constellation will impregnate very deeply his conception of method. Indeed, it allows Schleiermacher to derive from it the suggestion of a general form of philological and hermeneutic arguments.

Discussing a slightly different question, Schleiermacher remarks: "The understanding [*jedes Verstehen*] of a given statement [*Rede*] is always based on something prior [*gründet sich auf etwas früheres*], of two sorts—a preliminary knowledge of human beings, a preliminary knowledge of the subject matter. (Note: In the case of a text, either by a study of the author or by a study of the subject matter.)" (ibid., Section 120). In this passage we find reiterated, in a different context, the core of Schleiermacher's main objections against both etymology and a privileged metalanguage, not so much in a particular thematization but rather in a movement: just as one can show (with the help of the history of language) that literal meaning is just an effect of lexicological amnesia, so Schleiermacher argues analogously that there can be no understanding without "something prior." And, indeed, the belief in hermeneutic immediacy (that Schlegel treated derogatorily as mystical interpretation) is a correlate of the belief in the self-evident nature of literality as revealed.

Whereas in "something prior" there are undeniably temporal overtones, which can be read indeed in a commonsensical way, to the point one could, instead of knowledge, use the word acquaintance, one must bear in mind nevertheless that constructions such as "jedes Verstehen" denote a concern with a form. And also that the example provided by Schleiermacher introduces another very important topic that would include the topos of the disparity in size and scale between what is to be understood and the prerequisites for understanding. As a matter of fact, the relation between the study of a text and the study of its author or of its "subject matter" is primarily the kind of metonymical relation we remarked on earlier as connected to Schlegel's emphasis on the ability of seeing something as a sign of something else; and, in the following aphorism, it is going to find its canonical formulation: "The understanding of the particular is always conditioned [*bedingt*] by an understanding of the whole" (ibid., Section 121). A few years later, Schleiermacher will make this same principle rise to the dignity of general epistemological prescription: "Complete knowledge always involves an apparent circle [*Ueberall ist das vollkommene Wissen in diesem scheinbaren Kreise*], that each part can be understood only out of the whole to which it belongs, and vice versa. All knowledge which is scientific must be constructed in this way" (3, p. 113).

In the earlier manuscript, however, the stress falls on the expressions of the whole, which is not entirely typical of Schleiermacher. In paragraph 122 we read: "In order to understand a given topic, one must start with what is written at the beginning where the special sphere is first identified from what is general" (1, Section 122). And, in paragraph 123, Schleiermacher summarizes, albeit restricting his epistemological concerns to the domain of history: "This is a general canon [*ein allgemeiner Kanon*] for pure historical study. —Indeed, it is a rule for understanding anything at all" (ibid., Section 123).

The methodological solution that Schleiermacher gave to this problem is famous, and perhaps a bit too often taken for granted. I am referring, of course, to the description of a mediation between the whole and its parts as compared to a circular shape. Moreover, it recalls to one's mind Schlegel's emphasis on cyclicality.

But what is maybe important to remark is that, whereas for Schlegel the so-called encyclopedic method began as an answer to the question of the movement of objects in their striving for a whole, in Schleiermacher circular metaphors have to do with something else: a description of the logical necessities involved in interpretation and, as we shall see later, a defense against problems of hermeneutic transit. Both authors, of course, confine themselves to the phenomenal aspect of interpretation (although, as we have seen, Schlegel's case deserves some additional qualification) and indeed portray the double-faced angel of phenomenality in a complementary way: Schlegel looks toward the development of possibilities, whereas Schleiermacher turns to the possibilities of development. That is perhaps why Schleiermacher's emphasis on the whole, which has led astray critics like E.D. Hirsch, is not really determinant. *Whole*, within his system, is a particularly misleading name for the moment in interpretation when necessity imposes itself. Indeed, it points to a description of the power of what is conceived to be a logical antecedent. Such a power, however, is rewritten under the more-or-less tacit assumption that there has to be a similarity between interpretation and its conditions of possibility, just as there is a similarity between language and the language of philology.

There is a very important connection, then, between the methodological definition of the task of hermeneutics (a method of transit between two points compared to a circle) and the more basic question of why it has to be a transit at all. Indeed, the arguments used to answer the second question (that is, 'because language *is* transit') are going to be inscribed in Schleiermacher's solution in a way that occasionally upsets the more methodological implications and indeed the applicability of the whole system: "So formulated, the task is infinite, because in a statement we want to trace the past and a future which stretches into infinity" [*Die Aufgabe ist so gestellt eine unendlich, weil es ein Unendliches der Vergangenheit und der Zukunft ist, was wir in dem Moment der Rede sehen wollen*] (3, p. 112). It would be too tempting to refamiliarize this last statement with the help of notions of infinity that would make it in a way an attribute (and a consolation) of temporality. However, as Schleiermacher's remarks on literality have suggested, it seems to be the very movement of seeing (either a past or a future) that is necessarily infinite; or rather, no perception of the infinity of the task of the interpreter is given a priori, and all glimpses at its endlessness (which, one should not forget, renders particularly awkward all kinds of pragmatic euphoria that go with methodological "attributable" results) are constituted within the very repetition of tracing. Once more, as in Schlegel, a text is what it is not (its past, its future); and then there is the ability to read both past and future. And finally, it contains the ability to see the outcome of reading as a momentary "ossification", which entails a doctrine of the historicity of literality.

Much later, in 1829, in his second address to the Prussian Academy of Sciences, Schleiermacher wrote: "The hermeneutical principle which Ast has proposed and in several respects developed quite extensively is that just as the whole is understood from the parts, so the parts can be understood only from the whole. This principle is of such consequence for hermeneutics and so incontestable that one cannot even begin to interpret without using it" (5, pp. 195-196). Passages like these raise two important additional problems that derive from Schleiermacher's method. The first is, of course, the problem of the organization of the fluxes of transit and, indeed, the coexistence within a single doctrine of two different discourses, each partaking of two different methods, a macrology and a micrology, and both conceived under a similar double methodological imperative. The second is the problem of what Schleiermacher called, in the same text, the presentiment of the whole [*Ahnung des Ganzen*] (ibid., p. 198). Given the qualitative difference between macrology and micrology, how does one learn to jump from one to the other? I shall now address these two problems in that order.

The double aspect of Schleiermacher's hermeneutics can be seen as a result of a general theoretical move made necessary by what one could call his deduction of the "transitory" nature of the task. Such a move consists in the determining of a methodological proportion: the proportion between analycity and syntheticity in interpretation. As a matter of fact, the peculiar status of historical explanation within his system cannot but shape a priori synthetic judgments as further analyzable entities. It might be equally helpful and misleading to try to see Schleiermacher's version of analysis as embodied in a micrology he terms grammatical interpretation; as to the version of synthesis, it fits the kind of macrology known as technical or psychological interpretation. But for the time being I shall retain both the analogy and the caveat.

Grammatical interpretation and technical interpretation correspond to different practical aptitudes of interpreters, and indeed, as

Peter Szondi pointed out, "Schleiermacher seems to view the relationship between the grammatical and technical interpretations as based on a division of labour" (1970, p. 106). The obvious problem is, of course, that the methodological proportion I have alluded to previously can never be seen as a properly theoretical question, but has to be seen instead as a problem of balancing practical aptitudes (rather than, say, investigating the question of their possibility). As a matter of fact, and within a theory of interpretation that purports to be an account of the latter's phenomenality, all methodological terms are in a good sense ethical terms (empirical, insufficiently theoretical terms), descriptions of practical abilities of interpreters inferred from their experiences. This is why Schleiermacher never alludes to a difference of faculties and prefers the expression "difference in talents".

Referring precisely to the "difference in talents" of interpreters, Schleiermacher writes:

> Linguistically-oriented interpreters try to comprehend a work by grasping how it is related to similar works of the same type. They focus on the forms of composition which arise from the nature of the language and of the common life which develops and is bound together with language.... The other [the "technical"] interpreters, however, want to determine from a composition what kind of person the author is. To do this they identify themselves as much as possible with the moments of creativity and conception which break into the fabric of the author's everyday life like higher inspirations. They seek a vivid insight into every facet of the parts that may illuminate the process of creation, including the secondary thoughts which were of no consequence for the idea of the work, in order to evaluate properly how the whole process of composition is related to the author's existence or how the author's personality develops itself in representations. Of course, for such interpreters the relation to the language mentioned above recedes into the background. (5, p. 204).

In passages like this we find a distinction between "parts" of interpretation, as Schleiermacher calls them, dealt with in a purely empirical way; as a distinction of talents. Two families of interpreters are characterized, and the predicates used in such a characterization are distinctive activities and represent, indeed, distinctive cognitive interests: to "focus on the forms of composition" and to "determine from a composition what kind of person the author is." Later we shall see how these are also logical predicates, in which they convey a distinction between two kinds of inference. But before we proceed it is perhaps important to notice how *this* exact distinction (which one must never forget is a practical one) seems to embody the very destiny of literary studies.

In the next two chapters I shall be discussing the metamorphoses of both authors and texts as arguments in literary studies. But the discussion in a way shares the assumption that such argumentative usages are one-sided remnants of Schleiermacher's project, or rather of Schleiermacher's basic taxonomy of empirical interests (indeed, I shall suggest that they both derive from the same side of Schleiermacher's project, although they correspond to different interests). One major trait of Schleiermacher's approach, nevertheless, will be maintained. Even in the most farfetched biographical theories of the last two centuries we are very removed from Plutarch and even from La Bruyère in that, for instance, the argumentative use of the notion of 'author' seems to be connected to textual explanations and not primarily to moral exempla. But this connection is again a double one, for the Schleiermacher genealogy indicates, perhaps, that the refusal of a moral exemplary value to texts can build itself only on an interest that is in some devious way equally practical (albeit empirical). Even when the moment of priority (the *cause* of a text, so to speak) is presented under logical categories, presented as our concept and not as my intuition, the very obviousness of strategies of causation ("the words of a poem, as Professor Stoll has remarked, come out of a head, not out of hat," Wimsatt and Beardsley would write, 1946, p. 4) betrays, in its consensual basis, an empirical interest, without which, for instance, notions such as the one of "interpretive community" would not be thinkable. What I am trying to suggest, then, is that in distinctions such as Schleiermacher's we find the 200-year-old program, from Sainte-Beuve to Hillis Miller, of an ethics of reading (as opposed to Kant's notion that, by being an exercise of free will, the discourse of reading derives its principles from practical reason alone).

Schleiermacher's hermeneutics, however, allows us to go beyond the mere obviousness of the acknowledgment of different talents and provide discreet insights on the constitution of the practical abilities of the interpreter, even if, as I said previously, the latter is never seen as part of a faculty. In what is known as the "First Draft of 1809-10", he refers elusively to the importance of "forgetting the author in grammatical interpretation and the language in technical" (2a, p. 68) and thus correlates the building of practical abilities to an essential forgetfulness. For one to be able to "focus on the forms of composition" one has to forget that there is an author, which suggests that the analycity we mentioned is made empirical by what one might call a suppression of syntheticity a interest. But even in the later texts Schleiermacher reiterates the point: "Grammatical interpretation: The person and his activity disappear and seem to be merely an organ of the language. Technical interpretation: The language and its determining power [*bestimmenden Kraft*] disappear and seem to be merely an organ of the person" (4, p. 161). That is to say that the possibility of either part of the project of hermeneutics is grounded on the refusal of the other part and, moreover, takes the form of an exclusive possession by it, as if the horizon of grammar would exclude all technical concerns and vice versa.

Before we go to this phenomenon, which a contemporary philosopher did not call the conflict of interpretations, it might be worthwhile to remark that Schleiermacher tries to sketch some criteria of pertinence for both parts of interpretation, that is, and because the latter derive from practical abilities, tries to imagine situations that require either a grammatical or a technical approach. At times, the criteria seem to be genre-oriented ones:

> A statement may be of maximum significance for one side of interpretation or the other. It is maximally significant for the grammatical side when it is linguistically creative [*produktiv*] to an exceptional degree and minimally repetitive [*wiederholend*]: classical texts. A statement is maximally significant for the psychological side when it is highly individualized [*eigenthümlich*] and minimally commonplace [*gemein*]: original texts. (3, p. 102)

On other occasions, however, the choice of the approach seems to be self-evident: "there is no technical interpretation for myth because it cannot be traced back to a single person" (ibid., p. 106). Finally, there are situations where the conflict of both methods is not dialectically relevant; namely, the case of "works of genius [*das Genialische*]" where "a maximum of both linguistic creativity and individuality" (ibid., p. 103) is achieved.

For us to probe a little deeper into the conflictuality of grammatical interpretation and technical interpretation, it will be necessary to mention another aspect of Schleiermacher's negative characterization of both. In his early aphorisms he writes "Just as the first side [grammatical interpretation] is the reverse of grammar, so the second side [technical interpretation] is the reverse of composition" [*Wie die erste Seite umgekehrte Grammatik so diese umgekehrte Composition*] (1, Section 135). Grammatical interpretation (or philology, e.g. 2a, p. 69) is here compared to a regulated system that nevertheless can only be a posteriori (that is, nongenerative). As to technical interpretation, it is said to resemble a composition post factum. Whereas the reverse of the former consists in a system of rules, the reverse of the latter consists in the very invention of a system. And Schleiermacher makes clear that the point is that both parts of interpretation are opposed because their reverses are mutually exclusive; that is, the negative of philology negates the negative of psychology. The efforts of the process of mediation described with the use of circular metaphors can be said to be identical, then, to the efforts to promote a system of contiguities between grammar and rhetoric. The fact incidentally suggests that Schleiermacher's conception of a grammar sees the latter under the species of syntax, just as his conception of rhetoric consists in an expanded portrayal of the virtues of *inuentio*. Rhetoric means thus *two* things here: the effective power of hermeneutics (what Wittgenstein, and not Schleiermacher, would term the attraction of certain kinds of explanation, 1966, p. 24) and an art of production, that, as we shall see later, will also have its fair share of problems with grammar. In what concerns the first meaning of rhetoric, there is a conflict between what one could call the two poles of the double status of rhetoric—its being a technique of construction of discourse on the probable *and* its being a technique of rendering acceptable the specific modality of its discourse; namely, by presenting the probable as necessary. To simplify, one could say that such a conflict is a conflict between a double attraction: the attraction of dialectics and grammar and the attraction of hermeneutics.

In this conflict one can find a particularly neat recurrence of Kant's idea that the fight against the rhetorical power of exegesis is certainly not a mere hermeneutic disagreement, but another example of the conflict of the faculties, instanced by the impossibility of a full hermeneutic reduction of rhetoric and fueled by a desire for the full grammaticization (and dialecticalization) of hermeneutics. But if such a dispute would ever reproduce in its procedures the rhetorical force of hemeneutics, one would have what Kant calls an illegality of form, in that at least one of the parties would rely "not on objective grounds directed to his adversary's reason [*auf die Vernunft des Gegners gerichtet*], but on subjective grounds, trying to determine his judgment through his *inclinations* [*Neigung*] and so to gain his assent by fraud (including bribery) of force [*Gewalt*] (threats)" (1798, p. 47).

On the other hand, a science of sentences deprived of contingency (grammar) would prove here to be philosophy's main ally in its conflict with the other faculties:

> since arbitrary propositions, though sanctioned by the supreme authority [*höchsten Orts*], may not always harmonize with the teachings reason maintains as necessary, there will be a conflict between the higher and lower faculties which is, first, *inevitable* [*unvermeidlich*], but second *legal* [*gesetzmässig*] as well; for the lower faculty has not only the title but also the duty, if not to state the *whole* truth in public, at least to see *everything* put forward in public as a principle is true. (Ibid., p. 53)

Schleiermacher's efforts to promote a system of continguities between grammar and rhetoric partake, nevertheless, of the methodological belief that there is a symmetry between a hermeneutization of rhetoric and a grammatization of hermeneutics and are consequently prone to conceptual incidents. Such incidents are possibly due to his treating the conflict as either a conflict of powers or a conflict of *equal* faculties: in the "Compendium of 1819," Schleiermacher starts from a conception of hermeneutics as a summa of all arts of reception of speech, whereas grammar and rhetoric are considered to be the (indistinct) elements of a *tekhnè poietikè*. And "since the art of speaking and the art of understanding stand in relation to each other, speaking being only the outer side of thinking [*die äussere Seite des Denkens*], hermeneutics is a part of the art of thinking, and it is therefore philosophical" (3, p. 97). The general model, thus, in this first moment, points to a dominance of dialectics (which is the discipline that is able to grant philosophical status to hermeneutics). However, for dialectics to be conceivable in this way, the oppositions between both the subingredients of hermeneutics and the subingredients of an art of production have to be neutralized. As a matter of fact, no general art of thinking could survive as a product of the harmony of sets of arts which in their turn would be in conflict: that is to say that no conception of dialectics could accept non dialectical procedures (such as possession or forgetting) as a way of organizing the inner balance of its ingredients.

And although the circle would seem to perform the role of unifying mutually exclusive activities, the fact is that in Schleiermacher's terminology the process of unification reflects the same non dialectical procedures it tries to replace; namely, possession and forgetfulness. It is quite evident in Schleiermacher's terminology that both the arts of reception and the arts of production (especially the latter) are going to be methodologically identified with only *one* of their ingredients:

> Speaking is the medium for the communality of thought [*Gemeinschaftlichkeit des Denkens*], and for this reason rhetoric and hermeneutics belong together and both are related to dialectics.... Hermeneutics and rhetoric are intimately related in that every act of understanding is the reverse side of an act of speaking [*die Umkehrung eines Aktes des Redens*], and one must grasp the thinking that underlies a given statement....Dialectics relies on hermeneutics and rhetoric because the development of all knowledge depends on both speaking and understanding. (Ibid.)

In passages such as this, rhetoric becomes clearly the epitome of all arts of production, with the obvious elimination of grammar (as if the hermeneutization of rhetoric we remarked on previously would carry, on a second level, a rhetoricization of grammar). One should ask whether the direction of this elimination does not render understandable the much-debated evolution of Schleiermacher's thought, in that it would tend to emphasize increasingly technical interpretation over grammatical interpretation. There is, furthermore, a likely connection between this switching *and* the assumption of a principle of indifference between language and thought ("A person thinks by means of speaking. Thinking matures by means of internal speech, and to that extent speaking is the only developed thought [*gewordene Gedanke*]", ibid.), as if the rise of the concept of thought would be paralleled by both a rise of rhetoric and a fall of grammar. However, the resultant rhetoric is not a general rhetoric anymore, in the sense that such a project managed to survive perhaps up to Fontanier. The reason is because it works here primarily only as a theory of the creation of idiosyncratic systems of rules and never, for instance, as a theory of *dispositio*.

The very concept of hermeneutics, as the model of a general art of reception, is going to be profoundly affected by the disappearing of grammar from the realm of the arts of production. I remarked earlier that one of the consequences of the latter would have been the decline of grammatical interpretation. But it might be said that the principle of indifference between language and thought does not promote any corresponding conceptual consequence and indeed undermines the ideal partition between the field of subjectivity and the field of objectivity by reducing the latter to the status of consequence of the former, thus identifying what in 1805 Schleiermacher termed the "objective side" of interpretation with technical interpretation. The question is not so much that of the collapsing of internal distinctions between the domains of hermeneutics: in a 1828 note to the passage I am discussing, Schleiermacher still maintained that "general hermeneutics is related to criticism as well as to grammar. And since there can be no communication or even acquisition of knowledge without all three, and since all correct thinking is based on correct speaking, all three are related to dialectics" (ibid.). Rather, the question is that of the image of a hermeneutics whose exclusive methodological reverse would be rhetoric, or at least rhetoric and a rhetoricized grammar. The correlative of a rhetoric of *inuentio* cannot but be a hermeneutics of creation. And if it is perhaps true that the parallel traditions of philology and *Geistesgeschichte* seem to derive from Schleiermacher's general project of a double hermeneutics (and that for a long time critical discussion in literary studies would mean belonging to either of the two domains), it is also true that, implicitly conceived as the reverse of rhetoric, philology would always tend to remain confined to the domain of affectivity. It is not surprising, then, that the kind of appeal to the text we are going to be dealing with in Chapter 4 achieved a different kind of literality only after the emergence of a science of unrhetoricized grammar, that is, linguistics. And, even then, considerations of effects and affects would emerge periodically, as in the case of versions of stylistics that derived very obviously from linguistics (such as Bally's).

IV

The conflict between the two parts of hermeneutics that we find in Schleiermacher has, also, some specific methodological implications, in which it presents itself as a conflict between two models of inference. Peter Szondi (1975) traces such a conflict back to the dispute, in patristic hermeneutics, between the Alexandrian school and the school of Antioch and sees the two poles around which it is organized as two methodologically opposed ways of dealing with the temporal distance between the text as perceived by the interpreter and the text that the text perceived by the interpreter has to suppose. Both sides of the dispute (the allegorical side and the grammatical side) can be said to diverge on their conception of the methodological process of deriving an absent meaning from an allegedly present text. A moment of disturbance in Szondi's story however, could very well come from Kant's fight against literality *in the name of a first language* (the discourse of philosophy), through his reasserting that the only way of escaping the realm of interpretation is by the adoption of a principle of allegoresis that allows the reader to see in every text whatever is fit for purposes of edification; that is, only one thing, the maxims of practical reason. But then again, in this sense, the Kantian episode, by emphasizing the priority of "doctrinal" over "authentic" interpretation would not really belong to hermeneutics. Indeed, it is a good instance of a dispute that belongs to reading without belonging to hermeneutics, and hence an instance of the difference between the two.

Schleiermacher's hermeneutics is, up to a certain point, the heir to the conflict between the grammatical side and the allegorical side of interpretation, but with an important qualification: it tries to incorporate both traditions and, indeed, within the realm of his theory, one of the main methodological problems is going to become the problem of reconciling two kinds of inference. In Szondi's terms, these two kinds of inference are, as I have said previously, first and foremost, means of dealing with temporality. In a way, every operation of derivation cannot avoid seeing itself as the account of a contiguity, and in this sense a typology of inference is, up to a certain point, a typology of possible consequences, possible relations toward a past, propositional or otherwise. To borrow from Szondi's terminology, we can perhaps consider, then, a kind of inference that promotes "the abolition of the historical distance between text and reader" (ibid., p. 24) and a kind of inference that "sublates [*aufhebt*] the distance in the concept of prefiguration, in the difference between promise and fulfillment" (ibid., pp. 23-24).

Curiously enough, the main feature of Schleiermacher's enterprise of methodological unification consists, albeit acknowledging the inescapability of what he calls a twofold method, in relocating the duplicity of the method within each part of his hermeneutics. Grammatical interpretation thus ceases to be the exclusive realm of presentificational inferential devices, whereas technical interpretation is never considered the exclusive field of the allegorical revelation of what Dilthey would later call "life expressions".

Moreover, the circulation between grammatical and technical interpretation prevents Schleiermacher from ascribing to either one any exclusive method. As he puts it in "A Loose Page from 1810-11,"

> Twofold method. Immediate intuition and comparison. Each must aid the other. Comparison alone never reaches individuality [*Vergleichung allein kommt nie zur Individualität selbst*]. Immediate intuition can never be communicated [*Anschauung kommt nie zur Mittheilung*]. The two are mediated by a comparison with the totality of the linguistic sphere [*Totalität des Sprachgebietes*]. (2b, p. 93)

The fragment can be better understood in relation to what in the same document Schleiermacher calls the two tasks of hermeneutics: "determining the linguistic sphere of the author" (ibid., p. 92) and "determining the distinctive use of language from the linguistic sphere" (ibid.). The former corresponds to the task of grammatical interpretation and the latter to the task of technical interpretation. But even if one has to start by being a philologist, and thus, by comparison, the terms of such a comparison are not given a priori and have to be the object of an "immediate intuition." Conversely, the intuition of the individual that grounds, so to speak, technical interpretation, the intuition of the uniqueness of a usage, in order to be communicated (and thus made eventually the object of comparisons that in their turn would be the core of *geistesgeschichtliche* activities) has to be "mediated by a comparison with the totality of the linguistic sphere." We find here perhaps a somewhat devious gloss of the Kantian theme of the relationship between intuition and concept, not only because of the communicability of data is made possible by comparison, but especially because, if we like, such a dialectics is put into motion and rewritten by Schleiermacher as a phenomenology of interpretation.

In the "Second Address," Schleiermacher will make clear how the twofoldness of the method is a matter of duplicity of inferential procedures and indeed how both comparative and intuitive procedures are forms of inference. Philologists "try to comprehend a work by grasping how it is related to similar works of the same type" (5, p. 204) whereas "the other interpreters...want to determine from a composition what kind of person the author is...[and] they identify themselves as much as possible with the moments of creativity and conception" (ibid.). Indeed, comparison seems to be primarily a form of inductive reference and as such it does not offer any major theoretical problem (although, as we have seen, the intuition of the comparable is a different story). But intuition (which perhaps presents at this point closer ties to its allegorical past) is literally a form of deriving something from something *else*, that is, a form of inference in which the laws of propositional connection are momentarily broken. Where the syntax of propositions is broken, we see a very general principle of tropology that grants a priori that things like texts are replacements of things like authors. The question then would be that of knowing whether or not a principle of tropology can be a strict matter of propositional inference, as the moment of replacement is indeed the moment where a chain of propositions is necessarily seen as an illusion. The question resembles very much Novalis's reading of Kant's question of the possibility of a priori synthetic judgments: "Kant's question 'Are *a priori* synthetic judgments possible?' can be expressed in many specific ways. For instance:...Is there an art of discovery without data [*eine Erfindungskunst ohne Data*], an absolute art of discovery?" (1799, Section 98). In a very strict sense, all judgments about an individual that conveys knowledge is, for Schleiermacher, the product of a moment of identification, and thus the very energy of identification replaces the propositional mediation: a desire to become one with the author, indeed to become the total structure, is, in Schleiermacher's hermeneutics, the synonym of a desire for true knowledge. And even though it can bring consequences *from* (in the etymological sense of *inferring*), when it is seen with the glasses of the Concept, it resembles the bringing-from of something ex nihilo. It is perhaps not by chance that Novalis, in the same passage of the *Brouillon* we just quoted, mentions, as another equivalent for Kant's question (and thus for the problem of discovering without data), the problem of whether or not magic is possible.

V

This last expression could be read as a tongue-in-cheek (and Millean) description of Dilthey's project. But it is clear that one of Dilthey's dominating concerns in the methodology of the *Geisteswissenschaften* is going to be the fusion of Schleiermacher's double method in a single mode of inference that can accommodate the event of intuition with the historicity of the concept. Such an enterprise would, of course, reformulate the traditional partition of inference between induction and deduction, and it is perhaps important that we turn to it now.

There is a curious homology between the methodological solutions Dilthey gave to the problem of understanding, namely, in his revision of theories of inference, and his being, in Patrick Gardiner's words, "an impossible stylist" (1959, p. 212). Moreover, it is perhaps more than a simple coincidence that a comparable revision was sketched around the same time by an equally impossible stylist: Charles Sanders Peirce.[2]

In an essay published only after his death, belonging to the outline for the completion of the *Aufbau der Geschichtlichen Welt,* Dilthey's revision is made to derive from what he calls "the natural limits of the logical treatment of the understanding": "in every understanding, there is something irrational, as life itself is irrational; something is incapable of being fully represented by a logical formula. So a final, though wholly subjective certainty...cannot be established by any examination of the logical validity of the reasoning by which the process of understanding can be presented" (1927, p. 223). Such a point has a history and a posterity, which Gadamer summarizes as "the claim to truth of all formal argument" (1960, p. 309). Gadamer's point, apparent in his reading of Plato's *Seventh Letter* is, of course, that "there is no argumentatively adequate criterion to distinguish truly between philosophical and sophistic discourse" (ibid.); that is, "the formal refutability of a proposition does not necessarily exclude its being true" (ibid.). Whereas for Gadamer this is the basic and the only metatheoretical assumption that allows him to deal with the value of the conjunction in the title of his 1960 book, that is, to suppose that one has to decide between "truth" and "method" in favor of the former, for Dilthey such an assumption, albeit less refined, engages him in an intramethodological debate that would eventually lead him into a revision of a traditionally accepted doctrine of inference.

The quest for a method for hermeneutics, the *science* of philology, as he calls it, within Dilthey's arguments, has, then, the ambivalent status of the quest for a formal method that would incorporate a principle of independence from the laws of logical validity. However, seen from a purely practical point of view, such a method also appears to be the justification of the three main tasks of the interpreter; namely, the projection [*Hineinversetzen*], the reproduction [*Nachbilden*], and the reliving [*Nacherleben*] in the striving to "discover a life-complex in the given" (1927, p. 220). In this particular situation,

Dilthey's problem is strikingly akin to Freud's, inasmuch as the previously mentioned justification would require the elaboration of schemata of validity ruling over a process Dilthey terms "the transference of the self into a given complex of life-expressions" (ibid.). The tasks of projection derive from a principle of anagnoresis ("The soul travels along the accustomed paths by which in earlier, similar situations it suffered and loved, desired and achieved," ibid.). As to the *Nachbilden*, it is dependent on the principle of the "enactability" of past events ("To relive is to create in the same direction as the original events" [*Nacherleben ist das Schaffen in der Linie des Geschehens*], ibid.). And, finally, the process of reliving derives from the teleological ability of seeing data as stimuli, which is to say, from the interpreter's ability to be properly stimulated: "Every lively visualization of a milieu *or* an external situation stimulates a reliving process in us, while fantasy can strengthen or weaken the emphasis of the forces, feelings and aspirations which are contained in our own life-complexes and so allow us to reproduce the mental life of others" (ibid., p. 221).

Although the basic epistemological problem Dilthey shares with Freud in this occurrence has to do with the status of posteriority of the scientific subject (apparent in the prefixes used in his designations for the three tasks of the interpreter), he does not have, unfortunately, the equivalent of the pragmatic criteria of validity Freud's metapsychology has; namely, a notion equivalent to the Freudian notion of "cure." Dilthey's interest in theories of inference can thus be seen as a replacement for the effectiveness of *Nachbildungen* in Freud's theory, and indeed, within an area of science that is primarily concerned with the rules of the epistemological debate, it is the only possible way to defend "the certainty of the understanding against historical skepticism and subjective will" (ibid., p. 223).

It is not so much the inevitable a-posteriority of explanation in hermeneutics as the not less inevitable a-posteriority of the relationship between hermeneutic facts and hermeneutic explanations that leads Dilthey into the conception, for which he is famous, of the hermeneutic methodology as a methodology opposed to that of what he calls the other "part of the science":

> If we see that there are laws and forms of thought for each part of the science, and that they are related methodologically through their perceptions of reality, then we must begin to see methods of investigation which are in no sense analogous to

> those of the natural sciences. These methods, however, rest on the relations between life expressions and the inner reality expressed by them. (Ibid.)

But since the problem now is only the problem of replacing life expressions [*Lebenäusserungen*] by what they do express, Dilthey's hermeneutics cannot but be the organon of an art of allegoresis confined, in Szondi's terms, which I have quoted, to the inevitable dialectics of promise and fulfillment that the concept of expression rewrites. Life expressions can then be said to be the allegory of an inner reality precisely inasmuch in them, as Szondi puts it, "the temporal incline is indeed preserved as the difference between promise and fulfillment while at the same time it is leveled in [a] preestablished harmony" (1975, p. 24) between expression and thing expressed.

Understandably enough for a system that tends to turn allegoresis into its dominant explanatory device (but that, at the same time, does so in a way precisely opposite to Kant's; that is, by refusing to acknowledge the transcendence of the maxims of practical reason), the role of what Schleiermacher called grammatical interpretation (and the kinds of inference that would simply abolish all temporal distance) is demoted here to the status of an auxiliary (or propaedeutic, at most) activity: "The first elements which separate themselves out of the mental process of understanding are the grammatical and historical preliminaries, which serve *only* to put the reader of a work from the past, a foreign country, or an unfamiliar language, into the position of a reader from the author's time and *milieu*" (1927, p. 224; first emphasis is my own). Grammatical interpretation acquires, then, the paradoxical dignity of both being below methodological consideration and dealing with the raw strangeness of the so-called life expressions. And the very attribution of the predicate of expressivity derives, indeed, from its familiarizing maneuvers. This is to say that the *Hineinversetzen*, and the *Nach-* of *Nachbilden* and *Nacherleben*, are made possible only insofar as there has been a moment of constitution of a text, a *Bildung*, an *Erlebnis*: and such a moment, revealed by grammar (still maintaining the function of organon of the lower faculty), is discreet enough not to upset the status of expression, but is, even so, inescapable.

Contrary to Schleiermacher, however, for whom the burden of comparison tended to be associated with grammar (although, as we saw, both comparison and intuition are part of his dual theory of hermeneutics), Dilthey's method and the kind of inference he has in mind are exclusively meant for the transit between life expressions and inner reality. In the terms of his doctrine of inference, this fact means that the synthesis of induction and guessing, which seemed to be the desideratum of Schleiermacher's circular adventures with mediational devices, is ruled out a priori.

Indeed, the inductive procedures of analogical reasoning could never work within a theory of expressivity, because such theories have to presuppose necessarily a hierarchy of levels (the meaning of the expression being the outcome of the expression of a meaning and 'becoming meaningful' meaning here something like 'becoming meaningful differentially'), and hence cannot operate within the strict contiguity of analogy. That is to say, analogy cannot deal with discovery (be it the discovery of the meaning of a life expression or otherwise). Dilthey remarks that "in such reasoning, there is always the tendency, since in any structure the various items are connected with one another, to draw conclusions from a particular series of cases so as to reinforce others" (ibid.). The problem then is that "when applied to new instances, reasoning by analogy becomes a sort of reasoning by induction": "The distinction between these two forms of reasoning, in the process of the understanding, has only a limited validity, and in general one has the right to use only a certain limited degree of expectation of the occurrence of the new case" (ibid.). Dilthey's methodological question will, then, become something like, How can a case possibly be recognized as a *new* case? And the methodological crux, consequently, would lie in the possibility of learning to recognize an unexpected occurrence, that is, an occurrence about which "the degree of expectation is one about which no general rules can be given" (ibid.). Put in these terms, the other traditional candidate in terms of traditional theories of inference, that is, deduction, is also ruled out, rendering Dilthey's methodological alternative simultaneously incompatible with induction *and* deduction.

Dilthey still calls his solution *induction* (ibid.). Such a procedure would consist in the a posteriori building of contexts of pertinence (that would therefore be correctable contexts), each one being, in his own words, "a structure, an ordered system...which gathers the separate instances into a unity" (ibid.). The correctability of such structures would derive, of course, from the sheer unexpectedness of new cases, in that each new case can potentially lead to modifications in the general structure of accepted explanations. But then, as Dilthey does not fail to notice, "induction of its sort is common to the human studies and to the natural sciences" (ibid.). And the embarrassing consequence is that Dilthey's methodology for the human sciences, triggered by a particular awareness of intrasystemic disturbances, leads to the abandonment of the central thesis of his epistemology; namely, the one about the difference of procedures, validation devices, and metavocabularies between *Natur-* and *Geisteswissenschaften*. The essay I have been quoting from ends on that precise note:

> Kepler discovered the elliptical orbit of Mars through such a process of induction. And *just as* he imposed a geometrical structure [*geometrische Anschauung*], which extracted a simple mathematical regularity from observations and calculations, *so* must any investigation of the process of understanding give individual words their sense, and give structure to the meaning of the individual components of the whole. (Ibid., p. 224, my emphases)

It is very important to recognize that, at this point, whereas it is probably due to the more or less devious virtues of the *individuum*, Dilthey's solution points to the precariousness of the notion of structure and, indeed, presents a version of the notion of 'whole' that is simultaneously independent from the empirical version that induction offers and from the other, undisturbed, version that presupposes unchallenged principles. The hermeneutic circle, here, portrays not the circularity, the transit, between two points but rather acknowledges that at least one of them is the effect of the very process of circularity, which has to be taken for granted only so long as it remains unthreatened by new events.

VI

In the last part of Schlegel's "Rede über die Mythologie," after urging the audience to study physics, "from whose dynamic paradoxes the most sacred revelations of nature are now bursting forth in all directions," Ludoviko concludes:

> And thus let us, by light and life, hesitate no longer, but accelerate, each according to his own mind, that great development to which we were called. Be worthy of the greatness of the age and the fog will vanish from your eyes; and there will be light before you. All thinking is a divining, but man is only now beginning

> to realize his divining power. What immense expansion will this power experience, and especially now! It seems to me that he who could *understand* the age—that is, those great principles of general rejuvenation and of eternal revolution—would be able to succeed in grasping the poles of mankind, to recognize and to now the activity of the first men as well as the nature of the Golden Age which is to come. Then the empty chatter would stop and man would become conscious of what he is: he would *understand* the earth and the sun.
>
> This is what I mean by a new mythology. (1800a, p. 88; my emphases)

Ludoviko's conclusion, as far as a new mythology is concerned, is that such a mythology should finally be a mythology of the understanding. And, indeed, it shows indirectly that in this sense, even physics is a mythology of the understanding (one is reminded perhaps of Lichtenberg's sarcastic expression "Die Mythen der Physiker"). The human destiny seems, then, to be exclusively connected to the acknowledgment that understanding is the end (and the purpose) of thinking, and hence to thinking's invariably reproducing a process that is said to be distinctive of understanding: divination (Kant uses somewhere the word "Instinkt" to cover the same area, along with not altogether pleasant references to its relation to "die dümmsten Tiere"). But then again, the means of thinking, in Schlegel's sense, cannot but be the *Vorstellungen* provided by understanding itself: in Kant's words, "Äusserungsarten, die bloss auf sinnliche Dinge sich beziehen können," "modes of expression which can refer only to sensible things" (1798, p. 129). Such a characterization points to two important factors. The first is the connection between the development of hermeneutics and the verbal displacement that converted Kantian *Verstand* into Dilthey's *Verstehen*, in the sense that Dilthey's theory of understanding (but the same would apply to Schleiermacher and, partly, to Schlegel), before anything else, is a theory of the *Verstand*. It would then be possible to consider Dilthey's professed critique of historical reason as being primarily a critique of historical understanding, that is, of historical representations. But the second factor, that I shall try to follow now, is the inscription, in the hermeneutic tradition, of the very boundaries of *Verstand* and, indeed, of the presupposition that the human destiny is one-sided in the sense that it is contained exclusively within such boundaries.

The limitations of understanding provide, in fact, a rather

cogent reason for the process of restriction that made possible the constitution of Schlegel's, Schleiermacher's and Dilthey's hermeneutic projects. For them, the object of hermeneutics is always apprehended as a sensible object through a transcendental perception, that is, is always a *represented* object. In Paul de Man's words, and for this tradition, such an object is invariably "a phenomenal event that can be granted...[a] form of positive existence, whether as a fact of nature or as an act of the mind. It leads to...[a] transcendental perception, intuition or knowledge" (1971, p. 107).

Moreover, the positing of a text as the product of an intuition (and a rhetoric of representation could include here modes as different as the evidence of experience of the weight of tradition) carries, in Kant's terms, the equivalence between reading and the question of the 'is', that is to say, to the question of a nature: "In nature, everything *is*.... Since sensibility [*Sinnlichkeit*] and understanding aim only at determining what *is* and how it comes to be, they must have their function in nature, in the physical world, and so belong to it" (1798, p. 129).

Kant's conception of the human destiny is important here, not so much because of its thematizations, but simply because of its acknowledging of an essential duplicity in it. The conflict between reason and understanding, as a conflict between what Kant calls "*zwei ganz verschiedene Welten*", "two entirely different worlds" (ibid.) is, to take literally an expression used some years ago by Peter Strawson, a conflict on the bounds of sense and indeed a conflict that partakes of the belief that it is possible to transcend the realm of representation (and hence the realm of reference) and reassert the power of the "Vorstellungen der Vernunft, denen keine Gegenstände entsprechen"; that is, the power of what cannot present itself as sense and indeed cannot *present* itself at all: "reason as a theoretical power can have no objects in the sensible world; because the occasional causes of its action are not real things but only, perhaps, the play of understanding, it can produce only Ideas—that is, representations of reason to which no objects correspond" (ibid., p. 133). In this technical sense, the ideas of reason are not representations, because they create no objects, and as Kant does not fail to remark, "this is why reason cannot be used as a theoretical, speculative power here in this world of sense [*Sinnenwelt*] (and must, because it nevertheless exists as a power in it, be destined for another world)" (ibid.).

However, the emphasis Kant puts on the conflict of the faculties prevents him from considering that, in some way, the kingdom of reason does not belong to this world. Quite the contrary, in his description of the *bloss und allein praktisch* power of reason, one can find the sketching of a theory of reading that is *not* a theory of interpretation and is radically incompatible with exegesis: "its action [of free will] should not be a reaction but rather a pure objective act...the motive[s] [*Triebfedern*] and the object[s] [*Gegenständen*] of its volition should not coincide...it should, accordingly, act independently [*unabhängig*] of understanding's representations" (ibid.). This characterization works as a camera oscura vis-à-vis the self-representation of hermeneutics, and this is true of both Schleiermacher and Gadamer. In fact, three ongoing basic postulates of such self-representation are denied there in the name of the law of reason: the assimilation between text and reader, the interested nature of reading, and the representational nature of all meaning-constituting procedures.

In this respect Kant's maneuvers are particularly ambiguous, for it is precisely the fight against sense and representation and the positing of the contingence of the ascription of meaning that allows him to build the image of a subject that in the end is purged from understanding or rather purged from the physicalism and phenomenalism of understanding. "The moral law," he writes,

> guarantees us a specific characteristic that belongs only to man and distinguishes him from all the rest of nature: morality, which makes us independent and free beings and which is itself, in turn, based on this freedom. Thus morality, not understanding, is what first makes us men....Free will...is completely independent and should be determined solely by the inner law: in other words, man should be determined solely by himself in so far as he has raised himself to his original dignity and independence from everything but the law. Without its external things our understanding would be nothing—at least it would not be *this* understanding; but reason and free will remain the same in whatever realm they might carry on their activity. (Ibid., pp. 133-135)

It should be clear by now how such a subject could ever be the subject of hermeneutics. And indeed the subsequent development of hermeneutics would provide us with a collection of teratological incidents that correspond roughly to the project of maintaining the identity of the agency of perceptions while asserting that the outcome of perception is an untranscendable ground and thus there is no law but meaning itself. The development of post-Kantian hermeneutics presents then a collection of Kantian modified subjects: in this sense, lonely readers, implicit readers, impersonal readers, superreaders, archreaders, and ideal readers are simply instances of the reassertion of a model of reading as representation of perception. In this, they all exclude the possibility of a conflict of faculties. And in their exterior appendages they are all variations on the Schlegelian theme of the man with two stomachs.

3

The Appeal to the Author

> Soon after the publication of my analytic examination of *Gradiva* I attempted to interest the elderly author in these new tasks of psychoanalytic research. But he refused his co-operation.
>
> S. Freud (1912; p. 94)

I

There is a basic asymmetry in the way contemporary criticism and literary theory have dealt with the problem of the author. To simplify things I shall call this problem the problem of the disturbing possibility of one's not taking seriously some of the arguments one uses. In a number of its varieties, especially the biographical one, the appeal to the author usually coexists with a refusal to acknowledge its argumentative dimension, that is, with its being understood as a non-appeal. Another embarrassing thing has do do with some of its specific pragmatic virtues; for example, the use of biographical arguments often realizes the conversational utopia many theoreticians have been claiming for explanations (biographical explanations are not so much merely succulent as they are primarily *debatable*). And, finally and perhaps most important, the dismissal of the appeal to the author proceeded in most cases through a distinction between its thematizations (that were proscribed) and the maintaining of its function.

In this light it is certainly not surprising that versions of critical theory such as T. S. Eliot's, which have been feted for having claimed that "It is not in his personal emotions, the emotions provoked by particular events in his life, that the poet is in any way remarkable or interesting" (1917; p. 10), have kept the recourse to the author as the decisive centripetal factor, the cement indeed of their very structurality: "No poet, no artist of any art, has his complete meaning alone. His significance, his appreciation is the appreciation of his relation to the dead poets and artists. You cannot value him alone: you must set him, for contrast and comparison, among the dead" (ibid., p. 4).[3] In passages like these, in fact, all critical procedures are derived from the possibility of comparing unities, and the minimal unities of comparison are names of authors. And in Eliot, indeed, one finds that Curtius's description of the role of *auctores* during the Middle Ages still applies fully: "All *auctores* are of the same value, all are timeless" (1948, p. 51).

Curtius relates this situation almost exclusively to the pedagogic functions that the recourse to the author fulfills or makes possible. But even though it seems possible to relate such a recourse to the emergence of the teaching of grammar and rhetoric, to the point that it has become inseparable from the notion of literacy (and here one could call to mind that E. D. Hirsch's 1987 book on literacy presents as an appendix a list of authors, of course, but, perhaps more important, a list of names), the functions of *auctores* are not merely of a pedagogical kind. Related concepts such as 'authority' and 'authenticity' go well beyond the pitfalls of the transmission of knowledge and lie at the bottom of a whole area of argumentation, either, as in the former case, by delimiting its boundaries or, as in the latter, by conveying a doctrine of truth and establishing the limits of an allegation. In this sense, one does recognize a claim as an argument with the help of criteria of pertinence that are, first and foremost, criteria of authority and authenticity.

In Curtius's description of the function of the appeal to *auctores* throughout the Middle Ages, three families of implications can be detected, and up to a certain point, the lack of obviousness of the history of authorial evidences in literary criticism and literary theory might very well be ascribed to the fluctuation of the boundaries between such families.

We have, then, a set of technical implications, that belong both to the domains of dialectics and rhetoric and, as such, are connected to models of circulation of knowledge. As Curtius remarks, "not only for the entire Middle Ages but also on into the sixteenth century [*auctores*] are technical authorities" (ibid., p. 57). To this family are related the best-known varieties of author-invocation procedures. The main usages included there move along a continuum whose extreme points are, respectively, the allegation of propositional systems from which derivation is made possible without breaking the propositional link that is the substratum of a system of demonstration and the allegation of the insufficiency of such a system, either by ascribing an end to demonstration or by relocating it within such realms as the probable or the contingent. In this sense, the technical function of the recourse to *auctores* extends well over the boundaries of pre-Galilean science and, contrary to what Curtius seems to believe, is inscribed in the core of most (if not all) uses of language. My last sentence, for instance, is an eloquent example of the fact.

A second set of implications is clearly political. To quote again from Curtius (and I hope my uneasiness with the implications of authorized quoting will become increasingly evident), "*auctores*...are also a treasury of worldly wisdom and general philosophy" (ibid., p. 58). During the Middle Ages, however, there was only a very fine line between such implications and the third family I shall allude to later. But in any case, one can include here such modalities of invocation as the description of future states of affairs and the prescription of maxims of collective behavior. Worldly wisdom can mean here the ability to take texts like Plato's *Republic* literally and thus the ability to use Plato as one might today use, and not less literally, Friedrich Engels or John Rawls. To try to keep provisionally separate this family of implications, the important words in Curtius's quote are the adjectives "worldly" and "general".

But whereas political implications subsume an appeal to texts, eventually to be crystallized in a figure of authorship, there is a third aspect that instead subsumes an appeal to a narrativized account of an individual's life and thus provides individual maxims of behavior such as models of decision and of deliberation:

> the examples of human excellence and weakness that the Middle Ages found in antique authors served it for edification. *Exemplum (paradeigma)* is a technical term of antique rhetoric from Aristotle onwards and means "an interpolated anecdote serving as an example." A different form of rhetorical *exemplum* was added later (*ca*, 100 *B.C.*), one which was of great importance for after times: the "exemplary figure" (*eikon*, *imago*), i.e., the 'incarnation of a quality'...Familiarity with the most important exemplary figures remains a requisite for scholarly poetry in the Middle Ages. (ibid., pp. 59-60)

In this third sense, the recourse to an author is closely tied to the subsequent evolution of genres such as biography (as we shall see in Johnson). But the decisive point seems to be the mediation of the individual in this process of appeal, for the individuality of the incarnation and indeed the uniqueness of the icon correspond to a notion of private morality that, from Montaigne on, would become the literary equivalent of the solitude of the process of ethical deliberation itself. To this usage of the term belong expressions such as "auteur maudit" (with the massive consequences for criticism that soon followed), and indeed the usage made possible the emergence of the theme of the disproportion between the life of a person and his or her writings, which allows us to engage nowadays in activities from which follow inevitably morally enlightening conclusions either about Sallustius (the mean person with moral writings), Genet (the mean person with immoral writings), Tolstoi (the good person with moral writings), or Svevo (the good person with immoral writings).

In this chapter, unfortunately, I shall not endeavor to pursue a rehabilitational enterprise, either through a so-called theoretical reconsideration of the appeal to the author or through the displaying of signs of intellectual tenderness for the repressed component in criticism: my own maneuvers will resemble more a tentative mapping of the recourse to the author in literary discussions, occasionally discussing some of the features mentioned previously.

II

The case of Samuel Johnson is particularly illuminating as far as the emergence, as a literary argument, of a specialized discourse on the author is concerned. In his critical texts we can find several examples of the typical prebiographist (or postbiographist, for that matter) statement: "It is not difficult to conceive...that for many reasons a man writes much better than he lives" (1750a, p. 75). But we can also find the theoretical justification of biography in a way that allows for the justifiability of biographical arguments.

Johnson's understanding of the difference between living and writing as the preceding passage exemplifies, seems to be a moral one primarily: the writer is compared to the "Specialist," who "is only in danger of erroneous reasoning" (ibid.) whereas "the man involved in life has his own passions, and those of others, to encounter, and is embarrassed with a thousand inconveniences...He is forced to act without deliberation, and obliged to choose before he can examine" (ibid., pp. 75-76). In fact, through writing one can be eminently prudent, in the Aristotelian sense that one can more easily know how to conduct a deliberation within oneself. The very reflexivity of writing, which is closely connected to the positive existence of a set of rules or, as Johnson writes, "precepts...laid down in solitude, safety and tranquility, with a mind unbiased, and with liberty unobstructed" (ibid., p. 76), implies some sort of phronesis, made easy, of course, through the deferral of any urge to choose. The contrast is again that between a pathology of discourse (rhetorical or dialectical), which belongs to writing and which can be contained in a sophistic refutation such as Aristotle's, and a moral pathology, imprudence, which belongs to life: "Among the many inconsistencies which folly produces, or infirmity suffers in the human mind, there has often been observed a manifest and striking contrariety between the life of an author and his writings" (ibid., p. 74).

In this first version of the problem, writing is the model for moral behavior; that is, the rules of discourse production are seen as the ideal of the rules of morals. The disparity between life and writings, that is, after all, the very disparity between ethics on the one hand and rhetoric and dialectics on the other, is felt as a "folly," an "infirmity," or in any case, an "inconsistency": except for Milton, who "with great reason congratulates himself upon the consciousness of being found equal to his own character, and having preserved...that reputation which his works had procured him" (ibid.), "A sudden intruder in the closet of an author would perhaps feel equal indignation with the officer, who having long solicited admission into the presence of Sardanapalus, saw him not consulting upon laws, enquiring into grievances, or modelling armies, but employed in feminine amusements, and directing the ladies in their work" (ibid., p. 75). As long as writing remains the regulative ideal of living, the description of lives cannot be but disappointing pieces of information that, among other things, undermine the precise political power of poets that once constituted one of Plato's pet targets:

> Those, whom the appearance of virtue, or the evidence of genius, have tempted to a nearer knowledge of the writer in whose performances they may be found, have indeed had frequent reason to repent their curiosity...They have lost the pleasure of imagining how far humanity may be exalted, and, perhaps, felt themselves less inclined to toil up the steeps of virtue, when they observe those who seem best able to point the way, loitering below, as either afraid of the labour, or doubtful of the reward. (Ibid., p. 74)

It is crucial to bear in mind here that in a good sense the kind of disparity Johnson refers to is a specific product of the kind of biography he has in mind, namely the biography of a writer. The same kind of disparity would be unthinkable in apparently related genres such as biographies of men of action (let alone hagiographies). Such a disparity is perhaps tied to an important shift in the criteria of biographical evaluation. We would have to distinguish here two kinds of change. On the one hand, there is a kind of change propelled by the very "profanity" of the protagonists of Johnson-like biography. Unlike men of action, whose biographies were extensions of the hermeneutic ability to read actions and indeed were the symptom of a relation of *decorum* between action and literature, profane biographees could not be gracefully submitted to any *practical* evaluation. Moreover, the canons of practical evaluation were institutionally handed down and were not easily reconcilable with the description of contemporary action: here there is an aspectual difference, as it were, between the past of exemplary people of action and the more contingent past of other biographees. Such a difference, however, is not due exclusively to the temporal proximity of the latter. Apologies and eulogies were good examples of the usage of the rhetoric of a remote past applied to recent events. Rather, the kind of repented curiosity Johnson mentions in the preceding passage derives from applying to profane biographies a way of reading that could only see itself as the result of a practical prefiguration—and, so to speak, only *certain* actions could embody a destiny in biography.

On the other hand, in coexistent genres such as memoirs, the absence of a code of equivalence between actions and words becomes the primary trait of genre. Not only in memoirs is a typology of actions, with levels of hierarchy, nonexistent, but also the criteria of *decorum* seem to rest basically on the assumption that, instead of a mediating code of conversion, tendentially intersubjective, there are levels of access to data, which represent levels of authenticity (one could say that authority is figured there under categories of authenticity) and which are tendentially idiosyncratic. But then again, if they are so, no code of action would apply there, and disparities between practical codes and literary codes would be more than likely.

Finally, a biographer of, say, Montaigne, would be faced with the additional problem of having to make decisions in terms of a whole typology of access to consciousness and solving the truly epistemological question of deciding between competing writings (his own and Montaigne's), by granting them both a status within a paradigm of authenticity. The possibility of disparity, and thus of moral disappointment, derives here from the possibility of comparison, from the simulacrum of a truth-by-correspondence model, and is closely tied to the possibility of critical debate.

The preceding passage indicates how the biography of writers, by not being similar to the biography of persons of action, is bound to go beyond the felicitous outcome of prudent deliberations and, consequently, expose the very ambivalence of the deliberation as well as the several moral infelicities that accompany it. Such a question is connected to Johnson's opinions about the overall import of this kind of biography (which would have been of a political nature, at least in Plato's time)—sheer curiosity, disinterested curiosity, can never be apologetic, that is, the unselected material obtained from the intruding into an author's closet can hardly ever be flattering:

> It has long been the custom of oriental monarchs to hide themselves in gardens and palaces, to avoid the conversation of mankind, and to be known to their subjects only by their edicts. The same policy is no less necessary to him that writes, than to him that governs; for men would not more patiently submit to be taught, than commanded, by one known to have the same follies and weaknesses with themselves. (Ibid., pp. 74-75)

Johnson is particularly aware of the fact that writing (the oriental king's edict or the poet's writing) is a political expedient inasmuch as it is a technical device for maintaining a distance, and a very useful one at that. Biography, however, or, if we like, writing's becoming indiscriminate peeping, stands on the side of an undesired transparency, as if in it all *delectare* would prevent all *docere*. However, this standard classical version is not the only one we find in Johnson.

It is probably important to understand that the second version of biography, for which Johnson is famous (both as an author and a character), seems to be connected to a reformulation of the genetic question of writing. But, in so far as the latter is in its turn tied to a changing of the status of the rules of composition, it can be said that the second version of biography derives from the first one. As long as there are intersubjective rules of composition and as long as the *tekhnè poietikè* consists in the problem of the adequation to those rules, the theoretical question of the genesis can be solved by invoking the rules that one is supposed to imitate. Even if the problem of imitation is never at stake, however, Johnson tends to suspect that there is a basic difference between imitating rules and imitating non-rules: the basic difference lies, of course, in the fact that all imitation of non-rules requires a theory of the choice of the subject matter, that is, a theory of genesis, and that such a theory is already implied in any purely ruled system, independent of the character of the *institutiones*.

Writing about himself, Johnson seems to weaken the possibility of a purely ruled system of principles that would allow for a "deduction" of composition, due to its intersubjective nature, and to replace it by the idea of an idiosyncratic system of rules, stressing thus the difference between authors:

> An author has a rule of choice peculiar to himself; and selects those subjects which he is best qualified to treat, by the course of his studies or the accidents of his life; that some topicks of amusement have been already treated with too much success to invite a competition; and that he who endeavors to gain many readers must try various arts of invitation, essay every avenue of pleasure, and make frequent changes in his methods of approach. (1750b, p. 129)

The emphasis on difference and variety appears to reflect here a decisive primacy of *delectare* over *docere*: changing is a rhetorical device that requires a distinct basic attitude; that of the essayist, that of essaying "every avenue of pleasure." The joys of identification are somewhat forgotten (as if the classics were too classical to deserve even imitation), and consequently, the only possibility for the author seems to lie in the identification with oneself, that is, in the taking of oneself as the framework of all precepts. A theory of genesis would consist precisely in the elaboration of criteria of verifiability for such precepts, guaranteeing the grounding of every choice. Johnson seems to realize quite clearly that such a theory would involve a double strategy: the investigation of an author's "peculiar" choices would imply both the investigation of the "course of his studies" (a philological project) and the investigation of the "accidents of his life" (a biographical project). This is to say that a theory of genesis would include two distinct families of evidences, one of them corresponding to the formerly proscribed genre of biography. Such a basic bipartition is one of the most typical features of all controversies that have dealt with the author in the literary theories of the last two centuries, and it is at the same time the context against which Schleiermacher's efforts can be understood.

Johnson's rehabilitation of biography (or, rather, Johnson's "habilitation" of it, because in this respect he has no predecessors) could be seen very well as the formulation of an answer to a philosophical problem that, in a way, began and ended with Aristotle as philosophy, but has persisted as a problem ever since: the problem of grounding conceptually a discourse on the particular. The domestic metaphors I quoted earlier from Johnson's reference to Sardanapalus recur again, invested with an opposite value, in the famous number 60 of *The Rambler*: "The business of the biographer is often to pass slightly over those performances and incidents, which produce vulgar greatness, to lead the thoughts into domestick privacies, and display the minute details of daily life, where exterior appendages are cast aside and men excel each other only by prudence and by virtue" (1750c, p. 321). We witness here an apology for the leading of one's thoughts "into domestick privacies," opposed to "exterior appendages": such a conception of the true as a correlation between the inner and the private (as opposed to the outer and the public "appendages") will survive for a long time in the critical tradition and, as we will see later, will be one of the main concerns of Wimsatt and Beardsley's "The Intentional Fallacy."

But any grounding of biography as the discourse on the particular par excellence would have to face the problem of finding arguments for the dismissal of history, the traditional candidate to the place, at least since Aristotle's *Poetics'* Chapter 9. Johnson presents four arguments. The first could be considered a mimetic argument that is not without some resemblances to Plato's famous devaluation of poetry in the *Republic*: "We know how few can portray a living acquaintance, except by his most prominent and observable peculiarities, and the grosser features of his mind; and it may be easily imagined how much of this little knowledge may be lost in imparting it, and how soon a succession of copies will lose all resemblance of the original" (ibid., p. 323).

The second argument seems to be a somewhat ontological one: "The incidents which give excellence to biography are of a volatile and evanescent kind, such as soon escape the memory and are rarely transmitted by tradition" (ibid.). What Johnson appears to be aiming at here is the utter particularity of the particular; that is, the irreducibility of the particular to any transmission and thus to tradition. Curiously enough, this point would explain the emphasis on contemporariness in his own *Lives of the Poets* and also, of course, in Boswell's *Life of Johnson*. There is no particularity in the past, for the very way of transmitting the past (including the writing of history) presupposes the impossible permanence of a self-identical memory. The incidents of good biographies, that is, the incidents of the accidental, cannot be the object of a straightforward anamnesis; biography is the fragile way of arresting them, and a whole rhetoric of presence enacts such a process (that is very noticeable in the appearing of the equivalence, from Johnson and Boswell but also from Eckermann on, between biographer and witness).

The third argument seems to be a moral one:

> The general and rapid narratives of history, which involve a thousand fortunes in the business of a day, and complicate innumerable accidents in one great transaction, afford few lessons applicable to private life, which derives its comforts and its wretchedness from the right or wrong management of things which nothing but their frequency makes considerable, *Parva si non fiant quotidie*, says Pliny, and which can have no place in those relations which never descend below the consultation of the senates, the motions of armies, and the schemes of conspirators. (Ibid., pp. 319-320)

There are some paradoxical details in the argument that is, in fact, much more radical than seems to be the case: if the point is that only a discourse on the particular can be universally useful, that is, applicable to all individual situations, such a point echoes the rhetorical disproportion between the inadequacy of an elevated style and sublimity, stating that sublimity (and universality) is *in parvis* or rather that the absolutely small allegorizes the absolutely great. It is thus a process of rehabilitation of insignificance, of the descending below armies, senates, and conspirators into "things which nothing but their frequency makes considerable," into the realm of the "many invisible circumstances which...are more important than publick occurrences" (ibid., p. 321). Only the invisible can be universally and morally useful, precisely as what is defined within a system of descriptions of the world as the circumstantial, as opposed to the factual, and only that, appears to incorporate the pitfalls of moral deliberation.

Several decades later, Hegel would refer to this process under the topic of the "prosaic treatment of the objective world" (1842, p. 316). Such a treatment is marked by the envisaging of objectivity "as a pure externality" (ibid.). Even if Hegel connects such a treatment to the "restricted thinking of the Understanding [*Verstand*] and its categories [*Verständig Zusammenhang...[der] Kategorien des beschränkten*

Denkens]" (ibid., p. 974), he emphasizes the dubious commerce between externality and finitude on the one side and the circumstantial side of particularity on the other:

> In this way of thinking, every particular either appears falsely as independent or is brought into a mere relation with another and therefore is apprehended only as relative and dependent...[This] sort of conception...therefore gets no further than particular laws for phenomena; it persists in separating the particular existent from the universal law and in merely relating them together, and at the same time, in its eyes, the laws themselves fall apart into fixed particulars, while the relations between these are presented likewise under the categories of externality and finitude. (Ibid., p. 975)

Hegel is, of course, interested here in contrasting the kind of access to generality that the speculative thinking of reason provides with a first stage in the battle between spirit and immediacy, where the outcome of mediatization is total externality. But total externality amounts to an atomism of events, and in a very good sense, no consequences can follow from the prosaic treatment of the objective world, as there is no way of deriving universal laws from the "particular existent." Consequently, Hegel's poetics contain several cautionary prescriptions (e.g., "What has become prosaic in itself is not to be reshaped poetically; it can only be dressed up," (ibid., p. 423) from which the idea can be subsumed that all poetics of the prosaic amount to horticultural or decorative *localized* embellishments of objects apprehended as necessarily external and finite.

It is, moreover, particularly worth noting that, in Hegel's *Aesthetics*, the primal refusal of immediacy *is* the equivalent of a regime of immediate mimesis: "in no art should this definiteness go astray into the prose of actual nature and its direct imitation, nor should it overtower in partiality and importance the fullness of detail devoted to the presentation of the spiritual side of individuals and events" (ibid., p. 255). In fact, the consideration of objects in their pure externality obliterates their "spiritual side." That is to say that even arts of the detail (such as painting), in Hegel's view, should refrain from identifying their purposes and their procedures, for the "prose of actual nature" cannot but remain confined to the utter particularity that goes with the finitude and thus the perishableness of the objects of understanding. An art of such objects would mean both an art where the distinction between effects and procedures would not be possible (for finitude would be the only thematization of detail) and an art unfit for the traditional function of rendering its product as *aere perennius*, for Spirit would be absent from it, and ultimately such an art would not be able to evolve in time, that is, to have a posterity, a history. The direct imitation of the prose of nature has, then, deep temporal consequences, and ultimately the question that presides over Johnson's maneuvers is whether temporariness is worth imitating.

What at first sight could be no more than a series of injunctions toward an exhaustive mimesis of everyday life becomes, in fact, prisoner of the exhaustiveness of the process; that is, of the configuration of a situation as *one* situation, the structural model of the uniqueness of every situation. Such would be the difference between the kind of allegorical relation between metonymies that a poetics of the detail invariably produces, and a metonymical relation inside an allegory, supported by a code that converts either actions into values or particulars into consequences of generality, typical of the previous versions of biography.

Johnson's fourth argument for the grounding of a discourse on the particular could be called a political argument: "I have often thought that there has rarely passed a life of which a judicious and faithful narrative would not be useful...there is such an uniformity in the state of man, considered apart from adventitious and separable decorations and disguises, that there is scarce any possibility of good or ill, but is common to human kind" (1750c, p. 320). Any biography has a general use, as long as it remains close to the private. It is immaterial who is to be the subject of that biography. Again, this is the same argument of the generality in particularity, deprived of a rule for the choice of the particular: Johnson replaces instead some sort of aristocracy of the detail (only certain persons can acquire the function of significant individuals, only some particulars can become allegoretic, so to speak) by a democracy of the detail, which supposes that any person can become morally useful, that is, turned into a universal *exemplum*. Because there is "an uniformity in the state of man," anyone can represent humankind (and the kind of democracy that would apply to Johnson's concept of biography would be indeed a representational and a representative one, the political sense being derived here from a rhetorical one).

Such a complex mechanism, in addition to being one of the main points in Johnson's fight against history for the place of the best discourse on the particular, is also on the base of an implicit opposition sketched between biography, on the one hand, and poetry *and* history, on the other: "Our passions are...more strongly moved in proportion as we can more readily adopt the pains or pleasures proposed to our minds, by recognizing them as once our own" (ibid., p. 319). However, the process of recognition that biography entails, precisely because it stems from the most insignificant particular details, has more chance of achieving rhetorical success than the process associated with either history or poetry:

> Histories of the downfall of kingdoms, and revolutions of empires, are read with great tranquility; the imperial tragedy pleases common auditors only by its pomp of ornament and grandeurs of ideas; and the man whose faculties have been engrossed by business, and whose heart never fluttered but at the rise or fall of stocks, wonders how the attention can be seized, or the affections agitated by a tale of love. (Ibid.)

The recipe is again that of a radical, direct mimesis that in the particular would meet the universal: "parallel circumstances, and kindred images, to which we readily conform our minds are, above all other writings, to be found in narratives of the lives of the particular persons" (ibid.). The effect of such a radical mimesis would invert the contents of Aristotle's well-known remark that the contemplation of accurate imitations of disgusting objects does not provoke disgust (*Poet.*, 1448b). What seems to be the case here is rather the forgetting of the nature of reproduction; that is, the forgetting of all mimetic link: the pleasure and utility of absolute curiosity (a point that we can, for instance, find also in Burke and, before him, in Montaigne) is the Johnsonian correlative for the obsession with the insignificant detail. Biography would appear then to be connected to a particular process of loss of the self-identity of memory, not only, as we saw, through an emphasis on contemporariness, but also through an emphasis on immediacy; and we find here one of the main lines of much of the subsequent criticism: if we identify (with) the person in the person's particularity, we acquire thereby the idiosyncratic rules that would make the derivation of someone's works appear absolutely natural.

At this point it is perhaps important to emphasize the crucial distinction that seems to oppose lives of poets to memoirs. It is very evident that writers like Montaigne seem to incorporate in their works several procedures that are also typical of the Johnsonian doctrine of biography. But Montaigne's refusals of a practical code, for instance, are not backed by the awareness of the difference between lives of persons of action and lives of private citizens. Rather, they derive from a principle of indifference: "I set forth a humble and inglorious life; that does not matter [*c'est tout un*]" (III, 2, p. 611). Indeed, the stressing of the disparity of objects is analogously referred back to the source of an essential unity, that is, the subject: "all this fricassee that I am scribbling here is nothing but a record of the essays of my life, which, for spiritual health [*pour l'interne santé*], is exemplary enough if you take its instruction in reverse [*exemplaire assez à prendre l'instruction à contre-poil*]" (III, 13, p. 826). And even if the rhetoric has shifted from *exemplum* to *historia calamitatum*, as in the preceding passage, the use of a "record of the essays" presupposes a purpose for experience (and one should not forget that the word essay means precisely *that*), as well as the distinctive place for the protagonist.

In this sense (which is much more than etymological) memoirs cannot by definition be connected to a *loss of memory*. And what is sometimes taken to be the textualization of contradictory opinions (and thus a clear sign of the lack of self-identity of memory) resembles much more the rhetorical enactment of a movement whose literary name is perhaps memory, but that in any case is a movement where the identity of forms of enunciation makes up for the lack of thematic identity and, indeed emblematizes that supposedly absent thematic identity: "We think what we want only at the moment we want it, and we change like that animal which takes the colour of the place you set it on" (II, 1, p. 240).

The frequent protestations of moral nudity that one can find in the *Essais* ("I assure you, I should very gladly have portrayed myself here entire and wholly naked" [*tout entier, et tout nud*]" (Av., p. 2) are in fact manifestations of the nudity of a self-identical pronoun, and indeed, when Montaigne declares that "I am myself the matter of my book" (ibid.) he can perhaps be said to mean just *that*: the pronoun *I* (or, rather, *je*) is the matter of his book. In this respect, the omnipresence of memory denotes a shift on processes of authentication where it constitues itself as the guarantor of an authenticity: the regime of authorship where all the burden of proof would seem to rest on the possibility of inferring truth conditions from the use of deictics. And thus Johnson's amazing lack of memory (or, better yet, dissolution of memory), as we shall see later, belongs to a different story entirely.

III

Boswell's *Life of Johnson* can be said to be one of the few instances of fidelity to Johnson's radically mimetic project. Although he admired deeply Boswell's work, Macaulay, fifty years later, obviously felt very uncomfortable about such a project:

> Johnson grown old, Johnson in the fullness of his fame and in the enjoyment of a competent fortune, is better known to us than any other man in history. Everything about him, his coat, his wig, his figure, his face, his scrofula, his St. Vitus dance, his rolling walk, his blinking eye, the outward signs which too clearly marked his approbation of his dinner, his insatiable appetite for fish-sauce and veal-pie with plums, his inextinguishable thirst for tea, his trick of touching the posts as he walked, his mysterious practice of treasuring up scraps of orange peel, his morning slumbers, his midnight disputations, his contortions, his mutterings, his gruntings, his puffings, his vigorous, acute, and ready eloquence, his sarcastic wit, his vehemence, his insolence, his fits of tempestuous rage,his queer inmates, old Mr. Levett and blind Mrs. Williams, the Cat Hodge and the negro Frank, all are as familiar to us as the objects by which we have been surrounded from childhood. But we have no minute information respecting those years of Johnson's life during which his character and his manners became immutably fixed. (1831, p. 543)

The reasons for Macaulay's uneasiness had to do with an intermittent perception of some sort of essential disproportion between his admiration for Boswell's work and his awareness of the argumentative incompetence of it. In other words, this is the disproportion between Johnson's "outward signs that too clearly marked his approbation of his dinner" and the "information respecting those years of Johnson's life during which his character and his manners became immutably fixed", that is, between the fragmentary, albeit fascinating, results of a radically mimetic project and the urge for causation. In a very good sense, Boswell's *Life of Johnson* is neither history nor story: in Macaulay's own terms, in his famous essay on Hallam, it is neither map nor painted landscape. For "the picture," he writes, "though it places the country before us, does not enable us to ascertain with accuracy the dimensions, the distances and the angles. [And] the map is not a work of imaginative art. It presents no scene to the imagination; but it gives us exact information as to the bearings of the various points" (1828, p. 2). But when biographers get into someone's closet, it is as if their point of view would never appear to be capable of delimiting an area (cartographic or otherwise). Macaulay is keenly aware of such an ironical outcome, especially because Johnson's injunctions in favor of a biography of "invisible circumstances" were dictated by Johnson's belief that such circumstances were particularly fit for virtuous uses. In the remarkable last two paragraphs of his essay on Boswell on Johnson, he writes:

> The club-room is before us, and the table on which stands the omelet for Nugent, and the lemons for Johnson. There are assembled those heads which live forever in the canvas of Reynolds. There are the spectacles of Burke and the tall thin form of Langton, the courtly sneer of Beauclerk and the beaming smile of Garrick, Gibbon topping his snuff-box and Sir Joshua with his trumpet in his ear. In the foreground is that strange figure which is as familiar to us as the figures of those among who we have brought up, the gigantic body, the hugh massy face, seemed with the scars of disease, the brown coat, the black worsted stockings, the grey wig with the scorched foretop, the dirty hands, the nails bitten and pared to the quick. We see the heavy form rolling; we hear it puffing, and then comes the "Why sir!" and "What then, sir?", and the "No, sir!" and the "You don't know your way through the question, sir!".
>
> What a singular destiny has been that of this remarkable man! To be regarded in his own age as a classic, and in ours as a companion. To receive from his contemporaries that full homage which men of genius have in general received only from posterity! To be more intimately known to posterity than other men are known to their contemporaries! That kind of fame which is commonly the most transient is, in this case, the most durable. The reputation of those writings, which he probably expected to be immortal, is every day fading; while those peculiarities of manner and that careless table-talk the memory of which, he probably thought would die with him, are likely to be remembered as long as the English language is spoken in any quarter of the globe. (1831, pp. 561-562)

The singularity of Johnson's destiny, to borrow Macaulay's expression, becomes, however, the very singularity of Macaulay's prose, in which the latter becomes both a map and a painted landscape, where the topological situation of the characters described is the framework for the ethical conclusions he draws. In this sense the whole passage resembles an allegory on nations, where each territory has an emblem (spectacles, a smile, a snuff box, an ear trumpet) and where each emblem maintains a relation with the essence of its topological origin. Macaulay's remarks about Johnson's ironical destiny are, as it were, the object of the irony of the Boswellian undertones that his text takes. But such singularity is first and foremost the product of Boswell's Johnsonian biography of Johnson; that is, a purely literary singularity. When biography assumes clearly the function of a discourse on the particular, its subject becomes the object of a rhetoric of contingency, becomes a nonsubject, dissolved in a massive amount of unnarrativizable details. In a technical sense it cannot have any posterity (for no story can be told) but the very fragmentary posterity of its metonymies, that is, a posterity in discourse as opposed to a posterity of effect; to use Hegel's terms, this is not the realm of spirit at all. On other words, biography can become an argument only if it remains insufficiently biographical; that is, if it prefers subjects to objects and causes to closets.

IV

One of the main purposes of what is usually, and perhaps not too accurately, known as Sainte-Beuve's method is the formulation of a narrative grammar for biography or, at least, the formulation of a minimal functional system that, by establishing criteria of pertinence, would simultaneously protect biography from both the seductions of ancient rhetoric ("être le moins dupe possible des phrases, des mots, des beaux sentiments convenus," 1862, p. 19) and of particularity: "One day will come, which I believe I have glimpsed in the course of my observations, a day when science will be established, when the great families of the mind and their main divisions will be determined and known. Then, given the main feature of a certain mind, it will be possible to deduce from it several other features" (ibid., p. 18). Although keeping the basic postulate of the early Romantic tradition, from Johnson of *The Rambler* number 60 to Carlyle, Macaulay and Schleiermacher ("Literature, literary production cannot be distinguished to me from the rest of the man and the organization; I can enjoy a work, but it is difficult for me to judge it independently from the knowledge of the man itself," ibid., p. 17), Sainte-Beuve's procedure is basically a restrictive one. If the literary project is to be possible at all, one would have to establish grounds for the validity of biographical arguments; that is, one would have to design limits for the very possibility of biography. The first limit is the same historical limit we remarked in Johnson: the literary study of ancients is bound to reconstructive procedures emancipated from historical sources—one is reduced thus to commenting upon the work, admiring it, imagining the author and poet obliquely" (ibid.). Such a point would explain incidentally why the philological project, from Schlegel on, has constituted itself as a methodological alternative to the unavailability of a biographical project, the latter being seen as the symptom of theory's refusal to conceive any temporal gap between the interpreter and the text. In this sense, as we have seen in Chapter 2, both Friedrich Schlegel's *Klassicii* and the domain of Schleiermacher's grammatical interpretation, philology, are primarily the study of authorless (in Sainte-Beuve's sense) texts. But, as Sainte-Beuve does not fail to remark, "with the moderns it is a completely different situation; and criticism, that bases its method upon the means, has other duties here. To know another person, and to know him well, especially if this person is a prominent and famous individual, is a great thing that one should not disdain" (ibid.).

Biography is thus again a matter of contemporariness. But if contemporariness was to Johnson a consequence of particularity, it is to Sainte-Beuve a methodological consequence of the introduction of an intersubjective principle of verification in a striving for universality, that is, it corresponds to the region where a refusal of literary agnosticism can be shown to be tenable. Such a refusal, as I have remarked earlier, presents itself under the form of a set of narrative prescriptions:

> It is very useful to begin at the beginning and, when one has the means, by seizing the superior or distinguished writer in his native country, in his race. If one would know the race well, physiologically, the ancestors and forefathers, one could shed light on the secret and essential quality of the mind... (Ibid., pp. 19-20)

> When one is as properly instructed as possible on the origins, on the immediate and remote kinship of an eminent writer, an essential point is to be determined, after those related to his

> studies and his education: the first milieu, the first group of friends and contemporaries in which he found himself when his talent first blossomed, took form and became mature... (Ibid., p. 20)

> As long as one has not asked a certain number of questions about an author and obtained their answers...one is not sure of having grasped him as a whole [*on n'est pas sûr de le tenir tout entier*], even though such questions seem very removed from the nature of his writings: What were his opinions on religion? How was he affected by the sight of nature? How did he behave, women-wise? Money-wise? Was he rich, was he poor? what was his diet, what was his daily routine? Finally, what was his vice or his main weakness?... (Ibid., pp. 21-22)

It seems particularly worth noting that the use of biography is connected for Sainte-Beuve with the very possibility of introducing a principle of order in it. But, contrary to the ancient rhetoric he opposes, this is a project that fancies itself as a huge *rhetorica naturalis sive moralis*. In a much-quoted sentence, Sainte-Beuve wrote that "literary study leads me naturally into moral study" (ibid., p. 17). Biography, in fact, appears to be the genre for the mediation between the individual mind and a general science of the mind:

> Whatever may happen, one will get after some time, I suppose, to the broad establishment of the science of the moralist; such a science is presently where botany was before Jussieu and comparative anatomy before Cuvier, in an anecdotal stage...To a broader and brighter mind...will be possible one day the disclosing of the great natural divisions that correspond to the families of minds. (Ibid., pp. 18-19)

It might be important to notice that Sainte-Beuve's ordering of biography legitimates biographical arguments ultimately by distinguishing them from a project of total mimesis. Instead of a pile of contingent fragments, the model now is that of the harmonious whole of a subject, deprived of any particularity through an integration within one "family of the mind," that is to say, the model is now that of the total meaning:

> Every work of an author...after being situated in its own framework and surrounded by every circumstance that watched it

> appear, acquires its whole meaning—its historical meaning, its literary meaning—partaking its fair degree of originality, of novelty or imitation, and one does not run the risk, while judging it, of making up false beauties and devious motives of admiration... (Ibid., p. 21)

The prerequisites for a good biography can be seen thus as metaprescriptions or preliminary distinctions for a theory of meaning: a good story is, to Sainte-Beuve, a perfect (and true) explanation. And if the best stories are necessarily biographical, the very model for a perfect explanation that he propounds presupposes inevitably the becoming argument of biography; that is, a field of argumentativity dominated by the weight of biographical reasons.

The ideal of the perfect literary scientist, for Sainte-Beuve, is hence the ideal of a person who can make biography work as an argument, achieving a synthesis of the particular in the general: "I imagine, thus, someone having some sort of talent and facility to understand groups, literary families...someone that could distinguish them at first sight; seizing their spirit and their life; whose vocation would be truly this one; someone suitable to be a good naturalist in this vast field of the mind" (ibid., p. 19). This is to say that the ultimate universe of such a synthesis is that of a science of the mind meant to see in every individual story of a case (or case history) the example and the instance of a transindividual family, to see in each biography the pertinence to the biographical genre as grammaticized by Sainte-Beuve.

Sainte-Beuve's proleptic description or prophetic wish for "a good naturalist in the vast field of the mind" can be said to fit Freud quite well. As a matter of fact, there are striking similarities between the way Sainte-Beuve understands biography and the role of narrative in Freud's psychoanalysis (excluding, of course, its altogether different clinical aspect, where the criteria of verification are completely distinct). Such similarities appear to be particularly striking when we consider the emphasis on genesis in both "Sainte-Beuve's method" and some of Freud's writings on literature. These are possibly the latest example of a biographist theory of literary genesis, before the flood of the, in some ways, preJohnsonian theories of creation that one finds in Valéry and T.S. Eliot and before their metatheoretical acknowledgment, achieved in the moment when genetic arguments were first termed fallacious. I shall conclude the section, therefore, with some brief remarks on this aspect of Freud's theories.

A good example of the latter can be found in Freud's 1908 "Der Dichter und das Phantasieren." In the light of his theory of fantasies (that appears, in this essay, to be close to a phenomenology of fantasy) Freud proposes "to study the connections that exist between the life of a writer and its works" (1908, p. 151). Such a proposition is put in motion by a kind of curiosity similar to the one about which Johnson (in a pre-Johnsonian mood) once remarked leads invariably to disappointment: "We laymen have always been intensely curious to know—like the cardinal who put a similar question to Ariosto—from what sources that strange being, the creative writer, draws his material" (ibid., p. 143). The same basic sophistication of Freud's theory, when contrasted to, say, Sainte-Beuve's, is made possible by the introduction, in his own explanation, of the notion of 'unconscious' as an explanatory device. Instead of a causal relation between intersubjectively verifiable data and the fact of literary production, Freud suggests that "a strong experience in the present awakens in the creative writer a memory of an earlier experience (usually belonging to his childhood) from which there now proceeds a wish which finds its fulfillment in the creative work. The work itself exhibits elements of the recently provoking occasion as well as of the old memory" (ibid., p. 151). Such a point would reduce in the best of cases the narrative prescriptions of Sainte-Beuve's program to the status of methodological rules for the study of an intermediary process; that is, it would deprive of any significant factuality the kind of events Sainte-Beuve treats as primary causes for literary productions. The function of those events, in Freud's dynamic explanation, is a sheer memory-arousing one; that is, historical facts work not as causes but as anamnesical backgrounds. It is to the essentially undocumented (in Sainte-Beuve's very restricted sense of document) world of childhood that Freud's explanation refers. It has been remarked very often that the only way of individually validating such an explanation is by telling a story. But, and perhaps not by chance, the stories that work in psychoanalysis, although essentially biographical, belong to the family of Dr. Johnson's gastric-noises biographies and not to the family of Sainte-Beuve's cultural-milieu biographies. It is not the place here to discuss the resurgence of the theme of the Boswellian radical mimesis in psychoanalytic explanations: but it seems clear enough that the introduction of the notion of 'unconscious processes' in Freud's explanations undermines any attempt to establish a narrative grammar in Sainte-Beuve's sense; that is, to establish something like an ordered set of functions in a biographical narrative.

The second great difference would be a difference in the conception of the nature of the effect that the work is. For in both authors the work is seen as an effect: but whereas in Sainte-Beuve it is conceived as a pure manifestation of a tendentially identifiable cause, in Freud, because the latter is in itself a composite process, the work is seen as a compromise between the factors that integrate such a process and give it its composite character. Freud and Sainte-Beuve's disagreement would not be a disagreement about the cause of the work, but rather a disagreement about the nature of the cause. It is, if we like, the basic disagreement between incommensurable sciences of the mind: a metapsychology and a psychology. Both seem to require biography, but the regime of argumentativity, that is, the very function of biography, depends on the postulates of the broad genetic explanatory devices each one uses.

V

What for twenty years was thought to be the final settlement of the dispute between the anti-Romantic generations of the first part of this century and the Romantic theory of biography as we saw it in Sainte-Beuve is contained in the arch-famous essay by W.K. Wimsatt and M.C. Beardsley "The Intentional Fallacy" (1946). Instead of discussing the various argumentative incidents that appear to be part of the unmistakable flavor of the essay, I shall concentrate on what seem to be the basic implications for biographism contained in it, namely, the theorizing of a totally different partition of evidence, achieved through Wimsatt and Beardsley's distinction between internal evidence, external evidence, and a mysterious third kind of evidence, aptly termed "intermediate evidences".

Contrary to Freud's implicit disagreement with Sainte-Beuve, in which different conceptions of the nature of a cause were at stake, Wimsatt and Beardsley's essay expresses a disagreement about the very notion of pertinence of any causal explanation (under the somewhat more refined assumption that identifies cause with origin): "A poem does not come into existence by accident. The words of a poem, as Professor Stoll had remarked, come out of a head, not out of a hat. Yet to insist on the designing intellect as a *cause* of a poem is not to grant the design or intention as a *standard* by which the critic is to judge the worth of the poet's performance" (ibid., p. 4). The object of Wimsatt and Beardsley's indictment, then, is the sheer relevance of both psychological and metapsychological explanations, which seemed to be tied closely to the possibility of the argumentative working of biography. However, it would be overhasty to think that such an indictment is based on any intentionless theory of language. As a matter of fact, this is rather a genre-oriented indictment: "poetry differs from practical messages, which are successful if and only if we correctly infer the intention. They are more abstract than poetry" (ibid., p. 5). Some things can be said about such a distinction, namely, about the curious status of self-evidence that carries with it a dispensation of hermeneutic mediation, and that seems to be typical of Wimsatt and Beardsley's conception of poetry: as a matter of fact, "practical messages" presuppose, to be translated into meaning, an inferential operation performed by the addressee. Such an operation, which could perfectly describe the functions of both Sainte-Beuve's and Freud's naturalists of the mind, and indeed the argumentative working of biography, is said to be a process of abstraction. One of the main consequences of the partition of evidence I was referring to earlier is the unprecedented equation of abstraction with privacy and thus the legitimation of publicness under the unavowed assumption of its utter concreteness. The debt of American New Criticism to the English speaking empirical philosophical tradition is instanced here through a considerably revolutionary theoretical move: not through any vindication or rehabilitation of "common language" but rather by a redefinition of common language, that is, and now in a very Johnsonian mood, by considering that the commonest of all languages is poetry: "The poem is not the critic's own and not the author's (it is detached from the author at birth and goes about the world beyond his power to intend about it or control it). The poem belongs to the public. It is embodied in language, the peculiar possession of the public, and it is about the human being, an object of public knowledge" (ibid., p. 5).

The commonality of poetry seems to be, to Wimsatt and Beardsley, a tacit correlative of its self-evidence; and the self-evident, as we shall see, *is* the public, implying that the concept of public carries the theoretical dismissal of any actual audience, that is, of what is known as—the public.

All these points would appear to lead Wimsatt and Beardsley to an unequivocal condemnation of biographical arguments; and this is precisely what seems to happen for twenty lines or so. Their distinction between poetry and "practical messages" seems to confine the pertinence of biographical arguments to the latter and it seems, thus, to include the use of biography as a literary argument as a somewhat mild pathological case, under the general disease known as the intentional fallacy:

> There is a criticism of poetry and there is author psychology, which when applied to the present or future takes the form of inspirational promotion; but author psychology can be historical too, and then we have literary biography, a legitimate and attractive study in itself, one approach, as Professor Tillyard would argue, to personality, the poem being only a parallel approach. Certainly it need not be with a derogatory purpose that one points out personal studies, as distinct from poetic studies, in the realm of literary scholarship. Yet there is the fault of writing the personal as if it were poetic. (Ibid., p. 10)

It would be possible perhaps to see in this paragraph a particularly subtle rewriting of the methodological implications in Aristotle's distinction between poetry and history. Just as the method for a language of the universal (that is, poetry) would be criticism, the method for a language of the particular seems to correspond here to the scope of biography. As a matter of fact, the universal, in a very strict sense, is what "should not mean but *be*": implying, by the way, that criticism is not a question of means, either meaning or mediation, but rather a matter of ontological adequation. That is to say that the very task of biography consists in the basically inferential work of retotalizing the particular by rendering it intelligible (through the ascribing of an intention). Such a point implies perhaps that all knowledge of the particular would be of a biographical kind as long as it would reflect the necessity of an inferential mediation. And because the knowledge of the common (that is, poetry) is exempt from such a mediation, the pragmatic working of biography within poetry, by confusing criticism and biography, would identify poetry and history or, as Wimsatt and Beardsley called them, poetic studies and personal studies.

But then again, driven by the very logic of such a distinction, one would have to conceive a model for argumentative evidences applying to the general. The core of Wimsatt and Beardsley's essay consists precisely in their dealing with this problem; namely, by considering that only one kind of evidence does justice to the utterly general nature of poetry (this standard version, as we shall see, is considerably modified by the partition that follows from the previously mentioned necessity):

> There is a difference between internal and external evidence for the meaning of a poem. And the paradox is only verbal and superficial that what is (1) internal is also public: it is discovered through the semantics and syntax of a poem, through our habitual knowledge of the language, through grammars, dictionaries, and all the literature which is the source of dictionaries, in general all that makes a language and culture; while what is (2) external is private or idiosyncratic; not a part of the work as a linguistic fact: it consists of revelations (in journals, for example, or letters or reported conversations) about how or why the poet wrote the poem—to what lady, while sitting on what lawn, or at the death of what friend or brother. (Ibid.)

If one compares this distinction with Sainte-Beuve's criteria for the admissibility of evidences, one can easily realize an almost obvious inversion: to Sainte-Beuve's verifiability (and knowability) of the external, Wimsatt and Beardsley oppose the public nature of the truly internal, that is, language. The argument recalls at least some of the versions of Wittgenstein's famous private language argument (which he was developing around the same period in what was later to become his *Philosophical Investigations*). But both Sainte-Beuve and Wimsatt and Beardsley seem to rely on the distinction between internality and externality, privacy and publicness, and they both seem to argue that only what is public is knowable. The real reverse of the two positions would perhaps be found in Dr. Johnson's idea that a discourse for the private is not only useful, but also possible, and in Boswell's emphasis on the multiple signs of privacy (one could speak of a whole rhetoric of privacy in his *Life of Johnson*) to the point that the otherwise recognizable syntax of a diegesis becomes impossible.

Wimsatt and Beardsley's typical objection to the use of literary external evidences would be that of saying that in a very good sense nothing defined a priori as external could ever work as evidence and thus that, if we assume the medium of a poem to be linguistic, "we have no excuse for inquiring what part is intended or meant" (ibid., p. 4) But then again, their own division between poetry and "practical messages" would carry the paradoxical conclusion that, for the latter to become public (that is, practical), one would have to infer private elements.

I believe that the function of the third kind of evidence introduced by Wimsatt and Beardsley is precisely that of trying to cope with such elementary objections as well as that of, pervasively though, justifying a posteriori the prevalence of a practice within the institutions of criticism, and surrendering partially to the undeniable charm and rhetorical power of investigations such as those on "how or why the poet wrote the poem" (ibid., p. 10):

> There is (3) an intermediate kind of evidence about the character of the author or about private or semi-private meanings attached to words or topics by an author or by a coterie of which he is a member. The meaning of words is the history of words, and the biography of an author, his use of a word, and the associations which the word had for *him*, are part of the word's history and meaning...The use of biographical evidence need not involve intentionalism, because while it may be evidence of what the author intended, it may also be the evidence of the meaning of his words and the dramatic character of his utterance. (Ibid., pp. 10-11)

The central assumption required for the grounding of this family of arguments seems to be the equivalence and, indeed, the identification between the "biography of an author" and "his use of the word." The pertinent biographical arguments then would be those that could be related to linguistic aspects of a work. But such an assumption blurs the very notion of argumentability and indeed that of argumentativity by identifying the nature of an argument with its function: it implies that, no matter what, any argument is acceptable provided it accomplishes a desired function. If Johnson's preference for fish sauce and veal pie with plums would clear his use of expressions such as 'Addison was not similar to fish sauce', the so-called external argument would be admissible. But if the question had never arisen, the appeal to such an evidence would not be argumentative and hence legitimate. The problem is that the second situation is patently absurd: the existence of a disembodied arsenal of available evidence to be called forth by "concrete" textual problems seems very hard to justify and would lead us indeed into the conclusion that the solution to every problem is guaranteed a priori by a stock of timeless arguments. But then if the problems create the arguments there is no way, within Wimsatt and Beardsley's theoretical framework, of distinguishing between admissible and inadmissible evidence.

In a way that is very similar to Sainte-Beuve's, Wimsatt and Beardsley are led to such an aporetic situation precisely because the ultimate ground of their prescriptions is a moral one. The 'ought to' implied in their recommendations, although never justified (and could that ever be possible?) defines in the end an all-encompassing situation that undermines all criteria for evidential relevance: for if one were to follow it one would have to follow it blindly, including everything that would contribute to the fulfillment of the initial moral prescription—"internal," "external," "public"," "private," whatever. This is perhaps the sense of Kant's remark that moral prescriptions are to be followed *blindly*. There is, moreover, a second similarity between Sainte-Beuve, Freud, and Wimsatt and Beardsley's third group of evidence: in all such cases we are in the presence of very clear narrative prescriptions; that is, in the presence of the problem of organizing a legitimate, discriminating biography. Such an organization is made possible by the supposition of an end for that story and thus an aim for argumentation; psychological, metaphysical or logological, those ends enable us to tell the difference between proper pertinent stories and Boswell's closet-peeping narratives.

The ultimate import of the existence of narrative prescriptions for biography is of a temporal nature and allows us to connect procedures of demonstration with their temporal consequences. The kind of inference that supports Wimsatt and Beardsley's reallocation of biography, by being assisted by criteria that make possible a distinction between legitimate and illegitimate pasts, so to speak, that is, pasts that are fit to become causes and pasts without posterity, reproduces in itself the very structure of choice that narrative embodies. It is then relatively easy to understand why the narrative structure of biography would derive directly from a given partition of evidence (and would eventually incorporate the disturbances that are likely to affect the latter).

Johnson's emphasis on contemporariness, on the other hand, seems to be connected with some sort of refusal of inference. Such a refusal would mean the refusal of a past from which consequences could be extracted. But the possibility of organizing narrative prescriptions, and indeed the possibility of using as an argument "the general and rapid narratives of history," fall with such a refusal. What one finds instead is the belief in a kind of eloquence of the object that would yield its meaning by its simply being shown, demonstrations being here the mere act of showing objects that are contiguous in some way to the life of the author. In this sense, the adoption of a noninferential model of demonstration (which, by the way, would betray a shift from dialectics to rhetoric or even poetics) necessarily presupposes a model of pan-contemporariness, that goes equally well with Johnson's classicism of principle and with Johnson's insistence on the "management of things which nothing but their frequency makes considerable."

In Montaigne we find, of course, a neater, albeit intermittent, formulation of a doctrine of the unreliability of inference:

> The inference [*consequence*] that we try to draw from the resemblance of events is uncertain, because they are always dissimilar: there is no quality so universal in this aspect [*image*] of things as diversity and variety. Both the Greeks and the Latins, and we ourselves, use eggs for the most express example of similarity. However, there have been men, and notably one at Delphi, who recognized marks of difference between eggs, so that he never took one for another; and although there were many hens, he could tell [*sçavoit juger*] which one the egg came from. Dissimilarity necessarily intrudes [*s'ingere d'elle mesme*] into our works; no art can attain similarity. (III, 13, p. 815)

On the one hand, inference is seen as a way of dealing with an incommensurability of events. Such a way presents itself under the shape of an art of attaining commensurability. But on the other hand, Montaigne's general principle is here precisely that "there is no quality so universal in this aspect of things as diversity and variety." The methodological solution, in the preceding passage, comes under the shape of an exemplum; such an exemplum, nevertheless, is presented as a major objection to Montaigne's general principle ("However"). The way in which it is exemplary is the way in which it tells us the short story of someone who can deal with dissimilitude without, for that matter, being able to reduce it to the form of a science. But because such an action would be self-contradicting, the solution of the Greek is, of course, his being able to tell differences in a purely practical way (and it is curious how my own sentence reacts to the form 'The solution is to have an ability'). Now the only way of doing this, once the deduction of actual features from a principle of eggness is methodologically refused, consists in reacting to eggs upon *monstratio*; that is, being able to read in their individual appearances the difference that makes judgment possible (*sçavoit juger*) only insomuch as it gladly remains within the limits of the contingence, within the limits of the "one" and the "another." If the ultimate reason why inference is unreliable is because every egg is a case, the practical acknowledgment that it is so constitutes a parallel process of demonstration meant for the *individuum*.

To get back to Wimsatt and Beardsley, it is perhaps possible to see now how the positing of an end for biography and the establishment of narrative prescriptions for biography make particularly evident the fantastic character of such a grammar: the choice of an "inferable" past defines a basic narrative movement that, in its own compulsiveness, contaminates the *parti-pris* of internality that allegedly characterizes Wimsatt and Beardsley's conception of criticism. Or, if one prefers (and I think I do), it links together criticism and compulsion and thus, in a somewhat devious way, identifies again good arguments, bad arguments, and hardly arguments: all arguments are good so long as they relate inferentially to the good past, to the past inhabitable by the spirit.

VI

Such a moral drive is quite surprisingly present in authors that, like E.D. Hirsch, Jr., believe that "only one interpretive problem can be answered with objectivity: 'What, in all probability, did the author mean to convey?'" (1967, p. 207). As a matter of fact, Hirsch writes,

> Since it is very easy for a reader of any text to construe meanings that are different from the author's, there is nothing in the nature of the text itself which requires the reader to set up the author's meaning as his normative ideal. Any normative concept in interpretation implies a choice that is required not by the nature of written texts but rather by the goal that the interpreter sets himself. It is a weakness in many descriptions of the interpretive process that this act of choice is disregarded and the process described as thought the object of interpretation were somehow determined by the ontological status of texts themselves. (Ibid., p. 24)

The function of the concept of author in Hirsch's *Validity in Interpretation* (1967) must be understood within the assumption that the first, grounding choice is a matter of values and not a matter of necessity. In a paragraph that understandably escapes the attention of anti-Hirschean commentators, Hirsch remarks that "no necessity requires the object of interpretation to be determinate or indeterminate, changing or unchanging. On the contrary, the object of interpretation is no automatic given, but a task that the interpreter sets himself. *He* decides what he wants to actualize and what purpose his actualization should achieve" (ibid., p. 25). And, indeed, Hirsch's basic distinction between "meaning" ("that which is represented by a text...what the author meant by his use of a particular sign sequence...what the signs represent," ibid., p. 8) and "significance" ("a relationship between that meaning and a person, or a conception, or a situation, or indeed anything imaginable," ibid.) is first and foremost a distinction between the realms of, to use the appropriate theological vocabulary, predestination and free will, with an important difference, however: because the principle of the possibility of choice that applies to the field of significance, that is, to criticism, is again reflected into the adoption of a basic normative principle, there is a sense in which, for Hirsch, predestination is a matter of free will. The dialectic between predestination and free will is very apparent in Hirsch's own terminology:

> So long as the meaning of his [an author's] utterance is our object, we are completely *subservient to his will*, because the meaning of his utterance is *the meaning he wills to convey*. Once we have construed his meaning, however, *we are quite independent of his will*. We do not have to *accept* any longer values and assumptions he entertained. We can relate his meaning to *anything we want* and value it *as we please*. (Ibid., p. 142; emphasis added)

Of course, the Thelemic overtones of the last sentence are mitigated subsequently by the imperatives of scientific inquiry ("we emancipate ourselves from the author only to be enslaved (if we are honest and percipient) by whatever reality it is to which we have chosen to relate his work. However, this is a new kind of subservience," ibid., p. 143). But, nevertheless, the "return to the author," for which Hirsch is famous, is dictated ultimately by moral reasons that are hard to distinguish from the voluntary enslavement of the honest critics.

Logical necessity is, then, a product of a choice of value or, better, of a primal evaluation:

> As soon as anyone claims validity for his interpretation (and few would listen to a critic who did not), he is immediately caught in a web of logical necessity. If his claim to validity is to hold, he must be willing to measure his interpretation against a genuinely discriminating norm, and the only compelling normative principle that has ever been brought forward is the old-fashioned ideal of rightly understanding what the author meant. (Ibid., p. 26)

'Author', to Hirsch, is thus the designation for what he takes to be the strongest norm of validity possible. At the same time, Hirsch achieves the formulation of a perfectly sharp criterion of argumentativity: the argumentational use of a proposition, its evidential character, depends on its relevance to the knowledge of an author's meaning, which Hirsch calls sometimes "author's will" (e.g., ibid., pp. 183-184). It is then as if no nonauthorial arguments were possible if we are to play at all the game of giving reasons in the restricted domain of Hirsch's "meaning": "to banish the original author as the determiner of meaning was to reject the only compelling normative principle that could lend validity to an interpretation" (ibid., p. 5).

Even if Hirsch's theory can be linked to a vindication of biographical arguments, which is achieved theoretically through his rereading of Wimsatt and Beardsley and de facto in the numerous examples of the settling of a controversy he presents (viz., 1960, pp. 239ff. on Wordsworth's "A slumber did my spirit seal"), it would be fairly inaccurate, I think, to say that the impossibility of no nonauthorial arguments is to Hirsch the same as an impossibility of no nonbiographical arguments. The word 'author' is used by Hirsch as synonymous with a principle of authority; that is, a metaempirical construct: "The speaking subject is not...identical with the subjectivity of the author as an actual historical person; it corresponds, rather, to a very limited and special aspect of the author's total subjectivity; it is, so to speak, that 'part' of the author which specifies or determines verbal meaning" (ibid., p. 243). In such a distinction we can perceive the full import of Hirsch's rereading of Wimsatt and Beardsley; for what is at stake is a distinction between the irrelevance of purely biographical evidence (Wimsatt and Beardsley's external evidence) *and* the legitimate evidence of an originary *Sinngebung* (close to Wimsatt and Beardsley's intermediate evidence). Incidentally, such a point would show that Wimsatt and Beardsley never realize the dependence of their theory of literary evidence on the conception of a meaning-attributive subject.

But even the remotely empirical connection between the protagonist of a *Sinngebung* and an "actual historical person," which is still present in Hirsch's 1960 essay I have been quoting from, is considerably shattered by some formulations of the work of 1967: far from postulating a synechdochical relation between speaking subject and historical person, Hirsch, in a resolutely antiempirical move, decides to stick to the very a-priority (and indeed to the transcendentality) of the principle of authorship he supports and, in a paradoxically much more radical way than Wimsatt and Beardsley's alleged "antiintentionalism" (which seems to me to be no more than a mild case of antibiographism propelled by a few basic terminological misunderstandings), writes that "even when the original author is rejected or disregarded, any construction of a text still constitutes a meaning that must have an author—though he be merely the critic himself. All forms of written interpretation and all interpretive goals that transcend private experience require that some author's meaning be both determinate and reproducible" (1967, p. 27). Such a position (which incidentally would become one of the favorite themes for the variations of critics such as P.D. Juhl, S. Fish, and S. Knapp and W.B. Michaels) carries the refutation of Wimsatt and Beardsley's notion of internal evidence. Hirsch's point is obviously akin to his own version of Husserl's: our making meaning of a sequence of signs presupposes that our dealing with the latter is based on the assumption that they are the product of intentional acts of attribution of meaning. Wimsatt and Beardsley's notion of internal evidence, hence, because it emphasizes the stratified decisions of what Stanley Fish later would call interpretive communities, "implies that the meaning represented by a text is not the *parole* of an author....But since only individuals utter *paroles*, a *parole* of the speech community is a non-existent, or what the Germans call an *Unding*" (1960, p. 234).

In short, one could perfectly well say that, seen with Hirschean glasses (which, it is good to remember, up to the recent "Against Theory" controversy, actually have prevailed on both sides of the fence), Wimsatt and Beardsley's partition of evidence is shown to be untenable: internal evidence is really intermediate evidence, intermediate evidence is simply pertinent evidence and external evidence is indistinguishable from pertinent evidence.

What makes P.D. Juhl's 1980 *Interpretation* a singular work in the current traditions of English-speaking criticism is, as Frank Kermode once remarked after a rather unfavorable review of the book, its having "the merit of not assuming a great deal that is often too crudely taken for granted" (1981, p. 210). Although supporting most of Hirsch's points and, indeed, participating in the same strategy of return to the author, Juhl's books present some major differences. The first one (which I shall not analyze) is, *grosso modo*, the replacement of a Husserl-inspired theory of signification by a Speech act oriented model, implying a somewhat different meaning of the word *intention*. The second, which carries direct implications for my discussion, is the assumption that the principle of authority we sometimes call *author* is necessarily imposed on an interpretation, and also that such a priority is strictly logical, independent from any moral choice. In other words, and contrary to Hirsch's theory, we cannot choose not having *the* author (whatever that might mean). In our little story of authors in arguments, Juhl seems to typify not only the impossibility of no nonauthorial arguments for restricted domains (such as Hirsch's realm of meaning), but indeed the plain impossibility of no nonauthorial arguments: it is the very status of argumentativity that appears to be inextricably tied—and logically so—to the notion of author.

The interesting thing about Juhl's book (and one in which it can be said to break away from the core of the New Critical tradition) is the deliberate nonexistence of a concept that mediates two universes acknowledged as distinct (such as Wimsatt and Beardsley's "external" and "internal" domains). Such a nonexistence expresses not only Juhl's rejection of all dialectics of interiority and exteriority that goes with most correspondence theories of truth, but also the rejection of notions such as Booth's implied author, textual author, and even Hirsch's opposition between "historical person" and "speaking subject." One of the central these of Juhl's book is precisely that

> if a literary work conveys or expresses certain propositions, then...the real author is committed to the truth of those propositions and to the corresponding beliefs; that is, the propositions of a work expresses or conveys are expressed or conveyed by, and hence attributable to, not the "implied author" but rather the real historical author. It follows that, in an important sense, literature is not autonomous, that the connection between literature and life is a good deal closer that the implied-author doctrine, or the view that (fictional) literary works cannot make genuine assertions, would lead us to believe. (1980, p. 13)

If by "making genuine assertions" Juhl means, as he himself acknowledges (e.g. ibid., p. 167n), what Searle meant in *Speech Acts*, that is, making assertions that satisfy the "rules governing the nondefective performance of an act of asserting a certain proposition" (ibid., p. 167), it is also true that the proof of this thesis can be obtained only on the basis of how critics and readers in general deal with literary texts. As a matter of fact, Juhl seems here to identify the text and its interpretation and thus hermeneutic suppositions and textual features. Perhaps for this reason the continuity between author and work is not grounded theoretically on an a priori principle of sincerity (as in Sainte-Beuve) or even on an a priori principle of determination (as in

Freud). The identification between a statement and a real person (although Juhl does not acknowledge this point) seems to be rather a matter of critical assumption; that is, a matter of the very way an alleged general game of critical argumentation is played. Juhl's demonstration of this point seems to me perfectly true, insignificant, and convincing. He basically chooses passages from critics recognized usually as adverse to his own thesis (namely, Empson, Crane, and Booth) and tries to show how the statement of the reverse of his own thesis presupposes their belief in the principle he defends, in a blindness-and insightish way that implicitly assumes that the discovery of a spot of blindness carries the dispensation of all further rhetorical incidents for the critical discourse of discovery. Incidentally, such a trait would be one of the major rhetorical ingredients of the "Against Theory" controversy, that I shall evoke later.

One cannot deny that there is a certain charm in the sight of an intentionalist Empson. But that is, after all, the charm of all processes of justification that tend to demonstrate that there can be no rhetorical alternative to them and thus that disagreement is a form of alienated or unavowable agreement, the figuration of an omnipresent literality that is, so to speak, single voiced. Rather, Juhl's arguments derive basically from his analysis of what Aristotle, with some contempt, once called the mere opinion (in which Juhl follows the English-speaking tradition that insisted on the identification of common sense and common language and produced most of what went by the name of analytic philosophy): "the force of the common argument that, say, a particular poem is not to be taken as an expression of certain beliefs (of the speaker) because those beliefs are, for example, plainly false, unduly pessimistic, unduly optimistic, immoral or biased rests on the implicit assumption that if the poem expresses those beliefs, the author is committed to them and to their truth" (ibid., p. 172).

But precisely because Juhl's arguments demonstrate that the belief in a real person is a matter of critical assumption (even though such are necessary) it is simply not possible for him to prove the existence of any essential connection whatsoever between the person of an author and the statements he or she produces. It is, then, as if Juhl's overly publicized primal granting of an innate authority to language games (even though metatheoretically cautioned by a "commonsensicality of principle," as Kant would have said, that would reassure that common language could never get wild) would bring as a rather awkward companion a principle of weakness for all explanations it makes possible. In fact, from the supposition that the existence of critical assumptions is logically necessary, or even that critical assumptions provide the ground for disputations and hence warrant conclusions, one cannot infer a principle of stability for the contents of such assumptions. In Sainte-Beuve and Freud there was the conception of something ontologically prior and topologically exterior to discourse and thus an essential gap to be filled by rules of connection that were both transcendental and a priori. But once one admits, no matter how timidly, that there is no autonomous field of language (and at this point one begins to feel the effects of the most radical consequences of Wittgenstein's later philosophy), or even that a thing such as conceptual analysis is possible, one must do away with every rule of connection and use contradictorily expressions such as Juhl's "real, historical person"—even if the use of language one relies on presupposes such a thing as real people.

It can probably be said, however, that, although he cannot accept any distinction between common sense and common language (and thus perhaps between mere opinion and theory), Juhl is intermittently aware of the ambivalence of his own conception of the author as being a "real, historical person," not in the sense that he ever doubts "the homely truth that poets do after all actually say things" (ibid., p. 195), but rather in the sense that the considerable sophistication of his theory of critical arguments prevents him from relying too much on the version of narratives that express a wish for a deduction of things poets say from something they define as poets, also known as biographical arguments:

> I am not arguing for a kind of biographical approach to the study of literature. Whether or not personal events in a poet's life play an important role in his poetry is an *empirical* question and obviously cannot be settled on *a priori* grounds. It may be a truism that a man's (personal) experience shapes his beliefs and values; but it evidently does not follow that a poem or a novel is about the writer's personal life or about his psychological states. (Ibid., p. 15)

In this respect, the authors I have been analyzing can be divided into two families, and it is not irrelevant perhaps that this division is a historical one. The difference between, say, Johnson, Sainte-Beuve, and Freud, on the one hand, and Wimsatt, Beardsley, and the others, on the other hand, denotes a decisive shift in the very partition of evidence we have been discussing. Such a shift would correspond to a shift in the status of biographical evidence, from a-priority to empiricity. Of course, Juhl, like most of his contemporaries and, in the end, most of those who now indulge in the indeed extremely pleasurable biographical explanations, believes that "biographical facts may...be decisive by showing, for example, that an interpretation is based on mistaken assumptions about the author's knowledge" (ibid., p. 89). But, he adds, "whether the biographical facts about a certain author constitute string or weak evidence, are or are not decisive, depends on the particulars of the case" (ibid.). It is as if contemporary criticism, in this instance, had kept the rhetorical powers of a-priority as a nonrule, as a merely empirical recommendation.

To this tradition belong perhaps Steven Knapp and Walter Benn Michaels's interventions in the "Against Theory" controversy. But such an appurtenance does not lie primarily in the actual positions they appear to support. As a matter of fact, the specific difference of their opinions is, throughout the whole controversy and as could be legitimately expected, the object of a quite straightforward rhetoricization. Rather, Knapp and Michaels's relation with the questions I have been discussing has more to do with the form of the problems they inherited. And if it can be inferred from the occurrence of such words as 'author' and even 'intention', there are less obvious levels of appurtenance that are related for instance to Hirsch's ethical concerns. A good way of opposing them to both Hirsch and Juhl but, at the same time, making manifest how oppositions are literally grounded by similarities would be precisely by discussing the status of Knapp and Michaels's 'oughts'.

When Knapp and Michaels write that "all meaning is always the author's meaning" (1982, pp. 14-15) and, later, add that "Any interpreter of any utterance or text, within the institution of professional literary criticism or not, is...attempting to understand the author's intention" (1983, p. 105) they are assuming implicitly some form of propositional connection between the two statements.

Such a connection has perhaps the form of an equivalence: the equivalence between author's meaning and author's intention. And, indeed, such an equivalence has the somewhat awkward function, within Knapp and Michaels's arguments, of providing them with an indispensable metatheoretical claim: "once it is seen that the meaning of a text is simply identical to the author's intended meaning, the project of *grounding* meaning in intention becomes incoherent" (1982, p. 12). Because the latter operation is a possible form of "the attempt to govern interpretations of particular texts by appealing to an account of interpretation in general" (ibid., p. 11), it follows that if one (metatheoretically) supposes a principle of equivalence between meaning and intention, then no meaning-grounding operation can be theoretically justified. The argument is syntactically flawless, despite the facts of being an argument against the relevance of syntax and introducing surreptitiously a metatheoretical claim.

However, and at another level both statements can easily be rendered incompatible. In fact, whereas the first statement refers to something like an essential attribute of meaning, the second refers to a logical necessity of interpretation. The equivalence mentioned earlier can thus be said to subsume an identification: the identification between 'is' and 'does'.

Nevertheless, it is perhaps possible to say that, strangely enough, and for Knapp and Michaels's arguments to be true, such an identification cannot be a two-way identification. In other words, within their arguments it is true that an equivalence of meaning and authorial intention is supposed to be the cause (in Wittgenstein's sense) of certain (indeed of all) interpretive acts: but it cannot be true that the former is a side effect or a by-product of the latter. For if it were true, it would not become possible for Knapp and Michaels to rule out completely all forms of what they call theory, because there would not be any principle that could rule the project of grounding meaning in general. That is to say that as long as 'is' is the cause of 'does' there are no problems. But when one, shielded by the identification between 'is' and 'does', supposes (in a tempting pragmatist move) that indeed 'does' is also the cause of 'is', there is no possibility of, to paraphrase an obvious reference in these thorny matters, deriving an 'ought' from there.

The 'ought' question that we discussed earlier in Hirsch's formulation recurs in the major explicit metatheoretical thesis of Knapp and Michaels and is indeed brought to a level of prominence that suggests a very likely connection between it and the current use of terms like 'author'. But whereas in Hirsch the statement of such a question is surrounded by all the props of dignity (because Hirsch realizes that within his system it is a decisive question) and even in Juhl the question of choice still appears beautified by the sublimity of supposing that there is no choice (only logical necessity), in Knapp and Michaels it is, one would like to say, stated by understatement. As a matter of fact, the way of their positing it as a rule is ostensibly casual: "we do think that theory, like our arguments against it, will continue to have no consequences for the practice of literary criticism" (1983, p. 105).

One is tempted, nevertheless, to see moments of constricted nonchalance in all their uses of 'should': "If our arguments are true, they can only have one consequence...theory should stop" (ibid.); "the theoretical impulse...always involves the attempt to separate things that should not be separated" (1982, p. 29); "our thesis has been that no one can reach a position outside practice, that theorists should stop trying, and that the theoretical impulse should therefore come to an end" (ibid., p. 30).

The first of these two attitudes can be left on the account of a temporary supremacy of 'does' over 'is'. When Knapp and Michaels go strictly pragmatist they become oblivious to their more general move against theory: one does what one does, and there is no way of successfully prescribing (or grounding the prescriptions of) patterns of behavior. Moreover, there is no way of determining in this context whether the intentional shaping of meaning (and thus the entrance of the figure of the author) is made necessary by interpretation, unless one, metatheoretically again, assumes that all interpretive practices are a priori identical. I have, however, some problems in imagining the formulation of such an assumption outside of an attempt to rule over practice.

The second and more constricted attitude reveals, meanwhile, a no less temporary supremacy of 'is' over 'does'. And then the ontological statement, placed in a position of anteriority, of course, can justify prescriptions in a metatheoretical way: one does what to do *is* and one ought to acknowledge all the implications of such a procedure. But unfortunately, it leaves the door open to an obvious question, invented perhaps by one of Richard Rorty's most controversial fellow pragmatists, Friedrich Nietzsche, Why ought one to acknowledge such implications?

The 'ought' question mediates then, in Knapp and Michaels's theories, all relations between 'is' and 'does' and fuels indeed a to-and-fro movement that consists in a sort of alternation between two attitudes and two language games: a game in which the unimportance of rhetoric is rhetoricized (and where all metatheoretical propositions including the identification between meaning and intention are literally inconsequential, all practices made irrelevant); and a game in which the importance of rhetoric is unrhetoricized (and where prescriptions derived from metatheoretical claims are exempted from debate). And what is curious is that the notion of practice allows for both treatments. In the first version it stands for reality, for something that passes irrevocably aside from the dreams of theoretical ghost seers. But in the second version it stands for the embodiment of matter-of-factuality itself, which imposes a shape on things or, rather, which inscribes and prescribes the shape of actions. In this context it is relatively easy to understand why practice as reality needs to be built as an object of a figuration, whereas practice as matter-of-factuality needs to be seen as literality itself: do not think, because things are not what they seem, and act, because things are exactly what they seem.

My reference to the "Against Theory" controversy was not merely the reference to another (probably the latest) installment in the story of the author, itself part of a story of the theoretical construction of effects of homogeneity in literary studies. The first of these two stories, at least (as to other possible stories, see Chapter 4), would have to incorporate in a perpetually awkward way the very heterogeneity of the position of writers like Johnson. In Johnson, as I have tried to show, the homogeneity embodied in the concept of 'author' is achieved in fact through a multiplying of signs of heterogeneity. I wonder however, if *that* can be called an achievement.

It should be apparent by now how the "Against Theory" controversy also relates clearly to a distinctive way of using last arguments in current debates in criticism. In fact, the alternation between the supremacy of 'is' and 'does' in the texts of Knapp and Michaels, as well as the role 'ought' plays in them, are at this point another instance of keeping the rhetorical powers of a-priority as a nonrule, as a merely empirical recommendation (and an ethical recommendation, at that). For Knapp and Michaels, the author is both there, independent from and oblivious to the interpretive chores of the readers, as a moral law that sees itself under the species of logical necessity, *and* here, as a compelling source of precepts that readers are supposed to follow. Such a double stance or, better, the circulation between its poles, with the dialectical incidents that go with it, renders impossible its "syntactically" working as an a priori principle of argumentation. But the strength that keeps doubly disjoined allegations working together achieves in fact the function of a metacritical principle. That is to say, the very infelicities of the heterogenization of the concept of author are converted into a homogenizing factor. And then (but are we prepared to deal with that?) such a moment is perhaps the major consequence of what one could call Knapp and Michaels's will to refutation that would go with the very possibility of controversy. It is ironic enough that the theoretical justification of the concept of author, the entrance of the word in activities of justification, has taken

taken place only at a moment when theoreticians have been left alone with a pure will to justification. But, more ironic perhaps, is that the burden of proof would come to rest on professed antifoundationists, of all people.

4

The Best Part of Language

I

The circulation of the word *literature* (or, rather, the Latin misspelled form *literatura*) had a curious swerve in the latter part of the seventeenth century that has remained within the horizon of the discussion of some of the most vexed questions of literary studies. Such a swerve is connected with a persistent fascination with China. It is well known how the Chinese metaphor contaminated conceptions great and small of literary studies. But the fascination with both China and the word 'literature' precedes historically the fascination with both literature and the word 'China'.

China and 'literature' come together under the question of the Chinese language or, to be more precise, under the question of knowing whether Chinese *is* a language at all. The first sinologists could not decide, and the notion used to denote their indecision was precisely the notion of literature (one might recognize here the roots of a widespread conception of literature: what one cannot tell if it is still language). Chinese, even if not a language proper (or even in spite of being a language proper), presented itself as what was called a *litteratura*; that is, a set of characters. Conversely, the characteristic (in a sense used by Leibniz that I shall address in more detail later) nature of Chinese, by raising the problem of its own institution in a very explicit way, seemed to be opposed to the kind of "naturality" that traditionally went with the *proper* of language. That is, literatures were, here too, beyond the opposition between natural language and artificial language, in that they did not allow for a positive verdict on their institution.

The question of how a language can be seen as a *characteristica* is of considerable interest to my discussion, in this chapter. That Chinese was thought to be a characteristica meant that, if Chinese was really a language, then, some languages, by being characteristic languages, were combinatory products of a finite number of letters, that is, were *litteraturae*. The notion of 'literature' appears here in a tight opposition with a never fully specified notion of historical corruption: the difference between literary languages (sometimes called, as we shall see, deaf languages) and other languages is simply a difference in modes of historicity. Literature behaves toward temporality in such a way that the characteristic nature is never threatened by linguistic change and, indeed, by usage: even if characters can and indeed do change, they never wear out, let alone wear off (the metaphor conveys a story perhaps as old as Horace).

The discussion of the virtues of Chinese language, that, in the seventeenth century, fascinated writers such as Gohl, Müller, Kircher, and Leibniz, led eventually to severe conceptual disappointments. When Leibniz discovered that after all the Chinese language was like the others (that is, it *did* wear out) he also renounced the project of salvaging any *actual* characteristic for the project of building one and, finally, after some further mishaps that need not concern us here, he turned to the question of the universals of existing languages. Be that as it may, the literary nature of Chinese conferred on it the title of best empirical predecessor of Leibniz's characteristic efforts. Indeed, it emphasized a point, which proved to be determinant for the emergence of literary studies as an autonomous discipline: the idea that there is a connection between the degree of felicity of a given linguistic combination and its charateristicity, that is, its being recognized as a combinatory product. Such was, incidentally, the ground principle of both rhetoric and poetics (as opposed to the motley doctrines of inspiration).

But, and perhaps even more decisively, some of the key concepts of literary studies were equally derived from a metarhetorical and metapoetical notion of literality deeply tied to the allegations of "deafness" vis-à-vis Chinese. Such is the idea (which gained extended currency in recent developments in literary studies) that literature's mode of appearance is cut away from a voice, that is, that the materiality of a literature is deaf; from its very inception, indeed, philology had to assume the purely *characteristic* identity of its object. The notion through which such an assumption was (and still is) conveyed is the notion of text.

One can understand thus what might be termed the literary substratum of the notion of text: the ways in which this latter notion was used, primarily, but not only, by philology, denoted not just an emphasis on the attributes of perenniality (here too, "Was bleibet...stiften die Dichter") but also, furthermore, the attributes of a *characteristic* combination (which eventually would cause stylistics to be torn between the two senses of the word: in Spitzer's terms, which were also his crux, the search for the letter and the search for the etymon) and, finally, the attributes of a certain kind of severance (which would originate the opposition between the deafness, sometimes rewritten as autism, of literature and a model of referential continuity associated with common, "natural" languages). In this chapter I propose to follow the argumentative implications of the notion of an appeal to the text, bearing in mind the decisive moment of its "Chinese" conception.

II

In his *China Monumentis, qua Sacris qua Profanis, Nec non variis Naturae & Artis Spectaculis, Aliarumque rerum memorabilium Argumentis Illustrata*, better known as *China Illustrata*, Father Athanasius Kircher, S.J., translates the Latin version of the second commandment (*Non nominare Dei Sanctum nomen ad proferendum inane juramentum*) as "Lh́. uû hu tien chù xiḿ mím ỳ fa chái xí" (1667, p. 127). The text is included in a catechism (*"Divinae Legis compendium"*). Kircher uses a coeval system of transliteration ,heavily burdened with all sorts of diacritics. As a matter of fact, later in the book, he assimilated the five tones of Chinese to the first five notes in the Western hepetonic scale (ibid., p. 236). And, five years later, Andreas Müller added a musical staff to his own transliteration of the alleged Nestorian monument of Sianfu (cf. Lach, 1940, pp. 566-567). Immediately before the catechism, Kircher remarks to the reader that "Chinese language...differs from our Latin language in the way in which it is spoken [*in modo loquendi*]" (1667, p. 121). And he adds: "do not be surprised if the Latin translation word to word [*Latinam interpretationem de verbo ad verbum*] is thus made devious and awkward [*tortam & inconcinam*] (ibid.).

The predicaments of seventeenth century sinologists allegorize only too well not so much the anthropological problem of the translation of the other as a peculiar conception of translation as transliteration. For that process, Kircher uses the Latin word *interpretatio*. An interpretation, in this sense, is nothing more than the automatic conversion of one system of notation into another and presupposes thus the existence of what was then known as a *clauis*, a key. To all appearances, there was a mythical *Clauis sinica*, allegedly invented in 1667 by Andreas Müller, never published and eventually destroyed in the early 1690s by Müller himself. The key had become an important piece of intellectual gossip from the late 1670s on: it was said to contain a sort of generalized algorithm and thus would embody the very project of an *interpretatio recta*, as opposed to Father Kircher's *interpretatio torta* (Kircher was himself the author of a famous, albeit empirical, *Polygraphia*, published in 1663).

The polygraphic efforts of person like Kircher and Müller denote a very untimely conception of language. Such is the conception according to which *certain* (though not all) natural languages are conventional constructions, with the subsidiary metaphor of language as a piece of architecture (that is, of something that is perceived with a purpose). In his *China Illustrata*, Kircher, in fact, slides swiftly from a description of the Great Wall of China and the merits of Pekinese bells into a discussion of the "Chinese Hieroglyphic Characters" (ibid., pp. 225-236). In this latter section, aptly entitled "De Sinensium Literatura [sic]," the word "literatura" is used as a collective noun for "theory of letters" or, rather, "survey of characters." The discussion of a *literatura* for Kircher depends thus both on the existence of letters and on the possibility of a point of survey. The former is dealt with as an empirical, anthropological fact. The latter condition, though, carries the belief in a general key to the diversity of literary phenomena and thus a principle of interliterary equivalence. The question was certainly not a peaceful one. In his *Unterricht von der Reformirten und Lutherischen Kirchen*, published in 1678, Elias Grebnitz, in D. F. Lach's words, "attacked the Chinese language as a product of the devil...[and] insisted that as soon as the name of God should be used in this picture-writing a sin would be commited against the second commandment" (1940, p. 573). In a good sense, then, Kircher's interpretation mentioned earlier can be considered, in Greibniz's eyes, as a metasin: for by transliterating the commandment according to which, in Greibniz's interpretation, transliteration itself is regulated, Kircher would be indeed placing a command between quotes, that is, intentionally rewriting as infelicitous or at least "calculable" the will of God (Paul de Man discussed once Greibniz-like objections under the topic of "resistance to theory").

The fact that, for literary studies, the notion of text became increasingly the ambiguous notion through which is denoted the access to evidence of the other of language, namely, through the philological circumvolutions discussed in Chapter 2, determines perhaps the fundamental ambiguity of all appeals to such evidence: on the one hand, they invariably presuppose a standard common to language and its other (comparable to Kircher's notion of literatura) and a discipline of that commonness (comparable to Kircher's polygraphy); but, on the other hand, they invariably tend to gloss the pitfalls of *interpretatio torta,* that is, of the torture of interpretation and hence of the ultimate incompetence of any and every key. In this latter sense, the appeal to the text is the appeal to some sort of *incalculable* authority that cannot know but an *interpretatio torta*: not anymore the conversion of grammars presupposed by the existence of a key but rather the kind of interpretation that is required, indeed forced on the interpreter by the modes of incalculableness themselves, by the shortcomings of an empirically given key. In other words, the allusiveness (and the elusiveness) of the text becomes in this model the very source of the latter's authority and represents a transitional case toward the displacement of the very possibility of a key, eventually to be replaced by an equivalent of what Augustine called a rule of faith (which, incidentally, he never adopted entirely).

It would be important at this juncture, then, to dissociate the previously mentioned kind of torture (whose reason is interpretation alone) from the purely "keyless" conception of the sublimity of the other as the cause of one's present mishaps. Such a conception was discussed at some length in Chapters 1 and 2, and, for brevity's sake, I shall ignore it now. Kircher's discussion of the difference between Chinese and Egyptian hieroglyphs (and of the superiority of the first), as indeed all the subsequent efforts in the sense of the construction of a flawless *clauis sinica,* are, in fact, a very clear instance of what one could call the secularization (and desublimization) of the cognitive interests of a *literatura.* The reasons for Kircher's efforts are primarily empirical and pragmatic. Indeed, the major difference between Egyptian and Chinese hieroglyphs is that the former "denoted mysteries...[and] implied whole ideal concepts [*integros conceptus ideales*]" (1667, p. 234) whereas the latter "indicated simple concepts" and "no other latent mystery was instituted beneath them" (ibid.). With some qualifications that I shall indicate further on, this last point became eventually Pound's slogan "Get your 'red' down to rose" (1937, p. 202). Be this as it may, the projects of both Müller and Kircher of a Chinese *literatura,* that is, their concept of *interpretatio,* were characterized by the predominance of epistemological over aesthetic or moral grounds (even the ultimate conversion of the Chinese people was configured as a scientific or at best a political feat). And, of course, the serious defense of the possibility of a key, by including explicitly a metalinguistic vantage point, seemed to be incompatible with the correctability of such a key, that is, with the existence of cases that would upset the metalinguistic vantage point (such would be the status of a mystery in an investigation). Kircher's *interpretatio* is never, in this context, either a hermeneutics or a hermetics.

III

On June 24, 1679, G. W. Leibniz wrote to J. S. Elsholz a series of fourteen question directed to Andreas Müller and concerning Müller's *Clauis Sinica*. Among those

1. Whether such a *Key* is unfailing and certain as in our reading our a, b, c's or numbers, or whether from time to time one is in need of help, as often happens in reading hieroglyphics.
2. Since Chinese writing, as well is known, is worked out not on the basis of words, but rather on objects [*nicht auff die worte sondern auff die dinge gerichtet*], so I should like to know if the characters are always made according to the constitution of the object [*nacht der dinge Natur gemachet*].
3. Whether the whole language is based on certain common elements, or a basic alphabet from which the other characters are evolved.
4. Whether inanimate objects are expressed [*außgedrucket*] in terms of the animate.
5. Whether the Chinese language was artificially constructed [*durch Kunst gemacht*], or whether it has grown and changed by usage like other languages.
6. Whether the Chinese language was also artificially constructed on a certain *Key* [*durch Kunst gemacht, undt auff einen gewissen* Clavem *zubringen*].
7. Whether H. Müller therefore believed the Chinese to be unconscious [*ohnbewust*] of the *Key* to their own language.
10. Whether the characters take notice of such natural objects [*Natürliche dinge*] as animals, plants, and stones, and whether thereby the characteristics of objects [*der dinge eigenschafften*] differentiate one object from the other [*eines vom andern unterschieden beziehen*].
11. Whether and to what extent is the bare nature of objects [*die Natur des dinges*] added to... (M:568-9)

Leibniz's questions can be divided in two groups. Certain questions (such as 1, 2, 3, 4, and 7) deal with empirical features of Chinese and thus belong to the history of anthropological curiosity. Some of them (namely, 3 and 4) had already been addressed by Father Kircher in the *China Illustrata*. However, a second group is formed by *literary* questions properly speaking; that is, questions that presuppose a unified point of view as to the construction of *all* languages.

Among these, question 5 is particularly important, because it opposes two modes of origin and assumes, hypothetically, that Chinese has a constructed origin. Later, in the *Nouveaux essais*, Leibniz would still echo approvingly the theories of J. Gohl, according to which Chinese is "an artificial language...invented wholly by some ingenuous man in order to establish a commerce of words [*commerce des paroles*] between the number of different nations which inhabited...China; even if such a language now could be altered by its long usage" (E, p. 274). In the 1679 letter, however, question 5 admits the partly converse possibility of some languages' growing and changing by usage without being "durch Kunst gemacht," that is, articulates usage (and *usure*) with absence of artifice. The reconciliation of these two formulations is perhaps to be found in a third undated fragment, where Leibniz remarks that although "there ought to be a reason why certain words are assigned to certain things, " "it cannot be said that this was a result of design [*ex instituto*]" (O, p. 189). Such a point is decisive in a revision of the notion of construction and in dispelling Gohl's opposition between Western language and artificial language. Leibniz proceeds thus to argue that the loss of a memory of the origin of nonconventional languages is tied to their actualizing of a state of mutilation of an Adamic language (to use Jakob Boehme's term), "ubi artificium deprehendere difficile est" (ibid.). But the point does not preclude a commonness of origin of all languages—quite the contrary, "languages," he writes in the same fragment, "have a certain natural source [*originem naturalem*], namely the harmony [*consensus*] between sounds and affections which the sight of things excites in the mind" (ibid.). The difference between Chinese and other languages is not a difference in origin but rather a difference in the degree of intelligibility of the origin. And the importance of Chinese lies in its allegedly being a case for a *literary* ground: the principle of the construction of a consensus "sonorum cum affectibus."

But even at this level Chinese presents a special problem that comes from its being conceived of as a language *sub specie* of writing. On the one hand, the signs of writing "need not refer to to a voice necessarily, as it is shown by Chinese characters" (T, p. 497). On the other hand, though, and in Kircher's terms, the reason for the difference *in modo loquendi* between Chinese and Western languages is that "Chinese writing...could seem to have been invented by a deaf person" (E, p. 137) (Leibniz also describes a "Caractere Universel" as opposed to the Chinese characteristica as something that would "provide less deaf and more verbal thoughts," ibid., p. 398). Chinese, then, is simultaneously made the object of a suspicion of artificiality and, in Leibniz's *literary* conception of it, removed from any possibility of expressing a consensus between sound and affects; that is, removed from any possibility of being grounded on a construed consensus. The problem, of course, is that if a given language is *given* as writing, its origin can no longer be evaluated in terms of an opposition between natural and artificial.

It is not then so much that, to Leibniz, the example of Chinese as the other of Western languages betrays an opposition between *Kunst* and *Natur*, as it is that it shows that the nature of those languages whose origin was forgotten is itself an *artificial* production (albeit not *ex instituto*) and thus that *any* language is the actualization of certain possibilities of language in general, which is to say that language has no *other*. The key of a given language (alluded to in question 6), the trace of a constructing intention, of what Leibniz calls an *artificium*, is thus comparable to a poetics of certain combinations. This means that the principle of consensus admits of a multiplicity of applications and thus that concurrent applications cannot be evaluated in the terms of such a principle (à la Grebnitz) but rather in terms of poetic criteria, which is to say, in terms of their effects and their intrinsic systematicity.

Questions 10 and 11 address details of construction of a given *literatura* (and in Leibniz the term can be assimilated to 'characteristica'; that is, a given set of characters or *litterae*) and point therefore to the possibility of a semiotic critique of certain combinations; that is, a critique of the consequences of certain *artificia*. Question 11, for example, concerns the nature of the constructed relation between sign and thing, whereas question 10 concerns the possibility of a systematic homology between signs and things (the question of whether it is possible for a system of things to articulate its internal differences as if it were a system of things).

The construction of a well-formed language, for Leibniz, implies nevertheless the formulation of a poetic criteria, criteria of construction that would assure a ground for a semiotic critique. Leibniz's distinction between any characteristica and a *characteristica realis* is decisive in the formulation of such criteria: *real* characters are characters that represent the concept of the thing *immediately*. In this sense, the characters of phonetic alphabets are not *real*, because they represent the sound of words. Leibniz associates representational mediation with some sort of entropy of signification, which is to say that there is an inverse proportionality between the usefulness of a semiotic system and the number of instances of representation. "Signs," he writes, "are the more useful the more they express the concept of the thing they denote [*quanto magis notionem rei signatae exprimunt*]" (S, p. 181). And in this respect Marcelo Dascal remarks that, for Leibniz, "the highest degree of expression is attained by a sign from which all the predications deducible from the essential concept of the thing denoted can be directly deduced" (1987, p. 185n). This first criterion one might call, following Leibniz, a principle of "autarchy of characters" (cf. Leibniz, C, p. 284, also partly translated in Dascal, 1987, p. 185n). But it is clear that the justification of such a principle entails a further distinction, as the degree of immediacy of all real characters cannot be said to be identical.[4] In fact, some real characters are not even representative (numbers, or instance), and thus their usefulness is exclusively absorbed by their functions within a system. Chinese, in this sense, would represent an intermediate case between Western languages and a totally autarchic characteristic. And Leibniz's doubt as to the possibility of building a *Clauis Sinica* (cf. for instance Lach, 1945, pp. 437-438) can better be seen as doubts about the usefulness of an imperfect algorithm.

As is well known, Leibniz would eventually renounce the project of building a characteristica *ab ovo* for the less adventurous activity of establishing universals for existing languages. The fact remains, nonetheless, that the theme of the imperfection of (existing) words, to use the title of a chapter of the *Nouveaux Essais* (Chapter 3), would remain a constant reference and a reason not only for his particular treatment of Chinese but also for his justification of what he calls "the use and the extent of Criticism [*Critique*], little considered by some Philosophers, very ingenuous otherwise, who allow themselves to speak with contempt of Rabbinage and in general of Philology" (E, p. 337). Philology, one would like to say, is borne by combinatory imperfection, by the impossibility of *certain* models of writing.

Independent from its epistemological status (a priori or a posteriori), the project of building an autarchic characteristica could never quite free itself, in Leibniz's case, from the metaphor of Chinese *literatura*, perhaps because a Chinese characteristica existed already. As

Louis Couturat remarks, Leibniz's using of Chinese hieroglyphs as examples of a *characteristica realis* "shows that a characteristica realis is to him an *ideography*; that is, a system of signs which represent the things (or, rather, the ideas) immediately and not words, allowing every people to read them and translate them into their own language. It would be a writing and a language at the same time" (1901, p. 61). Because, as Couturat also remarks (for instance in ibid., p. 77), the model of the characteristics is, for Leibniz, grounded in a combinatory principle, Chinese would seem to acquire thus the status of the most prestigious empirically verifiable existing combination of signs or, rather, combinatory system of signs (that is, system of signs where there is a relationship of deducibility among an important part of its elements). In this sense, the model of a characteristica is the model of the combinatorily determined appearance of the other as the best part of the same: Chinese is, as it were, a felicitous combination that denotes language at its (empirical) best. And that the problem of the origin of Chinese can be answered only poetically perhaps points to a general notion of knowledge that refuses to attribute to chance its best results. In this chapter I shall try to suggest that in some decisive respects *that* is still an important use of notions such as text and literature.

IV

Ernest Fenollosa's *The Chinese Written Character as a Medium for Poetry*, published in 1920 and in 1936 with a foreword by Ezra Pound, remains the most typical example (albeit by no means as colorful as some of the subsequent *Tel Quel* adventures) of an articulation between the Chinese's language and a model of poeticity: in a sense, it has to do with what I called in section I the fascination with both literature and the word 'China', which, as it seems to be the rule for these cases, presents itself as an infatuation with both China and the word 'literature'. It is not by chance that Pound added to Fenollosa's title the subtitle "An Ars Poetica."

Pound's Foreword to the work is a convenient allegory of the sorts of problems of what one (in a Saïdian mood) could call far orientalism. Discussing Ogden's notion of Basic English, namely, the examples of "their sixteen verbal activities" (Pound, 1936, p. 6), Pound proceeds into the following exercise of collapsing *simplices*:

> To *seem* is the false case of *be*. It is the passive of the verb to *see*. To *do* is the more active mode of to *be*. To *let* is the permissive of *do*. To *make* is the formative of to *do*: it is a doing that leaves a concrete result. To *say* is a kind of making, leaving but a trace in the air.
>
> *Come* and *go* are opposites of motion.
>
> *Get, take,* are almost doublets; *have, keep,* also almost doublets. To *take* is more active *getting,* to *keep* more retentive *having*. And, to these, *put, send, give,* are relinquishings, standing in the possessive gamut, as *go* to *come,* in relative motion. (Ibid.)

The description of the conditions of success of the exercise I just quoted is: "All this will seem very simple to anyone trained in ideogram" (ibid.). In such a light, 'ideogram' denotes a technique of construction of simplicity, which is to say, a technique of reduction. And one would expect at least the customary (and not less rhetorical) "looking aside" of some uses of Chinese (which might be quoted in Pound's use of blank spaces between paragraphs). Instead, one finds, to one's considerable surprise and dismay, that the whole exercise has been performed with the help of a batch of fundamental terms (and some of the more pervasive oppositions) of far occidentalism: appearance=essence, falsity=truth, active=passive, action=essence, act=potency, concrete=abstract, motion=rest, one=multiple, internal=external, relative=absolute. If one adds to these the only collapse that actually takes place in Pound's text (the collapse of the opposition between use and mention), one realizes that the whole exercise is dependent moreover on the ontologizing of certain words that allows for the full flavor of statements such as "To *seem* is the false case of *be*": it is part and parcel of this kind of exercise that one might never be sure whether its protagonists are referring to the word *seem* or to the notion of appearance.

Passages like these raise a problem that I shall not address at all. In fact, I am not so much interested in the question of the ideology of the ethical sublimity of Chinese (which takes for granted, in either Leibniz's or Pound's case, the availability—in Cavell's sense—and, more, the ethical nature of Confucius's and Mencius's works) as I am in following the circumvolutions of the theoretical treatment of a principle of combination as the grounds for language effects or, as Pound writes, the principle that "prose and poetry are but an extension of language" (1913, p. 50). The formulation of the problem, I shall argue, does not differ significantly from Leibniz's. But for me to make this latter point it is important to show, also, how Pound's rhetoric (and Fenollosa's, for that matter) obeys a grammar that is, mutatis mutandis, Leibniz's.

In the beginning of his book, Fenollosa writes: "My subject is poetry, not language, yet the roots of poetry are in language. In the study of a language so alien in form to ours as is Chinese in its written character, it is necessary to inquire how these universal elements of form which constitute poetics can derive appropriate nutriment" (1920, p. 10). The passage argues for a causal connection ("roots") between poetry and language. However, the difference between the two terms in the connection is evaluated with the help of a concept that is used to inaugurate the possibility of a dialectic between identity and difference: the concept of 'form'. This all-encompassing concept ("universal elements of form") allows for poetry to be conceived *as a different appearance of language*. Moreover, 'form' is the notion through which the threat of incommensurability is dispelled; in other words, a comparison between Chinese and English can be operated only in terms of form. Later in his argument, however, Fenollosa will hypostatize the very notion of form in the more prestigious notion of genius; namely, by remarking that "the likeness of form between Chinese and English sentences renders translation from one to the other exceptionally easy. The genius of the two is much the same" (ibid., p. 20). 'Form' then is used to denote the quality of a *certain* connection between language and appearance, over and above the difference of Chinese's "written character" (ibid., p. 10). In this kind of expression one finds again the ambiguity in the use of such terms as *character*. The ambiguity is perhaps what makes possible Fenollosa's reenactment of Kircher's and Leibniz's remarks on the peculiar *modus loquendi* of Chinese: Chinese notation (which is, after all, the metonymical understanding of 'Chinese' that Fenollosa shares with most of his colleagues and predecessors) is said to have *"no basis in sound"* (ibid., p. 12). And, just as in the other cases, one finds at this point the familiar dialectic of deafness and insight: "a verbal medium consisting largely of semi-pictorial appeals to the eye" (ibid., p. 10). If Chinese is taken as a writing, deprived of its genius, there is no way the category of form can render it commensurate with anything else—but then again there is no way of fulfilling the project of a medium for "poetry" based in the Chinese character.

The universality of form, in Fenollosa's argument, raises the problem of the grounding of the *form of form*; that is, the grounding of universality itself. The point is obviously critical to the justification of the notion of 'poetry', which, needless to say, is one of the pillars of Fenollosa's whole enterprise. Form, then, is conceived of as the result of a mimesis of thought (seen under the species of "imagination", which would raise the problem of the ideality, in a Kantian sense, of poetry); but what is imitated in the process is the whole linearity of phonetic writing ("a regular and flexible sequence, as plastic as thought itself," ibid., p. 11). When Fenollosa claims that "poetry is a *time art*" (ibid., p. 10, a venerable claim exemplified in different respects by both Hegel and Schopenhauer), he is really arguing for a radically antiideographic—even in the Leibinzian sense—notion of poetry, because the latter is described as "weaving its unities out of successive impressions of sound" (ibid.). Fenollosa's poetry thus imitates the "phoneticity" of thought under the rhetorical excuse of temporality (there is, to be sure, a sense, and such would be Derrida's if not even Bloom's, in which temporality seems to be pneumatically engendered here).

But, of course, the order of thought is finally just a representation of the order of things and events:

> Perhaps we do not always sufficiently consider that thought is successive, not through some accident or weakness of our subjective operations but because the operations of nature are successive. The transferences of force from agent to object, which constitute natural phenomena, occupy time. Therefore, a reproduction of them in imagination requires the same temporal order. (Ibid., p. 11)

At this point, Pound interrupts with a footnote on the expression "same temporal order": "Style, that is to say, limpidity, as opposed to rhetoric" (ibid.). The mimesis of transferences of force (which the opposition Pound establishes between style and rhetoric helps perhaps to see in terms of generation and corruption) is thus said to be incompatible with rhetoric. *Rhetoric,* literally, denotes in Pound's note the dark side, the nonlimpid side, of style: but the full argument of Fenollosa lies on the necessity of doubling the order of things by imagination or thought and thus on the exclusion of the possibility of darkness in thought. Reading this argument *with* Pound's footnote, one realizes how the notion of rhetoric is taken there hyberbolically for the notion of chiasmus, and how the notions of thought and style are connected to a refusal of deafness, embodied in the linearity of phenomenal appearance. It is not surprising that Fenollosa's poetics (or necessary absence thereof) is in more than one sense a poetics of the "naturalness" of an order: his attacks on the uses of *is* as copula are supported by the argument that "there is in reality no such verb as pure copula" (ibid., p. 19), just as the supremacy (ethical, aesthetic, or ontological) of uninflected languages (such as English and Chinese) comes from their sentences' meaning having to presuppose an order of words, which is "the *natural order*—that is, the order of cause and effect" (ibid., p. 17): Pound's opposition between style and chiasmus reproduces, then, an opposition between nature and artifice based upon a conception of the former as an undisturbed contiguity between sign and referent.

That Chinese has the function of an *example* in Fenollosa's argument means that a choice between nature and artifice, in the terms of their mutual opposition, had to be argued for. The supremacy of Chinese (and of English, or of Chinese *for* English; in a complicated sense Chinese reveals the essence of English, for both Pound and Fenollosa) is a supremacy of nature. But what, in their conceptions, distinguishes the two terms of the supremacy is in fact a different regime of translation: if, as Fenollosa writes, "all truth is the *transference of power*" (ibid., p. 16), the natural order of things represents, semiotically speaking, the less costly transference possible; that is, the conception of an absolute identity between power and *force*. The force of a sentence ("A 'part of speech' is only *what it does*," ibid., pp. 20-21) is therefore definitely not the use of a sentence (as, say, in Austin) but rather (not unlike as in Leibniz) a function of the semiotic integrity of its components, its lack of semiotic deviousness, one could say (deviousness here would come with context, perhaps). This is probably the reason why both Fenollosa and Pound refuse emphatically the notion of 'grammar' (that is, the notion of a science of force that would have to justify the preferability of force) on the grounds of its unnaturalness: "Nature herself has no grammar" (ibid., p. 20), writes Fenollosa. And Pound adds, in a footnote:

> Even Latin, living Latin, had not the network of rules they foist upon unfortunate school-children. These are borrowed sometimes from Greek grammarians, even as I have seen English grammars borrowing oblique cases from Latin grammars. Sometimes they sprang from the grammatising or categorising passion of pedants. Living Latin has only the feel of the cases: the ablative and dative emotion. (Ibid.)

Grammar is adventitious and, moreover, it is "borrowed," which means that it cannot be evaluated in terms of a semiotic transference of cost. Nature seems here to be on the side of "emotion". The grammarian's funeral is a natural event, one could say. However, the fact that Pound (inaccurately but significantly) eliminated from his examples of "natural cases," say, the accusative and the genitive, just means that, for him, those cases cannot be described in terms of an economics of emotion or, rather, that the accusative and genitive are irreducible to stylistic (in Pound's sense) transferences of force: they are (even to Pound) irreducibly chiasmatic.

It is in this context, perhaps, that Pound's frequent attacks on what he calls nineteenth century philology should be understood. Philology is accused by Pound of "relegating everything to separate compartments, creating specialists capable of writing monographs or articles for encyclopaedias without the least understanding of their import of relation to the total problem" (1942, p. 66). Philology is in his theory replaced by an apology for a *Kulturmorphologie*; that is, for a science of the linearity of forms. In (his) other words, "not the document, but the significance of the document" (1938, p. 221). But the same context is also useful in understanding Pound's concerns with the mechanisms of money exchange and with the problem of the control of the whole economy of exchange. China plays a part in this argument, too:

> Until the seventh century after Christ, when an Emperor of the T'ang Dynasty issued state notes (*state* notes, not bank notes, mind you), the world was practically compelled to use as money a determined quantity of some commonly used commodity, such as salt or gold according to a decree of sophistication. But since A.D. 654, at least, this metal has no longer been necessary for trading between civilized people.
>
> ...the note measures the price, not the value; or, in other words, prices are calculated in monetary units. But who supplied these notes? And, before the present war, who controlled the issue of international money? If you want to discover the causes of present war, try and find out who controlled *international* money and how it came under such control. (1944, pp. 108-109)

In this passage, as in an uncounted number of other examples, the question is never the question of the transition between different systems of exchange (roughly between, in Pound's terms, a system based on "value" and a system based on "price") but rather the question of the internal economy of the second of these systems. Because, as we saw earlier, this particular notion of system seems to derive from a positional notion of force, semiotic economy cannot help being thought of as an economy of *control*; that is, an economy of the exercise of force. Pound's whole economics distinguishes, then, necessarily different uses of force: in China, force goes stylistic and one has—China. In Europe, force goes chiasmically devious and one has—war. Following the preceding passage, Pound proceeds by saying that "the enemy is ignorance (our own)" (ibid., p. 109). And, in fact, in his own premises, ignorance is, ultimately, the impossibility of holding a collectively accepted semiotic conception of economic control, which is to say, the impossibility of establishing rules of pertinence (of property and usage). In this sense "borrowing" (creating nonexistent money, endowing money with nonempirically verifiable ontological status) is a symptom of semiotic ignorance: "*pecuniolatry*, or the making of money into a god...was due to a process of denaturalization, by which our money has been given false attributes and powers that it never should have possessed" (ibid., p. 114). Again, one finds here the articulation between 'control', 'knowledge', and 'nature' as opposed to the relinquishing of powers (or creation of prosopopeias) that defines ignorance.

The opposition between semiotically efficient and semiotically inefficient systems in Pound and Fenollosa, however, cannot be reduced to an opposition between, say, style and rhetoric. It is rather the case that certain rhetorical procedures seem to be excluded. But the supremacy of Chinese (and hence the supremacy of limpidity) comes from its incorporating (in the rhetorical sense of the word) certain figures of a *rhetorica naturalis*. "Nature," writes Fenollosa, "furnishes her own clues. Had the world not been full of homologies, sympathies, and identities, thought would have been starved and language chained to the obvious" (1920, p. 26). The process of mimesis of the *rhetorica naturalis*, which is after all the process of translation authors like Kircher considered interpretation to be, Fenollosa calls *metaphor*. As far as Chinese is concerned, metaphor represents the moment of the triumph of insight over deafness:

> You will ask, how could the Chinese have built up a great intellectual fabric from mere picture writing? To the ordinary Western mind, which believes that thought is concerned with logical categories and which rather condemns the faculty of direct imagination, this feat seems quite impossible. Yet the Chinese

> language with its peculiar materials has passed over from the seen to the unseen by exactly the same process which all ancient races employed. This process is metaphor, the use of material images to suggest immaterial relations. (Ibid.)

In a footnote to the passage, Pound quotes (in a debatable translation) the same passage of the *Poetics* with which I began Chapter 1. But, translational disagreements aside, it seems important to me that the passage is again used to claim rights of exemption, to conceptualize the moment where the chain of interference is broken, in short, the moment of the *Aufhebung*. In the notion that languages change through metaphor one finds, of course, a consecrated topos. What Fenollosa calls "the ordinary Western mind" is just a result of "the feeble cohesive force of our phonetic symbols" (ibid., p. 28); that is, the forgetfulness of a past and the inability to *translate* it into a present. But the Chinese written language, contrary to "all ancient races," "has not only absorbed the poetic substance of nature and built with it a second work of metaphor, but has, through its very pictorial visibility, been able to retain the original creative poetry with far more vigour and vividness that any poetic tongue" (ibid.). The theoretical space is thus opened to what Gérard Genette once called mimologism and thus the whole landscape of ideography is populated by an arsenal of resources of "pictorial visibility" or, rather, and because one is still dealing with China, picturesque visibility: logs, smiling children, fires, moons, and of course, dragons. Moreover, mimology becomes "how to read." Discussing three ideograms, paraphrased respectively by "Sun," "Rises," and "East" (and having already had to add a preposition and an article, alas), Fenollosa produces a good example of the previously mentioned genre:

> The sun, the shining, on one side, on the other the sign of the east, which is the sun entangled in the branches of a tree. And in the middle sign, the verb "rise," we have further homology; the sun is above the horizon, but beyond that the single upright line is like the growing trunk-line of the tree sign. This is but a beginning, but it points a way to the method, and to the method of intelligent reading , (Ibid., pp. 36-37)

Because "in the beginning simple words were enough" (Pound, 1913, p. 50), this whole rhetoric of simplicity (with the correlative analogy for the "simplest" possible combination) is reenforced by the self-assuredness of anagoresis (an analogy for simplicity is an analogy for the remembrance of the origins). But, most important perhaps, it shows how deeply the principle of combination that rules the "ideogrammatic method" has to rely on the (other) principle of the stability of its own universe: in the previous passage such a reliance is exemplified perhaps by all the terms that rewrite the givenness in terms of spatial organization: "one side, " "other [side]," "in the middle," "above," "beyond"—all the terms, in sum, that convey the possibility of *looking at a text*. This catachresis assumes a constitutive position there and thus, by implying the ultimate reliability of the vocabulary of perception, attributes to perception itself the strategic function of both ground and horizon of every occurring combination. It is in this sense that, for both Fenollosa and Pound, the Chinese language as the idea of the best existing combination and, indeed, the idea of Chinese poetry as the ideal of every possible combination entailed a belief in the stability in the universe of all combinations. In section V, I shall analyze a theoretical formulation of ideas like poetry, literature, and text as versions of the best possible combination available. In section VI, I shall connect that belief to the notion of the objectivity of the givenness of a language. In section VII, I shall analyze the possibility of a universe of combination at odds with a principle of combination and thus with the very notion of universe.

V

In a 1934 essay, Roman Jakobson, claimed that "the borderline dividing what is a work of poetry from what is not is less stable than the frontiers of the Chinese empire territories" (1934, p. 741). The comparison denotes somewhat a shift away from the uses of Chinese limpidity I remarked earlier on. I take it to be a hyperbolic comparison and hence to assume the instability of the frontiers of the Chinese empire territories. Nevertheless, Jakobson's work is polarized around the question of such a borderline or, in the terms of the Chinese comparison or of the well-known Wittgensteinian concern, the question of the possibility of fuzzy boundaries. Poetry, just like China, can subsist and, indeed, be identified, in spite of its shifting boundaries: "Can you give the boundary? No. You can *draw* one" (Wittgenstein, 1953, Section 68). Moreover, Wittgenstein remarks that the drawing of fuzzy boundaries is achieved through exemplification, rather than definition. Philology, for Jakobson, is the discipline where the purveyance of examples is dealt with.

The notion of a combinatory is central to Jakobson's theory of the identification of poetry, in that the identity of poetry is seen conceptually (and, as I shall try to show, at two different levels) as the product of a combination of factors. As such, it presupposes a universe for all possible combinations (roughly defined as "language") and, at least in theory, a principle of stability of such a universe (although Jakobson explicitly question, at times, such a principle, as we shall see). Be this as it may, the semiotic organization that corresponds to the term *poetry* is envisaged as the combinatory product of rules of selection and, eventually, as the product that represents the best the nature of the universe of those operations. Whereas the latter position can be predicated on Jakobson's theory of parallelism (there is, if we like, an ontological dimension to it, which I shall address in the last part of this section), the former postulate is conceptually grounded on a theoretical doctrine of language and on an empirical doctrine of poetry (the two levels I allude to earlier).

One of the tensions that inhabits Jakobson's writings is precisely the tension between the exemplifying work of philology—where, in Wittgenstein's words, "giving examples is not an *indirect* means of explaining" (ibid., Section 71)— and his doctrines of language and poetry—which, by assuming the necessity of a stability of the universe of combinations (e.g., "any verbal behaviour is goal-directed," 1960, p. 19), fall back on the vocabulary used traditionally to describe non-Chinese (that is, Fregean[5]) boundaries: "*What makes a verbal message a work of art?*...the main subject of poetics is the *differentia specifica* of verbal art in relation to other arts and in relation to other kinds of verbal behaviour" (ibid., p. 18).

Jakobson's principle, according to which "the verbal structure of a message depends primarily on the predominant function" (ibid., p. 22), belongs entirely to this latter stance, but it belongs to it only to the extent that it locates the *differentia specifica* of a message (translated in the notion of 'verbal structure') in the systemic position of a given function. His famous doctrine of the functions of language should be understood, then, as a metatheory of positionality or, if we like, as an inventory of families of *differentiae specificae* that proceeds through the ascription of a sense to particular configurations. The ascription is, of course, supported by the arsenal of philological examples: but for such examples to work, one has to presuppose further the identity of their universe (which, in Jakobson, as has often been remarked, is a principle of intentionality, of directedness). On the other hand, his notion of "predominant function" reinforces conceptually his metatheory of positionality, because the sense of a function is itself a function of a given configuration. Referring to the "poetic" function (that is, to the result of a position of functions that determine a certain quality), Jakobson writes that it "is not the sole function of verbal art but only its dominant, determining function, whereas in all verbal activities it acts as a subsidiary, accessory constituent" (ibid., p. 25). On the one hand, such a position (or thought of the *differentia specifica*, if we choose to phrase it Heideggerianly) blows away a certain conception of the distinction between, say, poetry and common language, in that it can indicate the possibility of their distinction being just a momentary result of a distribution of functions and not the result of the presence or absence of a distinctive trait (this is an interesting respect in which Jakobson's theory of poetry parts from his phonological theories). But, on the other hand, it implies the essentiality of certain features of a configuration, because it distinguishes between a position of dominance and determination and a position of subsidiariness and accessoriness. In this second respect, positionality becomes subject to a principle of distinctiveness akin to the one at work in Jakobson's phonology.

The application of such a principle of combination to his understanding of the categories of literary genre is a particularly vivid example of both the degree of sophistication of his doctrines and their dependence on combinatory assumptions:

> The particularities of diverse poetic genres imply a differently ranked participation of the other verbal functions along with the dominant poetic function. Epic poetry, focused on the third person, strongly involves the referential function of language; the lyric, oriented toward the first person, is intimately linked with the emotive function; poetry of the second person is imbued with the conative function and is either supplicatory or exhortativem depending on whether the first person is subordinated to the second one or the second to the first. (Ibid., p. 26)

The possibilities of the different verbal structures (assimilated here to genres) are connected to the general possibility of a combination of functions, topologically expressed. In this sense it can be said that, for Jakobson, and from a theoretical point of view, a verbal structure is determined within a combinatory. The universe of such a combinatory cannot but be envisaged in this respect as the set of potential combinations, whose cardinal number may be indeterminate but has to be determinable *in principle*. Nevertheless, poetics, and not just Jakobson's, has traditionally tended to express the utmost reservations as to the desirability of the theoretical enterprise of determination of the number of possible combinations (the situation, again, is one of "calculable incalculableness"). At the same time, though, and I believe for deep epistemological reasons, it has never forsaken explicitly the combinatory assumption itself, as that would mean perhaps the epistemological loss of the very notion of its field: the loss of a certain notion of objectivity (more about this in the next section).

As I remarked earlier, the importance of combination in Jakobson's doctrines implies specific consequences at the level of an empirical doctrine of poetry. At this level, it can be said that, for Jakobson, verbal manifestation is determined by rules of selection and principles of combination whose universe is constituted by actualized functions in a situation of concurrence. Although I believe that the procedure need not be an exclusive of the domain determined by the poetic function, I shall follow this case because it is not only Jakobson's best developed example but also has the advantage of connecting the question of the (combinatory) generation of a verbal structure with the question of the presupposed models of evidence of the givenness of such a verbal structure (to which I shall again turn in the next section).

As one might expect, Jakobson is going to derive what he calls "the empirical linguistic criterion of the poetic function" (ibid, p. 27) from a principle of concurrence of functions:

> What is the indispensable feature inherent in any piece of poetry? To answer this question we must recall the two modes of arrangement used in verbal behaviour, *selection* and *combination*...selection is produced on the basis of equivalence, similarity and dissimilarity, synonymy and antonymy, while...combination, the build-up of the sequence, is based on contiguity. *The poetic function projects the principle of equivalence from the axis of selection into the axis of combination.* Equivalence is promoted to the constitutive device of the sequence. In poetry one syllable is equalized with any other syllable of the same sequence; word stress is assumed to equal word stress, as unstress equals unstress; prosodic long is matched with long, and short with short; word boundary equals word boundary, no boundary

> equals no boundary; syntactic pause equals syntactic pause, no pause equals no pause. Syllables are converted into units of measure, and so are morae and stresses. (Ibid.)

One could say that the empirical linguistic criterion for the poetic function is recurrence (and that is the standard answer), but it seems more important to me to notice that there is here a decisive rhetorical analogy between the mode of production of such a recurrence and its actual production. In other words, just as recurrence is produced through concurrence, so the definition of 'concurrence' is described as the product of a principle of selection into the domain of combination is already an example of the production of a recurrence; something is repeated for repetition to be possible at all. One could then say that the definition of poetic function *is*, at the same time, a definition of a rhetorical notion of equivalence; that is, of 'trope'; the principle of equivalence, made to stand metonymically for the axis of selection, is displaced into the axis of combination. This taking over of similarity upon dissimilarity, in the end, is a paraphrase of 'projection'.

In a way that is simply too tempting to be merely true, the mode in which the last part of Jakobson's text is organized is a perfect echoing of his point (and one would have to ask if there is a possibility for the *abyme* of the *mise en abyme* to be more extended than its *mise*). The proposition "equivalence is promoted to the constitutive device of the sequence" is exemplified through a syntactical sequence where equivalence is the constitutive device: "one syllable is equalized with any other syllable of the same sequence; word stress is assumed to equal word stress, as unstress equals unstress...", and so forth. Then, of course, the equivalence between the recurrent examples is itself, again, the product of a projection. In the sentence "word boundary equals word boundary, no boundary equals no boundary" the predicate ("equals") is projected onto the second member. And the semantic description of a given procedure becomes rhetorically generated by that same procedure.

"The obvious fact that on every level of language the essence of poetic artifice consists in recurrent terms" (1966, p. 98) presupposes, then, a not so obvious moment of constitution. However, the empirical experience of obviousness reflects the consequences of concurrence in that moment of constitution:

> The superinducing of the equivalence principle upon the word sequence or, in other terms, the *mounting* of the metrical form

> upon the usual speech form, necessarily gives the experience of a double, ambiguous shape to anyone who is familiar with the given language and with verse. Both the convergences and the divergences between the two forms, both the warranted and the frustrated expectations, supply this experience. (1960, p. 37)

The poetic enterprise has, thus, in Jakobson, two distinct stages: in the first moment, it leads into an estrangement *from* perception; in the second moment, though, it conveys the very notion of the estrangement *of* perception: "the experience of a double, ambiguous shape." The possibility of the second moment, however, the moment where a distinction between sensory evidence and perception is accomplished, is the topic of the theory.

The relation between concurrent principles in language, as well as the idea, implied by his treatment of the poetic function, that the concurrence of principles always presupposes the metonymic projection of one principle onto the other (and hence that, in Jakobson's own words, "any metaphor has a metonymic tint," ibid., p. 42) is theorized in Jakobson's 1968 "Poetry of Grammar and Grammar of Poetry."

It should appear clearer by now that the principle of projection, because of its metonymic nature, implies the impossibility of a perfect symmetry of replacement or, in other words, something like the projection of *the* axis of selection onto the axis of combination. Consequently, even if there is no hierarchy of principle, there certainly is a scale of intensities. In the 1968 essay Jakobson extends to language his explanatory model for poetic function. It is not surprising, then, that his general conception of language would, in turn, reflect the basic asymmetry of principle involved in such a model.

The principle of selection and the principle of combination are going to be made to correspond to "two classes of expressed concepts" (1968, p. 87), that is, to two differently alterable aspects of language: the former embodies the lexical aspect of language (where alterations are vertical, so to speak), whereas the latter embodies what Jakobson calls the grammatical aspect of language (where alterations are horizontal). However, assuming implicitly that, for this domain, the concurrence between selection and combination is achieved by a partial application of the first principle onto the second, Jakobson stresses an asymmetry between those principles and, thus, a difference in their structural roles. Quoting from Sapir's *Language*, Jakobson remarks that "grammatical categories...reflect 'not so much our intuitive analysis of reality as our ability to compose that reality into a variety of formal patterns'" (ibid., p. 88). In other words, the condition of possibility of intuitive analysis is grammar, just as the lexical aspect of language is made possible by a compositional faculty. And, indeed, this question raises the problem of the impingement of grammatical structure on vocabularies of intuition and consequently the epistemological problem of the reliability of the latter, or rather of the reliability of the belief that the latter are the unmediated tenors of intuition. As Jakobson remarks,

> The indispensable, mandatory role played by the grammatical concepts confronts us with the intricate problem of the relationship between referential, cognitive value and linguistic fiction. Is the significance of grammatical concepts really questionable or are perhaps some subliminal versimilar assumptions attached to them? How far can scientific thought overcome the pressure of grammatical patterns? (Ibid., pp. 88-89)

Jakobson's formulation (with its Nietzschean overtones: here too it is question of "illusions whose illusionary nature has been forgotten"), even if cautiously protected by the undecidability of the status of his two questions (is "Can scientific thought overcome the pressure of grammatical patterns?" a rhetorical question? Incidentally, is *my* question a rhetorical question?) defines a decisive problematic that would be inherited by Paul de Man and to which I shall return repeatedly before the end of the chapter.

On the one hand, the implicit analogy between Jakobson's prior description of the poetic function and his current description of the supremacy of grammar over the word (the poetry of grammar) is going to be explicitly reasserted by his considering that the best example of such a supremacy is poetry (the grammar of poetry): "Certainly there is one domain of verbal activities where "the classificatory rules of the game" acquire their highest significance; ***in fiction,*** in verbal art, ***linguistic fictions*** are fully realized. It is quite evident that grammatical concepts...find their widest applications in poetry as the most formalized manifestation of language" (ibid., p. 89).

On the other hand, Jakobson's concept of rhetoric is going to be deeply affected by the role grammar plays in his theory. Not only does he remark some sort of inverse proportionality between lexical tropes and grammatical tropes (for instance, in 1960, p. 47) he also notes that such a tropology is essentially split between the often conflicting natures of the lexical and the grammatical aspects of language: "the imaginative, metaphoric vehicles of a poem may be opposed to its matter-of-fact level by a sharp concomitant contrast of their grammatical constituents" (1968, p. 94). In this sense, as Paul de Man remarks, "Barthes, Genette, Todorov, Greimas and their disciples all simplify and regress from Jakobson in letting grammar and rhetoric function in perfect continuity, and in passing from grammatical to rhetorical structures without difficulty or interruption" (1979, p. 6). And, indeed, de Man himself, in his account of the ever tempestuous relationships between semiology and rhetoric, elaborates what amounts to a repertoire of the figures of the opposition between what Jakobson called metaphoric vehicles and grammatical constituents; namely, the impingement of grammatical patterns on rhetorical structures (or "grammatization of rhetoric") and the possibility of the same grammatical pattern's supporting different, incompatible, and in any case undecidable rhetorical readings (or "rhetorization of grammar"). As we shall see later, de Man's notion of a return to philology can perhaps be understood as a defense of the priority of all modes of opposition between asymmetric systems against the supposition of the justifiability of an intersystemic contiguity. This latter supposition, by making rhetoric and grammar's relationships contiguous and nonproblematic (what de Man calls a "simply generative, i.e., dependent on a univocal origin" account of meaning, ibid., p. 9), would necessarily, *through its very self-representation as language analysis*, embody the methodological refusal of the contents of its self-representation, that is, would imply a doctrine of language impervious to all analysis, which is to say, an essential contiguity between language and values—aesthetic, ethical, or otherwise. Conversely, de Man's point can be interpreted as an argument that states that the refusal of taking language for granted (the refusal of assuming a generative relationship between rhetorical meanings and grammatical patterns) implies the priority of all modes of opposition between asymmetric systems.

One can understand thus that the estrangement from and of immediate perception (a major theme, as it is well known, of the theoreticians of the Prague Circle, namely Mukařovský) is, for Jakobson, and in a de Manian sense (again, more about this later), a philological topic proper: in fact, given the lack of continuity between perception and its origin, and to use Wittgenstein's expression once more, "giving examples" can never be "an *indirect* means of explaining"; that is, in a philological sense, the text *is* the explanation. Such an estrangement in relation to perception, that theory describes, summed up in the motif of the acquisition of a stereoscopic conception of sensory evidence (seeing words as grammar, seeing grammar as grammar), coincides, then, with the theoretical emergence of grammar patterns as the undoubtable evidence behind the appeal to a text. For Jakobson, even the lexical constituents can emerge only as always already grammaticalized. In consequence of this, "any sensitive reader...feels instinctively the poetic effect and the semantic load of these grammatical appliances" (1968, p. 93).

This notion of evidence is determinant in Jakobson's overall conception of literary studies. As a matter of fact, from the assumption that words can never be immediately perceived because one can never fully establish their presence, it follows that such tasks as ascribing meaning have to become subject to the mediating role of grammar and, moreover, to become perpetually adjourned or necessarily disfigured in the conflict between selection and combination. In this sense, the destiny of intuition becomes its own sacrifice. On the other hand, the problem of the metalanguage for literary and linguistic studies is considerably reformulated, in that it becomes the problem of the constitution of a metavocabulary for the description of grammatical structures. And, given the grammatical nature of all evidence, such descriptions, to borrow from Paul de Man, "may be boring, monotonous, predictable and unpleasant, but they are irrefutable" (1982, p. 19).

That Jakobson expresses some doubts as to de Man's first four attributes is connected to the ontological dimension of his doctrine of parallelism, to which I briefly alluded early in this section:

> Any unbiased, attentive, exhaustive, total description of the selection, distribution and interrelation of diverse morphological classes and syntactic constructions in a given poem surprises the examiner himself by unexpected, striking symmetries and antisymmetries, balanced structures, efficient accumulation of equivalent forms and salient contrasts, finally by rigid restrictions in the repertory of morphological and syntactic constituents used in the poem, eliminations which, on the other hand, permit us to follow the masterly interplay of actualized constituents. (1968, pp. 92-93)

Not just "symmetries" (and "antisymmetries"), "balanced structures," "accumulation of equivalent forms and...contrasts," "restrictions" and "eliminations" are the conditions of possibility of description, but also an a priori description of the outcome of description itself is contained in the expression "masterly interplay of actualized constituents." In other words, the masterly nature of the interplay in question (that is, the technical nature of poetry) is due to a set of features that can be summed up as figures of repetition. In this sense, the particular nature of the combinatory that poetry is consists in the particular role repetition (and exclusion) play in its organization. In its masterliness, poetry fulfills the very ideal of the universe of its own combinatory.

The point is not unlike certain presuppositions of Pound and Fenollosa, and, of course, Leibniz's ideas about the virtues of the self-containment of semiotic systems. But, contrary to this tradition, for which self-containment (as it would tend to a point of immediation of mimesis) was always thought to be a feature of the sign itself—more a matter of *Begriff* than a matter of *Schrift*, so to speak—the case of Chinese language and poetry becomes in Jakobson one of the principal philological examples of the ideal purpose of every combinatory aspect (cf. 1968, pp. 90-ff; 1966, pp. 100-103) and thus perhaps, of the origin and tendency of systems and indeed of modes of articulation of difference in general. This happens not so much in that it is an example of the best empirically manifested ideography, as in Leibniz—although a case could be made, I suppose, for an assimilation between Jakobson's notion of poetic function as the promoter of "the palpability of signs" (1960, p. 25) and some aspects of the treatment of Chinese writing by his predecessors—as in that it is a particularly vivid example of the systematic role of repetition. At this point one can understand Jakobson's claim that "the variform parallelism that is the most salient feature of Chinese verbal style" is perhaps "'matched by that of the logical structure' and assumes a 'potentially positive role in spontaneous logical thinking'" (1966, p. 102, quotes in the quote by J. Chmielewski). Because parallelism is repeatedly said to be the main empirical feature of the domain of the poetic function and "poeticity is present when the word is felt as a word and not as a mere representation of the object being named or an outburst of emotion" (1934, p. 750), repetition is never conceived as the guarantor of a mimetic bond (or as a symptom of its loss) but rather inaugurates the very syntax of language and hence the syntax of thought:

> Why is it necessary to make a special point of the fact that sign does not fall together with object? Because besides the direct awareness of the identity between sign and object (*A* is *A1*),

> there is a necessity for the direct awareness of the inadequacy of that identity (*A* is not *A1*). The reason this antinomy is essential is that without contradiction there is no mobility of concepts, no mobility of signs, and the relationship between concept and sign becomes automatized. Activity comes to a halt and the awareness of reality dies out. (Ibid.)

The repetitions, the limitations, and the exclusions denote in this case the very systemacity of a system and the possibility of its manifestation as, say, verbal structure. Which is to say that, in Jakobson's case, the combinatory function is created by the mechanism of combination or, rather, by the ontological instability that triggers combination itself.

VI

The first five sections of this chapter were structured around a quite simple idea that I believe is inseparable from the set of presuppositions that made the institutionalization of literary criticism and literary theory possible in the first place, namely that the notion of text tended to be employed in such a way as to denote the absolute other of language or, in other words, a particular combination of properties of language that modify in some sense the universe of its combination.

The strategic value of, say, Fenollosa's recourse to Chinese poetry is exactly that: Chinese language was said to contain in itself the proleptic destiny of language *tout court* and thus a potential attack on alternative combinations. The acquisition of this theoretical status of otherness tends to be connected, in general, to a decisive belief in the redemptory virtues of the other: such, for instance, is the case of the beliefs in the advantages of "literature" or "text," which have a rather dismally simple history, from P. B. Shelley to T. S. Eliot, from *Tel Quel* to Richard Rorty, from Walter Pater to Gyorgy Lukács (philologists, on the other hand, were always proverbially thriftier as far as such commitments were concerned). I am suggesting that the notion of otherness has perhaps a *recognizable* use (and not just in literary criticism). Of course, the attacks on otherness—and the attacks on "literature" ("Quis...has scenicas meretriculas ad hunc aegrum permisit accedere?")—differed only in the kinds of consolation they promised. The philosophical consolation of common language is perhaps one of the latest installments in the continuing story of a distrust of special combinations or, if we prefer, of a belief in the homeopathic advantages of reason.

In some cases (such as Jakobson's), theoretical activity consisted, in this respect, in the formulation of the a priori combinatory principles; that is, the principles that would rule the particular combination of properties such a consolation was supposed to have. As such, theoretical activity had to confront itself with the moment of occurrence; that is, with the establishment of what one could call a system of reference through which the appearance of a privileged combination could be recognized. The question that determines such a field is the question of *how* the other is constituted into evidence. In this sense, the consolatory belief in the best possible combination available is tied to a notion of the objectivity of the givenness of language. The appeal to the text is thus undistinguishable from the appeal to a *construction* of objectivity.

Now it seems to be possible to imagine a correlation between the combinatory postulates that tended to be employed as ground of the use of such notions as "text" and "literature" and their implication for the construction of a model of objectivity. In a sense, there is a link between the supposition of a combinatory origin of the other of language and its science as a science of a distinctive presence, a science of the acknowledgment of the distinctiveness of a certain appearance. And, in this respect, the unfolding of literary criticism as we know it reproduced procedures and predicaments of fields to which analogous postulates were not unbeknownst.

Whereas the consolatory uses of literature betray invariably the signs of what Heidegger once called "the natural conception of the world," in which the thing tends to be assimilated to a bearer of special qualities (even when those qualities are reduced to the quality of originating experiences), literary theory as a science of the acknowledgment of the distinctiveness of a certain appearance had to develop (or import, which is here the same) a whole vocabulary of perception for which the frame of reference tended to be constituted by a rewriting of the question of the contingency of the appearance in terms of sensation. Taken in this way, sensory appearance denotes the limits of description itself and determines eventually what Paul de Man once called the "hardening of the text into a sheer surface that prevents the stylistic analysis from penetrating beyond the sensory appearances" (1966, p. 27).

The problem is known to all those familiar with the epistemological cruxes of logical positivism; namely, with the question of the construction of protocol sentences. For what is at stake here is not so much whether "a sequence of words has a meaning only if its relations of deducibility to the protocol sentences are fixed, whatever the characteristics of the protocol sentences may be" (Carnap, 1931, p. 63)—for this was the traditional formulation of the question of the validity of a description in hermeneutics, literary criticism, and literary theory—as it is whether "every word of the language is reduced to other words and finally to the words which occur in the so-called 'observation sentences' or 'protocol sentences'" (ibid.). In other terms, the scope of the vocabulary of perception developed by literary theory has to presuppose axiomatically the reducibility of every statement to sentences that are moreover postulated to coincide with "sensory appearance" itself.

Even if the appeal to the text as sensory evidence seems to follow here closely what Heidegger characterized as the model of modern, mathematical , physics ("to interpret the fragment-things [*Splitterdinge*], the sensations, as effects of a cause", 1962, p. 209), contrary to philosophy of science, literary theory has never addressed the problem of its empirical ground or, rather, the question of whether its empirical ground would go without saying. In other words, the dogma of sensory appearance was never further developed and eventually undermined by a doctrine of what Hempel once called "experiential test" (1950, p. 108).

Although there seems to be no metalanguage for the obvious, the way of that impossibility was different in philosophy of science and literary theory. But, eventually, the doctrine of reducibility to protocol sentences of all sentences of a description carried a similar kind of misfortune for both literary theory and philosophy of science. Indeed, from the fact that shared obviousness is irreducible to a structure of second-degree suppositions (and therefore stops, so to speak, the infinite regression of justification) one cannot infer that it conveys an epistemological result. As Heidegger does not fail to remark,

> Where...the thing and the body are represented as extended and resisting tings, as in modern mathematical physics, the viewable manifold sinks to one of sensory givennesses. Today the given for experimental atomic physics is only a manifold of light spots and streaks on a photographic plate. Now fewer suppositions are necessary for the interpretation of this given than for the interpretation of a poem. It is only the solidity and tangibility of the measuring apparatus which gives rise to the appearance that

> this interpretation stands on firmer ground [*auf einem festeren Boden*] than the allegedly subjective basis of the interpretations of the poets in the arts [*Geisteswissenschaften*]. (1962, p. 210)

In this passage Heidegger not only repeats Dilthey's claim that there is no intrinsic epistemological superiority of the natural sciences' *Erklärung* over hermeneutic understanding, but also collapses Dilthey's methodological distinction between the two. The difference seems here to be rather a purely historical one (a result of a momentary configuration, one could say) and hence a pragmatic one. As a matter of fact, the solidity of consensus is figured in the preceding passage in the "Festigkeit und Greifbarkeit der Messapparatur"; that is, made to depend on the acknowledgment of predicates that allegorize the predicates of the representation of the thing whose correlate is sensory appearance. But from the general, trivial, principle that states that whenever we can represent what we agree upon we agree upon such representations it cannot be inferred that agreement can concern only *some* representations.

The presupposition of some sort of evidence of the sensorily apparent Heidegger called a certain conception of the thing, produced by a "matematische Ansatz":

> the opinion reigns that the comprehension of things as a mere manifold of sensory givens is the presupposition for the mathematical-physical definition of bodies...But the contrary is really the case. The mathematical starting point concerning the thing as something extended and movable in space and time leads to the consequence that the usual everyday given [*das umgänglich alltäglich Gegebene*] is apprehended as mere material [*als blosses Material*] and is fragmented into the manifoldness of the sensations. (Ibid., p. 211)

What is probably necessary to emphasize here is that there is no univocal correspondence between a mathematical starting point and mathematical sciences, in the sense that a *matematische Ansatz* is also a trace (*Ansatz*) of mathematicity that "reaches altogether beyond the sphere of things [*Bereich der Dinge*] into the sphere of the 'spiritual' [*Gebiet der 'Geistigen'*]...into the sphere of signification of language [*Bereich der Deutung der Sprache*], of history, of the work of art, etc." (ibid., p. 51).

The best examples of theories of literature that work from combinatory premises and thus have to incorporate a vocabulary of description of sensory appearance (such as Jakobson's) frequently are at odds with a purely empirical or consensual model of appearance. The influence of psychoanalysis and everything Jameson calls depth hermeneutics in literary studies contributed a great deal toward such a situation. But, on the other hand, the nonproblematic acceptance of a "matematische Ansatz" and thus the nonproblematic acceptance of the reliability of a vocabulary of description has to be understood against a model of literary knowledge (which was and still is largely hegemonic) that takes Diltheyan arguments as a regional dispensation of justification for the field of the "humanities" or that, in harder to-argue-against cases, infers such a dispensation (and a contiguity between language and values) from a conception of "depth." This is the sense in which Carnap refers to what he calls metaphysic as "a substitute" (1931, p. 80).

In Paul de Man's description of a class taught by Reuben Brower, written almost fifty years after Heidegger's and Carnap's texts, one can detect the full complex implications of the wager on sensorial mathematicity that was a major feature of Anglo-American New Criticism in literary studies:

> Students, as they begin to write on the writings of others, were not to say anything that was not derived from the text they were considering. They were not to make any statements that they could not support by a specific use of language that actually occurred in the text. They were asked, in other words, to begin by reading texts closely as texts and not to move at once into the general context of human experience or history. Much more humbly or modestly, they were to start out from the bafflement that such singular turns of tone, phrase and figure were bound to produce in readers attentive enough to notice them and honest enough not to hide their non-understanding behind the screen of received ideas that often passes, in literary instruction, for humanistic knowledge. (1982b, p. 23)

On the one hand, in this passage we have exemplified the emergence of a very determinate conception of 'thing', with its own levels of evidence ('actual occurrences' as opposed to 'pseudo occurrences') and its own quasi-Carnapian amount of inference. Legitimate inference is described as built from a level of sensory evidence ("a specific use of language that actually occurred in the text"), which, incidentally, is taken to be the cause of psychological states like "bafflement." Such a level, moreover, is conceived as being discriminating enough to atomize perceptions into "singular turns" and determinating enough to make perception necessary and effects predictable ("were bound to produce").

On the other hand, however, even if it is predicated on moral attributes ("honest," "attentive"), this kind of sensorial mathematicity is, properly speaking, a *critical* tradition, commited to the emancipation from "received ideas," defined as what "often passes, in literary instruction, for humanistic knowledge." The "axiom of reducibility" I have referred to has, then, perhaps important consequences for literary theory, in that it coincides with the idea of a poetics in opposition to a conception of the importance of literature where, *because the construction of protocol sentences is not taken for granted*, the structural place of sensory givenness is occupied and in a sense rescued back into a "natural conception of the thing" (I shall address this last allusion in the next section) by what Paul de Man calls elsewhere an ideology of the aesthetic (1984b, p. 264). That ideology (which is somewhat impatient vis-à-vis the problems an appeal to the text carries) I have tended to characterize here as the resistance to the possibility of describing the engendering of the other, accompanied by a belief in the perpetual "naturalness" of literature and language: for hermeneutics, China is a matter of fact.

VII

In 1697 Leibniz edited a collection of texts on China by several authors, published under the title *Novissima Sinica*. His preface is structured around a general program. Rhetoric knows that program well under the topic of *adynata* or *impossibilia*: "I consider it a singular plan of the fates," Leibniz writes, "that human cultivation and refinement [*humani cultus ornatusque*] should today be concentrated, as it were, in the two extremes [*in duobus extremis*] of our continent, in Europe and Tschina (as they call it), which adorns the Orient as Europe does the opposite edge of the earth [*oppositum terrae marginem*]" (1697, p. 68). But, as it turns out, the singularity of the plan of the fates happens to rest on the possibility of endowing both extremes with a tropological ability; that is, on the possibility of describing China *pro* Europe and Europe *pro* China. Leibniz's text is full of illustrations of this rhetorical predicament that expresses itself in every sort of hyperbole ("Dici enim non potest...," "Quis vero non miretur...?" etc.). However, before he gets down to comparing Europe and China he asks, "But what should I put down first by way of comparison?" [*Sed ut rem in summam conferam*] (ibid.).

The question (although in the original it is formulated in indirect speech) is one of those good Arché-DeBunkerian examples of undecidability made famous by Paul de Man. And the text does not help one in deciding whether it is *really* a rhetorical question: in a sense it *is*, as the whole preface consists of comparisons: but then again, in another sense, it *is not*, as those are comparisons between "the opposite edges of the earth," that is, (literally) comparisons between margins. Leibniz's strategy oscillates between these two poles. At one level, Leibniz tries to prove that Europe and China belong to the same family (and thus partake from a similar, comparable, condition). At another level, however, he is forced to admit the theoretical possibility of using things like hyperboles as predicates of the dissimilar, not because the dissimilar is supposed a priori to have any sort of ontological superiority, but simply because he is forced to recognize the inadequacy of his own descriptive vocabulary. In fact, for a writer who so often speaks in the name of the light of reason, it is a rather surprising move to admit as "cultivated and refined" a people "ignorant of that great light of the mind [*magnum illud mentis lumen*], the art of demonstration, and...content with a sort of empirical geometry which our artisans universally possess" (ibid., p. 69).

Paul de Man, in "Phenomenality and Materiality in Kant," draws attention to a passage of Kant's *Logic* in which the latter describes "a wild man who, from a distance, sees a house of which he does not know the use" as an example of knowledge through "mere intuition [*blosse Anschauung*]" (cited in 1984a, p. 134). In a sense, for Leibniz, the possibility of predicating the dissimilar or building on the inadequacy of one's descriptive vocabulary is connected to situations of conceptual failure, that is, to situations of break of vocabulary (analogously, in the *China Illustrata*, Father Kircher describes an unknown fruit in some detail and then goes on to call it "*fructus* [sic] *innominatus*," 1667, p. 190). Leibniz's becoming (intermittently, as it will have to be qualified) Kant's savage is, in a good sense, his admitting the possibility of a vocabulary *after* vocabulary.

Such things are, in Kant's expression, "wie die Dichter es tun." In the same article, Paul de Man quotes from a well-known example in section 29 of Kant's *Critique of Judgment*:

> If...we call the sight of the starry heaven *sublime*, we must not place at the foundation of judgment concepts of worlds inhabited by rational beings and regard the bright points, with which we see the space above us filled, as their suns moving in circles purposively fixed with reference to them; but we must regard it, just as we see it [*wie mann ihn sieht*], as a distant, all-embracing vault [*ein weites Gewölbe*]. Only under such a representation can we range that sublimity that a pure aesthetic judgment ascribes to this object. And in the same way, if we are to call the sight of the ocean sublime, we must not think of it as we ordinarily do, as implying all kinds of knowledge (that are not contained in immediate intuition)....To find the ocean nevertheless sublime we must regard it as poets do [*wie die Dichter es tun*], namely by what the eye reveals [*was der Augenschein zeigt*]—if it is at rest, as a clear mirror of water only bounded by the heavens; if it is stormy, as an abyss threatening to overwhelm everything. (Bernard translation modified, original inserted by de Man, cited in 1984a, p. 133)

Although Paul de Man recognizes in this passage an "apparent anticipation of many such passages to be found in the works of romantic poets" (ibid.), his use of Kant's example follows from the necessity "to distinguish it from these symbolic landscapes" (ibid.). He points out then that "the predominant perception, in the Kant passage, is that of the heavens and the ocean as an architectonic construct" (ibid.). In fact, the realm of the opposition between Kant's alleged emphasis on the architectonics of a landscape and the regime of symbolization in such poets as Wordsworth (de Man alludes to *The Prelude*) seems to be that of teleology. The reference is, of course, to Kant's notion of the relation between intuition and concept in that the latter is seen as the end of the former or, rather, as adding a purpose to it (intuitions without concepts, as the much-quoted saying goes, are blind: perhaps just as concepts without intuitions, like writing without sound, as in the characterizations of Chinese mentioned before, are deaf). Kant's archtectonics belong consequently to the realm of what de Man calls pure aesthetic vision (ibid., p. 134); that is, they point to the possibility of what would be in Kant's own terms a *blind* vision. Such a possibility (and perhaps the particular sense of 'architectonics' and 'architectonic' in de Man's essay, as applied to Kant) is described by Nietzsche (in his remarks, *im aussermoralischen Sinne*, on the use of concepts) as an ironical *zerschlagen* and *zusammensetzen*, a smashing and reassembling of the architecture of the concept itself:

> That enormous structure of beams and boards of the concepts, to which the poor man clings for dear life, is for the liberated intellect [*freigewordenen Intellekt*] just a scaffolding and plaything for his boldest artifices [*verwegensten Kunststücke*]. And when he smashes it apart, scattering it, and then ironically puts it together again, joining the most remote and separating what is closest [*das Fremdeste paarend und das Nächste trennend*], he reveals that he does not need the emergency aid of poverty, and that he is now guided not by concepts [*Begriffen*] but by intuitions [*Intuitionen*]. (1873, p. 255)

The architectonic perception of Kant's poets is in fact an aimless perception, in the sense that the reversion of symbol into symbolized thing, presupposing a direction, cannot be part of its features. "Kant's architectonic world, " de Man writes,

> is not a metamorphosis of a fluid world in the solidity of stone, nor is his building a trope or a symbol that substitutes for the actual entities. Heaven and ocean as building are a priori, previous to any understanding, to any exchange or anthropomorphism....There is no room for address in Kant's flat, third-person world. Kant's vision can therefore hardly be called literal, which would imply its possible figuralization or symbolization by an act of judgment. (1984a, p. 135)

Again it is clear why the word *literality* is not the good one: for what we have here is a *third* term that, like Kant's "flat third-person world," would be *beside* tropology (in this respect, and contrary to what de Man seems to suggest, the status of Kant's buildings is *not* a priori but, rather, transcendental). About such a raw and dull, unusable, architecture, Paul de Man writes, "the only word that comes to mind is that of a *material* vision" (ibid.).

Paul de Man's argument is that "the pure materiality of the *Augenschein*, of aesthetic vision" (ibid., p. 143) is a critique of the teleological mode of perception implied by the Kantian model of the synthesis of intuition and concept. A blind vision disrupts the purposiveness of phenomenal perception or, as Nietzsche writes, "from these intuitions no regular road leads to the land of ghostly schemata, of abstractions" (1873, pp. 255-256): Kircher's *fructus innominatus* is described architectonically in de Man's sense—and, then again, so is Chinese characteristic and probably *any* literature—-but the purpose of it (just as the predicative synthesis implied in its naming) becomes the object of the same family of stylistic procedures Leibniz uses for certain aspects of China: for "what should I put down first by the way of comparison?" remains there the same undecided question of the priority of an interpretation, just as Nietzsche's speaking "in sheer forbidden metaphors...to correspond creatively [*schöpferisch*] to the impressions of the mighty present intuition" (ibid., p. 256) points to a parallel way of rhetorization of the sublime.

That the "pure materiality of the *Augenschein*" is critical means, for Paul de Man, that its role is structurally analogous to the critical role transcendental principles play vis-à-vis metaphysical knowledge in Kant's formulation. For "Transcendental principles contain no knowledge of the world or anything else, except for the knowledge that metaphysical principles that take them for their object are themselves in need of a critical analysis, since they take for granted an objectivity that, for the transcendental principles, is not a priori available" (1984a, p. 122). Hence, it would be accurate perhaps to say that, if "the critique of the aesthetic ends up, in Kant, in a formal materialism that runs counter to all values and characteristics associated with aesthetic experience, including the aesthetic experience of the beautiful and of the sublime as described by Kant and Hegel themselves" (ibid., p. 136) then the rawness of seeing things *wie mann sie sieht* "is always the critical philosophy of metaphysics" (ibid., p. 122). This is the breaking point for Leibniz's assumptions about China, which partake from a general belief in the virtues of comparison and thus in a comparability of principle ("c'est tout comme icy," he writes about the vices of the Chinese, 1697, p. 71), in much the same way as, in a different respect, Kircher's botanic taxonomy has to introduce the category of *innominatio* in its procedures. In either case, these incidents denote an awkward imperviousness as to the possibility of a text's being *on* something entirely, as to the possibility of mediation (under the species of purposiveness, reference, adequation, correspondence, comparison, or else) being a natural attribute of language. In the terms of our previous discussion, this is the point where Jakobson has to ask himself the question of whether "scientific thought [can] overcome the pressure of grammatical matters" (1968, p. 89); that is, the question of the possibility of a universe of combination at odds with a principle of combination and thus with the very notion of universe.

For the supposition of a harmony of principle between what Walter Benjamin once called *Art des Meinens* and *das Gemeinte* is challenged not just by the metaphysical infelicities of both Leibniz and Kircher but by metaphysical infelicities *tout court*.

The idea of a return to philology in Paul de Man's later writings became a way of thinking the priority of "scientific thought" over "grammatical patterns." Philology, in this sense, is an equivalent of literary theory, as far as "literary theory raises the unavoidable question whether aesthetic values can be compatible with the linguistic structures that make up the entities from which these values are derived" (1982b, p. 25). The return (or the very activity of literary theory) is effected through the supposition not of a reversed order of priorities (which would have reproduced—and very unironically so—metaphysics) but of an impossibility to ground any priority whatsoever. It thus appears to be not so much an injunction toward the assuming of a *transcendentality* for the field of literary studies as an injunction toward the critique of metaphysical assumptions that have tended to constitute themselves as the greater part of that field (the tense in my previous formulation glosses de Man's never fully clarified notion of *return*). Such assumptions can be traced back to a constitutive ambition of the teaching of literature (and thus to its basic constitutive ambivalence): the ambition to go "beyond mere description" (ibid., p. 21); that is, the ambition of, in Paul de Man's expression, attributing "a reliable, or even exemplary, cognitive and, by extension, ethical function to literature" (ibid., p. 25).

What is taken for granted in that constitutive ambition, de Man remarks, is not the existence of an ethical function of literature but rather the compatibility between a philological and an aesthetic or ethical program, that is, a process of reliable inference that converts the very *Stoff* of philology into "values." This does not mean, however, as de Man writes, that it is

> an established fact that aesthetic values and linguistic values are incompatible. What is established is that their compatibility, or lack of it, has to remain an open question and that the manner in which the teaching of literature, since its beginning in the later nineteenth century, has foreclosed the question is unsound, even if motivated by the best of intentions. What also ought to be (but is not) established is that the professing of literature ought to take place under the aegis of this question. (Ibid.)

The passage repeats three times the verb 'to establish', and organizes three different claims. The third claim expresses the wish that the second claim be true and, thus, implies its falsity. The second claim follows from the first claim in the mode of necessity and, thus, implies its contingency. The first claim reads, as it were, the illocutionary mode of the third. Its circuitous organization is ultimately due to the impossibility of, in terms of the third claim, expressing the second one. For the third claim implies the falsity of the second claim, in that it precludes the possibility of "establishing" that "compatibility...has to remain an open question." In fact, the possibility of justifying legislation on "the teaching of literature" (second claim) would imply automatically a compatibility between "aesthetic [or ethical] values" and "linguistic values" (contrary to the first claim). This is why the first claim cannot be formulated in the mode of assertion but has rather to take the form of a wish (third claim). The point proves *à outrance*, against de Man's argument, the truth of his argument that the "pure materiality of the *Augenschein*" "is always the critical philosophy of metaphysics" if one considers, as he wrote with regard to Proust, that

> what is at stake is the possibility of including the contradictions of reading in a narrative that would be able to contain them. Such a narrative would have the universal significance of an allegory of reading. As the report of the contradictory interference of truth and error in the process of understanding, the allegory would no longer be subject to the destructive power of this complication. To the extent that it is not itself demonstrably false, the allegory of the play of truth and falsehood would ground the stability of the text. (1979, p. 72)

The analogy between language and metalanguage is then, for Paul de Man, the figure of the epistemological dispensation of literary theory: for when metalanguage becomes allegory in this sense it is no longer subject to the "power of...the contradictory interference of truth and error."[6] Indeed, methodological propositions otherwise tautological such as "reading texts closely as texts" (1982b, p. 23) become truly *critical* in the sense of Kant's suggestion that the experience of the sublime consists in a way of looking at things that takes them "merely by what the eye reveals" (cited by de Man, 1984a, p. 133). For de Man, this kind of sublime corresponds to what he calls elsewhere (1982b, p. 24) mere reading; that is, the refusal of taking for established the link between intuition and concept (which characterizes all sorts of hermeneutics). An appeal to the text, understood in this way, is no longer the appeal to something that is primarily given as a sensation, the distinct appearance of a combinatory product (even if the best part of it). Nor is it an *appeal* proper, because the confidence in the hermeneutic catachresis that assures us that texts answer back has been considerably shattered. Rather, it is the disquieting analytical disinterestedness (can one still read this word Kantianly and etymologically? For instance, "from which the legitimation of any transit is undecidable") of houses for savages, Chinas for Leibnizes and a *weites Gewölbe* for the rest of us. This is the point where philologist and poet coincide; that is, the point where reading and production might be said to be identical.

5

Manners of Interpretation and the Ends of Interpretation

I

If for a long time the idea of an imaginable discussion coincided with a constant reference to the procedures of the so-called hard sciences, to the point that the room for the *Geisteswissenschaften* was usually conquered by employing the weapons of the former (like an emphasis on communicable procedures and criteria of verification), it is also true that some of the strengths and most of the charms of contemporary philosophy of science derive from the constant reference to what is taken to be the procedures of the *Geisteswissenschaften*; namely, the procedures of literary studies. The situation is somewhat equivocal, for, as I have partly tried to show in the last two chapters, there has never been any general consensus about the latter's procedures.

It is, therefore, not very surprising that the theories of scientific debate and controversy in the literary studies that place themselves under the aegis of the question of validity in interpretation (to use E. D. Hirsch's famous expression) have proliferated. What is surprising, perhaps, is the proliferation of theories of controversy that refuse to place themselves under the aegis of the question of validity in interpretation. This happens not so much in the sense that they would refuse all doctrine of verification as in the sense that, for instance, they would tend to formulate such doctrines in a vocabulary imported from poetics and literary criticism, and replace the consensus about principles of verification by the supposition of a peculiar consensus concerning the properties of "literature" or of "literary procedures."

Throughout this chapter I shall be discussing one such situation in some detail, namely the case of the explanations by the virtues of narrativity. Indeed, the recourse to the virtues of narrativity, and not just within the field of the literary studies, seems to be often a gloss on the topic of validity and, in fact, the kind of gloss used when theories of controversy run out of more orthodox solutions (such as Hirsch's solution that validity can be ascribed only when there is a constant point of reference). Assuming that scientific explanations are narrative in their nature (and hence that scientific disagreements are disagreements between different stories) became in fact a way of asserting a model of commensurability that is no more a commensurability of the logical form or of the reference of explanations but rather a commensurability of the use of explanations. This is why the empirical notion of narrative we shall see later, as conveyed in the writings of authors like Dennett or Rorty, is neither the notion of a universal model of narrativity, such as in the models developed by narrative semiotics, nor the notion of a universal meaning of narrativity, as developed for instance by Paul Ricoeur (in fact, both these alternatives imply the possibility of either a commensurability of form, as in the first case, or a commensurability of reference, as in the second.) This is also why nonempirical notions of narrative used by authors like Fredric Jameson can be thought along the lines of a similar pattern of commensurability. Aside from a very general notion of storytelling (broad enough to encompass all uses of the word 'story'), the notion of narrative, I shall be arguing, is used in this and similar contexts first and foremost as a shorthand term for a doctrine of the continuity, the possibility and the limitation of debate and interpretation in spite of an incommensurability of either form or reference. In addition to this, the recourse to narrative is here usually connected with the assumption of an intrinsic debatability (of a "lack of convergence," as Putnam calls it), and such a debatability is often seen under the figure of interpretation.

It is thus plausible that in this family of explanations (which decided resolutely to join and increase the respectability of the clan of conversational hermeneutics) the theories of modalities of debate are affected by the form of the peculiar consensuses they suppose; namely, as to the permanent availability of literary forms. What takes place is not unlike the ways in which the explanations through the author and through the text proved to be affected by their own models of intelligibility (in the sense that 'author' and 'text' were sometimes used to denote both the ends—that is, the engendering—and the end of an interpretation), while at the same time being instances of a comparable relation toward intelligibility, which found perhaps its most explicit thematization in Hirsch's theory of validity. The difference, though, is that, as the times shift more and more toward narrative, softer versions of dispute, it is perhaps the very boundaries of the thinkable (and hence of imaginable discussions) that have now to be thought in connection with the increasingly shared assumption that description and narrative, history and story, are *naturally one*. What upsets a discussion what paralyzes an interpretation and ultimately causes it to stop, then, is not a mere problem of the old curiosity shop of the *Geisteswissenschaften*, let alone one of literary studies. Rather, it constitutes itself as the main (and perhaps the only) problem of every field that, for all the possible reasons in this world, invested lexical coincidences such as the preceding with a special power.

However, in this final chapter, my purpose is not epistemological proper. After trying to link the question of the unthinkability of consensus to the question of manners of interpretation, I shall be interested, rather, in the modalities of interference of such unthematizable consensuses in arguments. Such an investigation follows, in my text, from an analysis of several different explanations of agreement through narrativity. To close (and it will become increasingly clear how unfortunately ironical this last expression is), I shall come up with some suggestions concerning the ways in which unthematizable consensuses can affect the ends of interpretation, if not a full-bodied version of a theory of a nonconsensual dimension of forgetfulness in interpretation.

II

I have always relished the unfulfilled possibility of a very serious scholar writing in a very serious professional journal, disagreeing with another scholar on a very trivial issue, say, the number of verses in a sonnet. Such a disagreement is hard to imagine, unfortunately, perhaps not so much because certain forms of skepticism are intrinsically inconceivable as because our imagining of disagreements on sonnets brings about a burden of disagreement, so to speak. Often, indeed, what is taught about literature is precisely that burden; that is, the limits of doubting—to paraphrase Stanley Fish, thou shalt recognize a sonnet when thou seest one. I repeat, the point is absolutely trivial, but there might be a sense in which it is also necessarily so.

Paul de Man's return to philology, discussed in the last chapter, is in this sense a return to the absolutely trivial or, rather, to the special kind of triviality one has learned to detect and admire in other domains, in figures like tautology or perhaps in examples such as Tarski's "'Snow is white' is true if and only if snow is white." It would be then probably overhasty to assume, as for instance Hilary Putnam does, that the status of Paul de Man's poetics, like the status of his Kantian "pure materiality of the *Augenschein*," even if it does not correspond to any kind of objectivity (Putnam recognizes that "de Man [is]...far too sophisticated to be [the victim]...of what amounts to a vulgar fact/value dichotomy," 1984, p. 238), is dictated by the fear of interpretation's "lack of *convergence*" (ibid.). Indeed the project of a poetics is in this respect both the dream of an absolute convergence (and Putnam of course is right here, as far as it goes) *and* the dissolution of such a dream in the triviality of tautology. Analysis, in Paul de Man's sense, is always somewhat analytic; in Kant's sense, a domain where the connection between the subject and the predicate of a sentence is thought through such figures of identity (of course, de Man insisted on the fact that figures of identity are just that—*figures* of identity). And, moreover, analycity is the way in which the inevitability of the close reader's response to language structures is deployed; that is why the project of philology can never be properly a cognitive project.

The cognitive project, as Paul de Man has also seen, seems to be on the side of hermeneutics. Nevertheless, as we noticed in the last chapter, this is certainly not merely a matter of replacing hermeneutics with poetics, in that the very admission of an interchangeability would structure poetics as a version of hermeneutics (and not the other way around), for it would rely on the assumption that both disciplines perform a comparable function, and the notion of 'function' belongs to a hermeneutic project already, in that it presupposes, to borrow again from Kant, some kind of extensiveness. It is then, perhaps, the reluctance of ascribing to hermeneutics (and thus to a cognitive project) the totality of the field of literary studies that draws de Man apart from the very, very vast majority of his contemporaries, especially from those who concede, joyfully or not, that interpretation is not a term in an opposition nor an epistemological matter ("anymore," as the most naive would put it).

The difference between poetics and hermeneutics would be in this sense more like the difference between unimaginable and imaginable discussions (and I suspect that the replacement of the former by a doctrine of unthinkable discussions would run into serious and curious trouble); but again, *not* like the difference between consensus and disagreement. The word consensus, in fact, denotes a kind of positivity that it would be better to avoid, for reasons that I hope shall become more apparent later on. Moreover, the possibility of stating consensus in the language of disagreement makes it something of an endogenous outcome of disagreement, a topos of disagreement; taken in this way, although often commonsensical, consensus never has the kind of triviality of what resists the language of disagreement, of what there is no need to state (not because it is unspeakable but simply perhaps because it is temporarily uninteresting).

There might thus be an aspect of what I have called earlier the manners of interpretation in which the restrictive procedures in a debate, the question of the end of interpretation, could be linked to what upsets the very dichotomy between controversy and consensus, between what is open to question and the set of issues about which there is a common sense. That such is a grounding dichotomy is shown by the way in which a discussion of manners of interpretation can never be in this respect a discussion of the alternative for interpretation. In fact, there seems to be no instance in the name of which one would suppose a choice between the thinkable and the unthinkable. Nor can it have, in this sense, the form of a gloss on the theoretical coziness of incommensurability, that is, after all, a gloss on the theme of the choice of vocabularies. And, as Putnam remarked,

> When two theories conflict, then, although the common theoretical terms generally have different meanings and a different reference...that does *not* mean that there is no "common language" in which one can say what the theoretical terms of both theories refer to. In fact, if we have available the "old terms," that is, the terms which existed in the language prior to the introduction of the specific new terms characteristic of the two theories, and enough set theoretic vocabulary, we can express the empirical claim of both theories, and we can say what the admissible models of both theories are. (Ibid., p. 235)

III

There seems to be a connection between the good reputation currently enjoyed by doctrines of explanation that appeal to the notion of narrative, inside and outside the fields of literary studies, and the falling into disrepute of doctrines of explanation that appeal primarily to syntactic or semantic models of intelligibility. In fact, some recent developments in this direction in the philosophy of science are linked to a sometimes very explicit refusal of most forms of verificationism, together with a rejection of what is sometimes known as correspondence theories of truth. Analogously, in the study of literature, a similar movement can be detected and tied to an antiphilological trend, which includes a critique of the aspects of the nineteenth century philological heritage more connected with the question of verification, such as those developed by Formalism, together with the strongest versions of semantic models and theories, such as those developed by semiotics after 1950. The part of the philological project that survived in the mainstream of literary studies after the late 1970s was mostly the one that dealt with the treatment of history; that is, the properly hermeneutic component of the old Schleiermacherean project. And not even the extensive attention paid by semiotics to forms of narrativity prevented narrative from acquiring some sort of thematic autonomy, cut away from the original semiotic framework that determined its brief scholarly popularity in the first two or three decades of the second half of the century. It would be fair to say that the hyperbolic promises of narrative semiotics were ironically fulfilled not by semiotic theories, but rather by theories that promoted narrative to the role once occupied by protocol sentences and definite descriptions and, indeed, to the role a general observational language had played once in semiotics.

The rise of the narrative can be seen as the correlative of a modification in the procedures of verification in some activities. But the recent developments in both philosophy of science and literary studies also show that such a modification consisted chiefly in the methodological minimization of the problem of verification. The rediscovery of rhetoric brought in this respect, perhaps, an important, if unnoticed, consequence. Such a consequence has to do with an implicit reduction of rhetoric itself to a curious aggregate of lexis and hypocrisis, together with a minimization of the question of the status of both premises and proof. The terms of the opposition between dialectic and rhetoric were then dramatically changed, and eventually such an opposition got lost or neutralized in theories of the general narrative essence and regime of explanation. Philosophers of science, consequently, tended to feel free to borrow from vocabularies, terminologies, and procedures that once were exclusive to activities far removed from the dignified realm of dialectic.

This was also perhaps why, in most cases, the notion of narrative came to embody, indiscriminately, and often concomitantly, two different projects. On the one side, the correctability of and thus the continuity between what is considered at least partly commensurate, heir to the old dialectical topos of the possibility of genuinely true premises. On the other side, the irreducibility of mutually exclusive ways of worldmaking, heir to the equally old rhetorical belief in a "faculty of discovering the possible means of persuasion in reference to any subject whatever" (Aristotle, *Rhet.*, 1355b). T. Nagel's, impossible, account "What Is It Like to Be a Bat?" (Wittgenstein had used a lion for similar purposes in the second part of the *Philosophical Investigations*), Rorty's assumption that "each new language creates or modifies a genre" (1985b, p. 15), and Nozick's injunctions to "think of our world as a novel in which you yourself are a character" (1980, p. 461) are more than vaguely related by an identical trust in the virtues of a comparable allegory.

Such a trust, of course, is caught up very fast in the predicaments of allegory (which is to say, in the duplicity of narrative), and perhaps the dark side of Nozick's jovial tone is Dennett's utter seriousness when he writes that

> the storytelling side of science is not just peripheral, and not just pedagogy, but the very point of it all. Science properly done is one of the humanities, as a fine physics teacher once said. The point of science is to help us understand what we are and how we got here, and for this we need the great stories: the tale of how, once upon a time, there was a Big Bang; the Darwinian epic of the evolution of life on Earth; and now the story we are just beginning to learn how to tell: the amazing adventure of the primate autobiographers who finally taught themselves how to tell the story of the amazing adventure of the primate autobiographers. (1981, p. 460)

In Dennett's passage, there is an equivalence between "science" and "great stories." The function of "great stories" is "to help us understand." There is therefore a narrative substance ("the very point of it all") to understanding. However, Dennett adds, understanding itself is polarized around a double task: "what we are" and "how we got here." Both tasks invent, so to speak, the notion of a subject of scientific narratives and that in both senses of the word *subject*: the "we" of science and the themes of the "we" of science. Interestingly enough, however, there seems to be no rhetorical difference (or just a minor difference) between the invented subject of Dennett's scientific narratives and the insistence on both reflexivity and representation (reflection, mimesis) that had marked the system in which the narrative was just a peripheral, nondialectic, device; that is, the system that emphasized the possibility and predominance of a nonstorytelling side of science.

One finds a rigorous formulation of the contrast between the two systems in a "philosophical metaphor," as he calls it, at the end of an essay by Hilary Putnam:

> Kant's image was of knowledge as a 'representation'—a kind of play. The author is me. But the author also appears as a character in the play (like a Pirandello play). The author in the play is not the 'real' author—it is the 'empirical me'. The 'real' author is the 'transcendental me'.
>
> I would modify Kant's image in two ways. The authors (in the plural—my image of knowledge is social) don't write just *one* story: they write many versions. And the authors *in* the stories are the *real* authors. This would be 'crazy' if these stories were *fictions*. A fictitious character can't also be a real author. But these are true stories. (1978, p. 138)

In fact, the way in which Putnam understands the differences between Kant and himself makes it clear that, despite the ascription of the functions of Kant's transcendental subject to an empirical subject and the multiplication of "versions" of knowledge, the metaphor of 'representation' is never really at stake. The permanence of this latter metaphor explains the slippage, in Putnam's text, from "play" to "stories." Which is to say that the narratives on "what we are and how we got here" issue from a dramatic genre: the genre where both specularity and speculation, where reflection, in both senses of the word, is at home.

IV

Richard Rorty's use of the notion of narrative would appear to be an obvious counterexample to my suggesting that all such uses presuppose a model of knowledge as representation. One of the main targets of his *Philosophy and the Mirror of Nature*, in fact, is the conception of philosophy as "a general theory of representation, a theory which will divide culture up into areas which represent reality well, those which represent it less well, and those which do not represent it at all" (1979, p. 3). Even though Rorty does not often use the notion of narrative in that book (he prefers 'conversation'), in several of his subsequent essays the notion emerges nevertheless, and his attack on representation is not substantially weakened. Of these essays, "Texts and Lumps" has for us the advantage of discussing the status of literary theory or, rather, some of the activities performed under the assumption that there are texts, in relation to some of the activities performed under the assumption that there are lumps. Rorty's metasuggestion is that "we avoid Dilthey's suggestion that we set up distinct parallel metavocabularies, one for the *Geistes-* and one for the *Naturwissenschaften*. We should instead assume that if a philosophical doctrine is not plausible with respect to the analysis of lumps by chemists, it probably does not apply to the analysis of texts by literary critics either" (1985b, p. 2). The notion that blurs the distinction between metavocabularies for texts and metavocabularies for lumps is the notion of narrative: this is to say that, in Rorty's text, the function of the appeal to narrative is that of replacing the claim of a substantial difference (such as a difference in level) between the procedures of a *Klumpenwissenschaft* and the procedures of literary criticism. Rather, the "reputed hardness of facts" (ibid., p. 3) of the former is seen "as an artifact produced by our choice of language game" (ibid.) (we shall see witness a little later some incidents that upset Rorty's point here). The kind of language games that produce hard facts and indeed a distinction of facts according to criteria of softness are said to be epistemological; and, according to Rorty, an important feature of epistemology consists in its claiming that there is a correlation between the mode of constitution of an object and the kind of hardness and truth we can expect from it, in the important sense that objects constituted according to rules ("rules laid down by unavoidable concepts wired into our transcendental faculties," ibid., p. 6) acquire the kind of hardness that has made them traditionally more prone to the tasks of knowledge and science. Rorty's position is, of course, that "the object can, given a prior agreement on a language game, cause us to hold beliefs, but it cannot suggest beliefs for us to hold" (ibid., p. 7). The moment of constitution of the object is thus displaced into the conventions of a language game. And the only difference between epistemological and nonepistemological approaches is a difference in the awareness that it is so. Now narrative is precisely the discourse of such an awareness, that is, the rhetorical approach of those who discovered the utter conventionality of truth. But, as this last point is supposed to be true, narrative is also the substance of all rhetorical approaches; and indeed Rorty's position can easily be brought back here to an uncomfortable alternation between good conscience and bad faith: because there are only narratives, the sole difference is the one between narratives that know themselves and the alienated narratives of epistemology. This is the reason why the very mode of Rorty's own narrative is an ethical one: "the pragmatist," he writes,

> tells stories about how the course of Western thought has been stultified by the metaphors he dislikes. His own technique in philosophy is that same Homeric, narrative style which he recommends to the literary critic. His recommendation to the critic is thus not grounded in a theory about literature or about criticism, but in a narrative whose details he hopes the literary critic will help him fill in. (Ibid., p. 5)

It is not so much the casual tone of evaluation that interests me here (which is not probably the inevitable burden of the aesthetization of knowledge that follows from the demise of a distinction between modes of constitution of objects) as it is the justification of that tone. In Putnam's words, "it looks...as if Rorty says 'no more metastories' and tries to convince us by telling us a higher-level metastory of his own, a cultural relativist or cultural imperialist metastory" (1985, p. 74). In fact, the grounding function of theory is displaced into narrative, and the epistemological dispensation that prevents an infinite regression is again the ethical mode of self awareness, that is, of reflection if not of reflexivity.

The immense appeal of Rorty's suggestion, however and ironically enough, can be subject to Popper's criticisms aimed at what he calls historicism. Historicism, for Popper, in fact, is the confusion between interpretation and theory (cf. 1945, p. 151) also in the sense that it is an interpretation's acquiring of rights of exemption. And, as Putnam saw, this happens when your claim against metastories undermines itself by being a metanarrative claim. Thus, when Rorty writes that

> Time will tell, but epistemology won't—nor will philosophy of science, nor semiotics, nor any other theory which purports to give a taxonomy of all possible bright new ideas, all possible futures...In the future we shall have to redo our narratives of how scientific theories or paintings or poems or literary essays

> fit together just as often as somebody does something so original and striking that it won't fit into the stories we have been accustomed to tell. (1985b, p. 13)

his apparent Popperian point that one cannot predict the future (and thus that what one calls theories—or, at least, historical theories—is really hopelessly a posteriori) is upset by the prediction that the future will necessarily come in a narrative form.

I think it is possible to connect this last prediction to Rorty's conception of the origin of movement, indeed to his metaphysics: the point is tied to the very question of the origin of the inquiry. Rorty has to replace all the drivelike explanations (such as truth drive, money drive, good drive, pleasure drive, and so on) with the notion that inquiry takes place after action and, indeed, reabsorbs action: this procedure consists in rendering compatible local or general action induced changes with prevailing versions of possible change, and it sometimes involves (as in the case of "revolutionary science") the reformulation of the latter. The distinction is one of fitting (the notion of fitting being here the structural equivalent of ethical decorum, perhaps): stories are defined in terms of contextual relations (that is, either they "fit" in with other stories or they do not) and, more important than that, Rorty's metanarrative principle tells you that all stories *should* fit in with each other.

There is, of course, a very close relation between the contents of what Putnam calls Rorty's metastory and Rorty's own conception of the origin of movement and, indeed, that relation is thematized at another level by Rorty's emphasis on what he calls solidarity (for instance, in Rorty, 1984), as opposed to the kind of objectivity epistemologies promise. In Rorty's story, Putnam says, "there are people, cultures, and dispositions—including dispositions to agree" (1985, p. 74). But, he continues, "if the whole project of saying how the world is, as opposed to saying what sentences we utter, has collapsed, then why are *dispositions*, of all things, in better shape than *truth*?" (ibid.). And Putnam connects the relation between Rorty's metanarrative and its very contents with the problem of the dispensation characterized earlier:

> If we are allowed to go on using dispositional idioms without a metaphysical account of how dispositionality "emerges" in the world (without a "foundation"), then why should we be forbidden to talk of true and false, right and wrong, rational and irra-

> tional, in exactly the same way? The failures of metaphysics as an enterprise are not a proof of the correctness of...Rortian culturalism. (Ibid., p. 76)

The disposition to agree that Rorty relates to solidarity (as opposed to the drivelike explanations of objectivity) points thus to a peculiar application of criteria of fitting: not so much the well-formed nature of a narrative (whatever that might mean) that can be opposed to the well-formed nature of a conceptual explanation (whatever that might mean), which, in that case, would point to the possibility of a model for derivation of either narratives or explanations, as the general relations of sympathy between narratives. What Putnam calls Rorty's culturalism is precisely such an emphasis. Culture, as a matter of fact, for Rorty, is the expression of a fitting of not necessarily homogeneous narratives ("the test of philosophical truth consists neither in 'correct analyses' of individual concepts...nor in the internal coherence among hundreds of such analyses linked together in a philosophical system, but only in the coherence of such a system with the rest of the culture," 1985b, p. 14). Solidarity or coherence in this sense appears to be something like the commensurability of all thinkable in a given time, that is, the delimination of the boundaries of what makes the very thinking of solidarity possible in the first place. But such a commensurability is neither structural (not all narratives are narratively alike) nor semantic (not all narratives point to the same meaning): it is rather a commensurability of use, in the sense that narratives get discarded as they become useless. There is then an important relation between the "aggregational" moment of coherence and a "segregational" moment of temporality; and the inclusive drive of Rorty's notion of cultural movement is in fact, because it points to a situation of pragmatic commensurability, an essentially composite one, even if it defers forgetfulness onto the realm of history, instead of, as in the "objectivistic" conceptions, making it a result of a criterion-bound intentional decision.[7]

However, if Rorty's notion of narrative in the preceding case is the best possible image of solidarity (and thus reflects self-reflection, so to speak), there is another sense in which it is also constituted as a mimetic version. I will try to show that this is the sense in which Rorty's narratives have got to incorporate a level of correspondence, even if the latter is not a correspondence to the facts alone—in fact, Rorty's notion of facts seems to be simply that those are "the truth of sentences" (ibid., p. 4).

This last definition, however, suffers a considerable number of accidents. One of the causes of such accidents has to do with a certain reluctance to endure the possibility of autotelic agreement, which causes Rorty to admit that "the datum *itself*...is utterly real quite apart from the interpretation it receives" (ibid.). In *Philosophy and the Mirror of Nature*, Rorty provides us with a good pragmatic excuse for our respect for data when he urges us

> to stick to the classic notion of "better describing what was already there" for physics...because, when we tell our Whiggish stories about how our ancestors gradually crawled up the mountain on whose (possibly false) summit we stand, we need to keep some things constant throughout the story. The forces of nature and the small bits of matter, as conceived by current physical theory, are good choices for this role.... Our tough-minded "naturalistic" sense that spirit is, if not reducible to nature, at least parasitic upon it, is no more than the insight that physics gives us a good background against which to tell our stories of historical change. (1979, pp. 344-345)

The idea, very casually expressed, again, is that metanarrative data are *loci communes* designed to make life easier for us storytellers. However, although there is "no way of transferring this nonlinguistic brutality...to the truth of sentences" (1985b, p. 4)—a point that after all was already central to Wittgenstein's *Tractatus*—Rorty winds up by conceding in "Texts and Lumps" that "facts are hybrid entities; that is, the causes of the assertibility of sentences include both physical stimuli and our antecedent choice of response to those stimuli" (ibid.). Even if this is a quite vivid illustration of what Putnam calls Rorty's transcendental Skinnerianism, the point is that if "there is such a thing as brute physical resistance" (ibid.), then, on the one hand, facts are not as handy as it might have appeared in the first place and, on the other hand, the notion of 'fact', given its hybrid nature, is itself a partial replacement for such a lack of handiness, and thus it can be said to represent it, no matter how partially. The difference between the belief that there is a way of converting data into sentences and the belief that there is no such way is not, after all, a disagreement over the virtues of representation but rather a difference on the virtues of certain inferential procedures; that is, the kind of difference that exists between two tropes and *not* the one between the kind of contextual literality Rorty seems to be interested in and tropology. Interpretation, then, represents something that is not defined as interpretation but rather as "brute resistance"; and because such a resistance is what upsets the purely contiguous relationship between present interpretation and past interpretations, the relation of coherence we discussed earlier, it can be said without great dialectical agonies that there is a sense in which Rorty's notion of interpretation represents what upsets interpretation, that is, it represents good old hard facts.

When taken into discourse, though, such a sense is always the sense that truth cannot help but being correspondence, even if not perhaps so much in the verificationist's use of the word as in Baudelaire's. Indeed, de Man's statement that "Close reading...cannot fail to respond to structures of language" (1982b, p. 24) denotes a similar movement (and, as a matter of fact, Rorty's hybrid relation within facts is comparable to de Man's relation, which the conflicts between poetics and hermeneutics, reading and interpretation are about).

The resemblances between Rorty and de Man stop here, though. Rorty's uses of the word philology should make it clear (ibid., p. 8):

Texts	*Lumps*
I. The phonetic or graphic features of an inscription (philology is in point here)	I. The sensory appearance and spatio-temporal location of a lump (avoidance of perceptual illusion is in point here)

In fact, in comparison with the correlative lump-task, philology is here the activity in charge of correcting "perceptual illusion." And whereas the description of "the phonetic and graphic features of an inscription" seems to give a priority to structures of language, one is reminded, by the lump column, that those are the structures of a "sensory appearance" ("At Level I a text...is just the thing which is found on a certain page, has this visual form when printed in that font, and so on," ibid., p. 12). The moment of spatiotemporally located appearance is, then, the uncontroversial moment par excellence, which is to say that Rorty's model seems to turn around a discursive opposition between accounts of appearances and interpretation. At this level the representative movement of interpretation takes place. The process includes an explicit refusal of its being either a matter of meaning or a matter of interpretation (in Rorty's opinion, the difference between level I under "texts" and the other levels is that the former does not refer to "meaning," see ibid., p. 10); there is then a non-interpretive discourse (philological verifications or protocol sentences) on which interpretation properly speaking is grafted. The very notion of true appearance (vs. perceptual illusion) is thus confided to the care of a protocolar discourse (philology in this sense being one), which is to say that the object of interpretation is constituted by the only kind of discourse that cannot be interpreted. In *Philosophy and the Mirror of Nature*, Rorty referred to such a discourse by saying that "we *do* have a neutral, if unhelpful, observation language" (1979, p. 349). However, as it turns out, such a language is the discourse of representation, and such a language is the possibility for subsequent narratives to thrive.

V

The question is perhaps tied to the other and vexed question of the sense of words like *model* and *deduction* in narratological discussions in that it is also a question of construction and a question of derivation. But if the latter problem can be tackled with the help of precedents in other areas, the former question poses a problem that is unprecedented: the justification of narrativity as a universal model. It is by no means established that one needs a justification here, and some of the better-known solutions (such as Hegel's suggestion that historical narrative is a correlative of the existence of an organized State, or Barthes's more sibylline suggestion that the acquisition of an ability to narrate coincides ontogenetically with the Oedipal stage) are no more than philosophical demonstrations, in Friedrich Schlegel's sense of "military demonstrations," even if a great number of consequences is made to depend on them. However, it is, I think, very instructive to see how a justification would develop here.

Like most matters of necessity, the matter is not rewarding, and so justifications do not tend to be frequent. In Frederic Jameson's *Political Unconscious*, however, one finds a particularly strong theory of the conceptual mediation of necessary suppositions and narrativity. In fact, Jameson sustains that necessity itself is a narrative category. Referring to the writing of history, Jameson remarks that "the 'emotion' of great historiographic form can...always be seen as the radical restructuration of that inert material ['the sheer chronology of fact'], in this instance the powerful reorganization of otherwise inert chronological and 'linear' data in the form of Necessity: why what happened (at first received as 'empirical' fact) had to happen the way it did" (1981, p. 101). The point is, of course, a well-known topos, from Hegel's occasional Rortian moods ("what in our view is important and suited to our purpose is settled for us in advance, and the relation of the past to it involves a selection of the events to be recounted, a way of interpreting them, and points of view from which to arrange them," (1833, p. 6) to George Eliot's Hegelianism ("Rosamond had registered every look and word, and estimated them as the opening incidents of a preconceived romance—incidents which gather value from the foreseen development and climax," *Middlemarch*, Chapter 16). But Jameson's emphasis shifts somewhat away from the topos in his underscoring of what could be called the necessity of necessity; that is, a necessity deprived of an organizing point of view and thus independent of all thematizations. In this sense, for Jameson, necessity is not so much a trope or a theme for historiography or novel writing (although it also that) as it is what the act of historiography and novel writing stands for: "necessity is...represented in the form of...[an] inexorable logic" (1981, p. 102). The act of narrative writing becomes, moreover, the moment of the transition between what Jameson has to suppose to be the inertness of materials and the latter's narrative form; it is thus a moment of shaping. Indeed, for necessity to be considered a narrative form, it is indispensable that all that is nonnarrative be, in a sense, formless. That point, of course, leaves the door open for the argument, which for instance Hayden White (1980) or Louis Mink (1981) have made, that "chronological and 'linear' data" already correspond to constituted forms of historiography, namely those of the annals.

This moment of representation is the very moment when the mediation between a general model of narrativity and particular narratives is achieved. In other words, it is the moment that defines the criteria of pertinence to a class for particular narratives. However, because necessity itself is not seen as the product of an intentional choice, exemplarity cannot take the shape of a thematization, in the sense that, for Jameson, narratives are not "about" necessity:

> History is...the experience of Necessity, and it is this alone which can forestall its thematization or reification as a mere object of representation or as one master code among many others. Necessity is not in that sense a type of content, but rather the inexorable *form* of events; it is therefore a narrative category...a retextualization of History which does not propose the latter as some new representation or "vision," some new content, but as the formal events of...an "absent cause." (1981)

My description of Jameson's procedures can perhaps more simply be seen as the description of the catechresis that converts 'history' into 'story' followed by the allegory (as opposed to the metonymies of thematization) that converts 'story' into history (without quotes). And in this respect, Jameson's procedure, like Hegel's, and in the words the latter used to describe it, consists in the acknowledgment that "this union of the two meanings we must regard as of a higher order than mere outward accident" (1837, p. 60). The supplement the process introduces, nevertheless, disturbs the return-ticket imagery of the justification (from history back to history), for what really takes place is an itinerary that leads Jameson (and Hegel) from the word 'history' to history, that is, an itinerary of naturalization.

This itinerary derives possibly from the theoretical identification of historical process and narrative process. But such an identification implies necessarily the impossibility of any substantial distinction between the realms of the two processes; that is, of a distinction between, so to speak, the dialectics of nature and the dialectics of language. Indeed, in authors like Lukács, who is a major inspiration for Jameson himself, such an impossibility becomes even the refusal of admitting of any tropological relationship between the two terms (for then one would have to admit the theoretical moment of the positing of such a relationship). In *History and Class Consciousness*, Lukács claims most explicitly that "thought and existence are not identical in the sense that they 'correspond' to each other, or 'reflect' each other, that they 'run parallel' to each other or 'coincide' with each other (all expressions that conceal a rigid duality). Their identity is that they are aspects of one and the same historical and dialectical process" (1923, p. 204). Such a claim is very noticeably a claim *against* what Lukács calls a rigid duality (and this term is Lukács phrasing of the ultimate mutual irreducibility of terms of tropological relations), which sees itself as a claim *for* the constant reducibility of difference to the level of "aspects." This is to say that the identification between the dialectics of thought, embodied in language, and the dialectics of nature, embodied in history, is made possible by what one could call a certain conception of antagonism: a conception of "sublatable" antagonism (Lukács develops such a conception in another essay in the same book under the term "dialectical antagonism", as opposed to "contradictory antagonism", see ibid., p. 61).

Under that conception, the versions of history (that is, narratives) do not stand toward history so much in the position of determined reflection that is sometimes ascribed to Lukács's theories as they are seen as engendered by a particular process of self-reflection that, moreover, is the exclusive prerogative of the class endowed with the power of producing true narratives (that is, the proletariat). For, Lukács writes, "the dialectical method as the true historical method was reserved for the class which was able to discover within itself on the basis of its life-experience the identical subject-object, the subject of action; the 'we' of the genesis: namely the proletariat" (ibid., pp. 148-149). It is in this precise sense that Jameson remarks that the solution of the problem of the legitimation of a metalanguage for history (which is to sat, the problem of the access to the historical process in itself) is found, "for the Lukács of *History and Class Consciousness*...not in the nineteenth-century philosophical systems themselves, not even in that of Hegel, but rather in the nineteenth-century *novel*" (1971, p. 189). Jameson's argument is that "the process he [Lukács] describes bears less resemblance to the ideals of scientific knowledge than it does to the elaboration of plot" (ibid., pp. 189-190) (which is probably true in more than one sense). However, the underlying assumption, that Lukács's theory allows Jameson to omit, is that such a resemblance can be posited only if one admits the reliability of certain self-reflexive procedures, which is to say, the primacy of certain modes of consciousness. The problem, of course, is that such a primacy can be deduced only from an access to the truth of the historical process: and, by the very terms of the theory, such an access is what has to remain unthought. In other words, for a story to be a history the relation between story and history has got to be extracted from history alone. And either the latter is possible (in which case one would have nonnarrative history, in the sense of a dialectics of nature severed from the dialectics of discourse) or the former is improbable.

Be that as it may, the omission of the link between 'history' and 'story' (or the catachretical nature of such a link) is the result of the ultimate impossibility of conciliation within the realm of self-reflection between "language" and "reality," "language" and "metalanguage," "subject" and "object"—there is no substantial difference between the self-reflexive way in which Lukács proletariat discovers itself to be its own object (and *the* object, par excellence) and the way in which narrative, within Jameson 's formulation, is discovered to be the form of history. In the two cases, instead, one witnesses the same kind of conceptual solemnity that generally accompanies the taking of a catachresis for a ground: as if Lukács were always saying "Look, the proletariat's being an object is not a mere metaphor" and Jameson were always saying "Look, history's being a story is not a mere pun." The reason why for Lukács the proletariat is a *proper* object and for

Jameson history is a *proper* narrative is that there is a self-reflexive instance where the very regime of exemplarity that promotes such identifications is put into motion. Functionally, such an instance is what stops the genealogical regression of tropology. Rhetorically, such an instance promotes a conceptual identification between two kinds of dialectics and thus translates itself into a figure for non-awareness: what Lukács calls the "'we' of the genesis," the refusal of catachresis, is yet another catachresis.

VI

The fact that for Jameson narrative re-presents necessity, even as, for Rorty, narrative represents the stubbornness of texts and lumps, denotes in both cases a concern with the relationships created between the poles of representation. The exemplarity of representation lies here in the possibility of a repetition; that is, in the possibility of a narrative discourse's redoubling of, in Jameson's terms, "what hurts." But such is the possibility of a reliable attribution of a strategic, positional or essential value to the catachresis that identifies 'story' and 'history'. In both Rorty's and Jameson's theories this point has two distinct but interrelated consequences.

The first consequence is that, if the model is supposed to have a universal scope, narrativity itself appears to be the function of a cause of universal scope. Even when Rorty mentions ironically "all this masochistic talk about hardness" (1985, p. 5) he is not willing to give up totally the notion that stimuli are primarily translatable into ubiquitous (and unpleasant, at that) physical qualities; namely, stubbornness or pressure. Analogously, the pangs of history are a major metatheoretical theme of Jameson's. One is tempted to say that there is in both cases a whole pathology of universality, with roots as old as Socrates's maieutics. The second consequence is that all narratives appear to be up to a certain point narratives of a connection: in their being representational they recall their origin and, indeed, they define their pertinence through the accuracy of reminiscence. The model here is the repetition of a cause accompanied by the belief that its manifestation is reenactable, that is, that there *is* a repetition, but also that such a reenactability is determined by criteria of accuracy.

These two consequences have a different degree of consequentiality, however. As to the first, it can be easily reconciled with the notion that narrative can disappear or that not every explanation is essentially narrative. In fact, for Jameson to keep his theory of necessity intact it is sufficient to introduce a distinction between latency and manifestation that allows for narrativity to be always there even when not present; such is, for instance, the function of the notion of political unconscious. Analogously, Rorty would assert at this juncture that the difference that constitutes nonnarrative explanations is merely a case of institutionalized bad faith. The history of explanatory procedures that issues from there is consequently described as an alternation of figures of narrativity, which can easily include the refusal of the narrative.

However, the second consequence, which concerns the function of storytelling, can never be subject to a similar expedient. In fact, whereas presence can be turned into the reverse of presence (in the sense that alienation or bad faith can be said to be modes of presence), the notion of relation through repetition does not have a conceptual reverse (just as the contrary of a trope is still another trope). If, thus, one attempts to touch the rhetorical dispensation without which the previously mentioned catachresis would not be operational (i.e., if one attempts to see the relation between 'history' and 'story' as a *determined* relation), one is likely to affect the possibility of all criteria of representational accuracy, which is to say, in Hegel's words, all "on which Mnemosyne, for the behoof of the perennial object of the formation and constitution of the State, is impelled to confer perpetuity" (1837, p. 61).

Indeed, Hegel's presupposition of a coextensiveness between history and story implied in the structure of the State ("it is the State which first presents the subject matter that is not only *adapted* to the prose of History, but involves the production of such a history in the very progress of its being," ibid.) is first and foremost a presupposition of an essential link between both senses of the word *Geschichte*; that is, a refusal to submit such a relation to any further analysis. Affecting the rhetorical dispensation of the catachresis (and I concede that the expression is far from perfect) here consists basically in supposing that there *is* a catachresis; that is, that the links between the two senses of *Geschichte* have been laid down by tropology. This is perhaps why Nietzsche's famous (and *unzeitgemäss*, in more than one sense) attack on history and his injunction toward a therapeutic assumption of a "*suprahistorical* vantage point" (1874, p. 65) is an attack on the literality of historical discourse itself, which is to say on the reliability of the connection between 'history' and 'story': "the viewer from this vantage point could no longer feel any temptation to go on living or to take part in history; he would have recognized the essential condition of all happenings—this blindness and injustice of the soul of him who acts; he would, indeed, be cured forever of taking history too seriously" (ibid.). "Taking history too seriously" means seeing it as a story, seeing it as a process, and at the same time, seeing it as *the* story and *the* process: like a story, but more than a story. "The historical men," Nietzsche writes, "believe that the meaning of existence will come more and more to light in the course of its *process*, and they glance behind them only so that, from the process so far, they can learn to understand the present and to desire the future more vehemently" (ibid.). The ultimate import of the use of history, in this conception, consists in its localizing the moment of meaning (that is always an apocalyptic and often a kerygmatic moment, one might add) in the assumption that all givenness should be regarded functionally (in a very technical narrative sense). Inference, in this respect, is nothing more than the belief in a preestablished sequence of functions; that is, in the naturalness of a sequence.

Thus Nietzsche's remark that "history always inculates: 'there was once', morality: 'you ought not to' or 'you ought not to have'" [*die Geschichte prägt immer ein: 'es war einmal', die Moral: 'ihr sollt nicht' oder 'ihr hättet nicht sollen'*] (ibid., p. 105) is an ontological remark about the belief that the objects of history are prior to their story in the sense that the latter (under the name of history) is the authorized representation of the former, and *also* that in a sense all representation is of a moral nature. Consequently, the claim that "History understood in this Hegelian fashion has been mockingly called God's vicissitudes on earth though the god referred to has been created only by the history" [*Man hat diese Hegelisch verstandene Geschichte mit Hohn das Wandeln Gottes auf der Erde genannt, welcher Gott aber seinerseits erst durch die Geschichte gemacht wird*] (ibid., p. 104) can be understood as a tropological remark on the origin of the two meanings of the word *Geschichte*: God is there seen as a character created by a narrative, which nevertheless thematizes its own representative nature; that is, the fact that characters are preexistent. Such is the acknowledgment that 'history' has not only a catachretical genealogy but also that the refusal of such a genealogy is the very substance of a pathological use of history, one that coincided in the late nineteenth century with the very field of history and, some seventy years later, with what Popper called historicism. I think indeed that it would be possible to relate Popper's indictment of historicism (despite Popper himself) to Nietzsche's indictment of certain uses of history. When the former emphasizes the nonrefutability of what he calls the selective approaches of historiography, he is very obviously attacking the existence of an essential connection between the objects of history and historiographic discourse; that is, that the proximity between 'history' and 'story', for instance, is a lexical proximity and thus a coincidence in language. Historicists, writes Popper, "do not see that there is necessarily a plurality of interpretations which are fundamentally on the same level of both suggestiveness and arbitrariness" (1945, p. 151). Understandably then, Popper's recommendation that we should "write *that history which interests us*" (ibid., p. 150) is at bottom a recommendation for us to *use* history in a very Nietzschean sense; namely, as "an attempt to give oneself, *a posteriori* as it were, a past in which one would like to originate in opposition to that in which one did originate" (1874, p. 76). Popper, of course, believes that scientific objectivity can and should be saved here by deontological prescriptions ("This does not mean that we may twist the facts until they fit into a framework of preconceived ideas," 1945, p. 150); and this would mean that, although one recognizes the objects of history as narrative, "interested" constructions, the very activity of history (its point, one could say) depends on an attitude (which can be predicated only by an ethical discourse) that goes against the former principle. There is, if we like a certain interest to disinterest itself.

VII

Benjamin's idea that "the art of storytelling is coming to an end" (1936, p. 83) was soon followed by several theories of narrativity that, by often incompatible means, asserted that there is a sense in which storytelling can never properly come to an end. Seen in this way, one can relate current incompatible versions of the problem, such as Ricoeur's ("historicity comes to language only so far as we tell stories or tell history. In a word, if our historical condition requires...narrative genres, it is because of the very nature of our experience of *being* historical," 1979, p. 294) and Hayden White's ("narrative might well be considered a solution to a problem of general human concern, namely, the problem of how to translate *knowing* into *telling*," 1980, p. 5). What in Ricoeur is thematized as an existential and, indeed, ontological question, becomes in White a universal epistemological problem. But one thing, what one could call a certain kind of relationship toward universality and purpose, does not change: the occurrence of narrative, in its multiple cases, replaces or actualizes the meaning of narrativity, and that is an *endless* meaning, just as narrative is a timeless form.

Benjamin's point was nothing but an extension of a point made previously by Hegel himself while dealing with the "prose of history" (1837, p. 61), namely, that there are conditions for memory to appear (that is, "an *imperfect* Present," ibid.)—and so, likely enough, conditions for memory to disappear. It is noteworthy that, as remarked earlier, apropos of Jameson and Rorty, the model of narrative that has survived as a metaphor fit for export (which is to say the exemplum of what we call narrative explanations) is the kind of model that, by postulating a representative function for discourse, is capable of dealing with loss of memory only through the category of alienated presence. Benjamin again made a distinction once that can be invoked at this point between "the perpetuating remembrance of the novelist" [*verewigende Gedächtnis des Romanciers*] and "the short-lived [*kurzweiligen*, amusing] reminiscences of the storyteller" (1936, p. 98). Such a distinction, more than echoing Hegel's other distinction, which I shall mention later more explicitly, between memories worth being perpetuated and restricted memories of pre-State epochs, denotes, in the first term, a concern with totality that is indeed built on the forgetfulness of the necessarily evanescent, on what Benjamin called a dissociation between remembrance [*Eingedenken*] and reminiscence [*Gedächtnis*]. And notions, such as community of interpreters, existential condition, consensus or ideology, that many contemporary theories employ, convey, indeed, the very possibility of a therapy for forgetfulness that consists primarily in the postulating of dissociative criteria of pertinence for memory: remember only what can become general in remembrance. As such they are the products of the narratives of the novelist, rather than the narratives of the storyteller. Indeed, the metaphor of a narrativity of explanatory devices constituted itself as if the latter would always resemble if not the *Wilhelm Meister* at least the *Education sentimentale*: the characters that authors like Nozick, Ricoeur, or White want us to be like tend to be the protagonists of a *Bildungsroman* or, at least, do not tend to be characters like the Cheshire Cat or Long John Silver.

Jean-François Lyotard develops, in *The Postmodern Condition*, a theory of narrativity that, even if it was modified in some important and interesting respects in his subsequent book *Le différend* (cf., e.g., 1983, Section 219, in the light of the following discussion) seems to be both a theory of a distinctive end of storytelling (comparable to Benjamin's) and a theory of the pragmatics (and thus of the effects) of such endings. As to the latter point, he writes: "a collectivity that takes narrative as its key form of competence has no need to remember its past. It finds the raw material for its social bond not only in the meaning of the narratives it recounts, but also in the act of reciting them. The narratives' reference may seem to belong to the past, but in reality it is always contemporaneous with the act of recitation" (1979, p. 22). If nothing else, what is clear in passages like this one is that what is at stake is a conception of narrative where, in relation to Jameson's, there is a shift of the regime of exemplarity: for Lyotard these narratives are always self-referential in that they represent the act of their own production (they are, in Benjamin's sense, narratives of experience). In this, one might add, they are not just incommensurable but also they dissolve further into a multiplicity of what Lyotard calls language games. But, contrary to what Jameson's reading of Lyotard (cf. Jameson, 1984) appears to perceive (and Lyotard seems to suggest at times), their self-referentiality by no means *necessarily* implies what Nietzsche calls "das Vermögen...unhistorisch zu empfinden." The distinction here seems to be rather a distinction between the discourse's denoting of necessity (that is, its cause) and the discourse's recalling in its form the conditions of its possibility, which is to say its own effects. It is a distinction between modes of reference, not unlike perhaps the kind of distinction Aristotle established between dialectics and rhetoric.

The discussion could be organized around the opposition Lyotard formulates between what he calls meter and what he calls accent. Both notions are dealt with briefly in *The Postmodern Condition* under the topic of the effect on time of narrative knowledge. Lyotard writes:

> Narrative form follows a rhythm; it is the synthesis of a meter beating time in regular periods and of accent modifying the length or amplitude of certain of those periods...This kind of knowledge...exhibits a surprising feature: as meter takes precedence over accent in the production of sound (spoken or not), time ceases to be a support for memory to become an immemorial beating that, in the absence of a noticeable separation between periods, prevents their being numbered and consigns them to oblivion. (1979, pp. 21-22)

Maybe it is possible to build a consistent misunderstanding of Lyotard's use of such expressions as "consign to oblivion" from the adjective "immemorial": even if the latter has to do with that whose origin memory cannot grasp anymore, it certainly does not signify precluding the effort of grasping itself (it is not amemorial, so to speak) Indeed, something like an effort of appropriation is precisely what is conveyed through the repetition of meter: by being structured on metric repetition narrative can become a "mode of temporalization" of its own. For Lyotard, however, being structured on metric repetition means here being *poetically* structured; the recourse to the notion of meter signals perhaps, in his theory, the one basic opposition between discourses that from Plato on was constituted as epistemology, namely, the opposition between an intentionally accentuated discourse (the discourse of knowledge) and a discourse where the measure of the inherited form takes precedence over the individual accent. What is forgotten in meter is thus the relevance, one could say, of the accent (just as rhetoric has to forget the ideal of a purely demonstrative system of proof, purged of ethos and hypocrisis) rather than the possibility of an effect and thus the relevance of memory.

If in what Lyotard calls the accent is figured a relation of *renvoi* traditionally associated with memory (basically the kind of relation Jameson alludes to in his idea that history is the unforgettable), it seems nevertheless possible to understand Lyotard's opposition between meter and accent as an opposition between figures of *renvoi*. As a matter of fact, even in what Lyotard calls meter, the structural function of *renvoi* is preserved through repetition; in other words, what would allow for a story in a pre- or post-State stage to work would be the possibility of establishing a connection with its production; and such a continuity, Lyotard tells us, is assured by meter. In Hegel's terms, the difference between the temporalization of accent and the temporalization of meter would be the difference between the "serious remembrance" of history, exercised through accentuation (the inscription of "comprehensive and universally binding prescriptions," 1837, p. 61), and the other kind of remembrance typical of "constantly present and satisfying...profound sentiments" (ibid.). But it might be worthwhile remarking here that in both cases one still has a model of referential working (and thus of representation) that is ultimately incompatible with the more appealing aspects of a language game theory, in that it is a model that, although remaining commited to the conception of a general anamnesic working of language, asserts the precedence of a purely demonstrative discourse over poetic discourse. Indeed, when Lyotard mentions the "strange temporalization that jars the golden rule of our knowledge: 'never forget'" (1979, p. 22), typical of manifestations of what he calls narrative, he seems to be echoing the consistent distrust on the part of dialectics vis-à-vis the possibility of a nonaccentual art of building discourse, rather than taking seriously the possibility of narratives' being an organized form of forgetfulness.

Lyotard's arguments are complicated by the possibility of what he calls the "return of the narrative in the non-narrative" (ibid., p. 27). Indeed, he writes, "it is not inconceivable that the recourse to narrative is inevitable, at least to the extent that the language game of science desires its statements to be true but does not have the resources to legitimate their truth on its own" (ibid., p. 28). And in this light, understandably enough in a section entitled "Legitimation by Paralogy" (that is, a section written, so to speak, from the point of view of dialectics), Lyotard's remark that "the little narrative [*petit récit*] remains the quintessential form of imaginative invention, most particularly in science" (ibid., p. 60) should be understood. However the return of the narrative, in Lyotard's own terms, is also the return of a necessary "consignment to oblivion" inscribed in the core of the pedagogic and scientific projects.

We have seen earlier how, strictly speaking, the need to forget to which Lyotard refers is rather a need for dialectics to remember rhetoric as forgotten; that is, a need to ascribe to rhetoric the exclusive of an "immemoriality of the origin" (the converse image of Lukács's "'we' of the genesis" dialectics). This happens perhaps because Lyotard bases his whole pragmatics of narrativity on the notion of the extension of a repeated pattern; that is, on the possibility of an inaugural repetition (despite the oxymoron) and, indeed, on the transcendence of *metrum* vis-à-vis language. Knowledge in this sense is not assured by the repetition of an intentionally produced image anymore, but rather by that very extension: each occurrence of the same meter is thus seen as a *new* occurrence, as *more* occurrence (as Frederic Jameson remarked, e.g., 1984, p. ix). But, then again, the problem is that a pragmatics of narrative knowledge, as long as it remains just that, may have to rewrite its conception of reference (no longer in terms of a correspondence of images) but it can never avoid it. And, surprisingly enough, even when Lyotard is dealing with the kind of narrative language games that allow themselves easily to be "mythified" by the logos of knowledge, his very conception of meter betrays the figure of a transcendence of history vis-à-vis story that we had found in Jameson's theory, and ultimately seems, again not unlike Jameson's, to turn around the possibility of incorporating (that is, figuring) the historic into the narrative. The model remains thus predatory rather than "distracted." Moreover, it shows, perhaps, why a pragmatics of narrative knowledge (no more than a phenomenology of self-consciousness) cannot help thinking of the return of the reverse under the tropes of alienation, repeating, among many others, Aristotle's gesture of conceiving of rhetoric as an alienated dialectics, as an *antistrophos tè dialektikè* (*Rhet.*, 1354a, 1), which by the way is an excellent example of the undermining of a "dialectic" description by a rhetorical term.

From what has been argued previously, there appears thus to be a way in which a theory of the pragmatics (and thus of the effects) of storytelling, such as Lyotard's, cannot be a theory of a distinctive end to storytelling without supposing a moment of consensual transcendence for narrative (the moment when interpretation ends at the hands of reference's common sense by the means of representation, so to speak). In this, Lyotard's theory again is not unlike Rorty's or Jameson's. However, the interest of Lyotard's analyses for us lies in the fact that they make more apparent than the other cases in point that the possibility of a connection between the question of interpretation and the question of the end of interpretation, that is, the possibility of considering the question of the limits of interpretation independent from the categorial determinating opposition between controversy and consensus, can be related to a thought of the narrative that would deliberately avoid the constructive moment of reference, of the transcendence of history, indicating perhaps the complex way in which the difference between history and story is always necessarily neutralized by the normativity of what is invariably assumed to be its very literality. But, as this section has perhaps made clear, this is by no means a mode of beyondness, that looks to the multiplication of a gesture for the dispensation of an aporia. It seems, rather, to be a very sober moment: this is the moment of the distinction between things *unzeitgemässe* and things unpopular, between the unthinkable and the *impensé*, between the forgotten and the repressed. In sum, the distinction between the apathy of the superdog and the pathos of the underdog.

As in the case of the person with two stomachs and the ruminants in Chapter 2, I am inadvertently drawn again into the field of animal and teratological allegories. I can claim on my own behalf, though, that it has been a consistent vice if not a real tradition, at least from Hegel's *Phenomenology* on, when talking about forgetfulness, to use animals or, at least, the kind of animals literature has provided us with. In the beginning of the second *Unzeitgemässe Betrachtung*, Nietzsche writes:

> Consider the cattle, grazing as they pass you by: they do not know what is meant by yesterday or today, they leap about, eat, rest, digest, leap about again, and so on from morn till night and from day to day, fettered to the moment and its pleasure or displeasure, and thus neither melancholy nor bored. This is a hard sight for man to see, for, though he thinks himself better than the animals because he is human, he cannot help envying them their happiness—what they have, a life neither bored nor painful, is precisely what he wants, yet he cannot have it because he refuses to be like an animal. A human being may well ask an animal: 'Why do you not speak to me of your happiness but only stand and gaze at me?' The animal would like to answer, and say: 'The reason is I always forget what I was going to say'—but then he forgot this answer too, and stayed silent: so that the human being was left wondering. (1874, pp. 60-61)

The fable, despite its final twist, is built around an opposition that makes it impossible for it to be seen as a mere thematization of the delights of forgetfulness. As Paul de Man once remarked in relation to this same essay: "like most opponents of Rousseau in the nineteenth century, Nietzsche's thought follows purely Rousseauistic patterns" (1970, p. 146). In fact, forgetfulness is described as an impossible desire, in a way similar to the impossibility of a return to nature, whereas remembrance is described at the same time as the source of boredom and pain. Indeed, and to quote Rousseau, in Nietzsche's passage, and in a very literal sense, "l'état de réflexion est un état contre Nature" (1755, p. 138) (which is probably a devious way to assert the objectual, *gegen-ständliche* overtones of reflection itself).

In the fable, the impossibility of becoming cattle is signified by the impossibility of forgetting language. But because this is a fable, such an impossibility would mean the impossibility of the very figure that constitutes fable, namely, prosopopeia (that is, the impossibility of attributing speech to animals). The fable, indeed, thematizes what one could call the justification of such an impossibility; but because that justification can proceed only by attributing to the animal an intention to speak ("Das Thier *will* auch antworten, " I emphasize), it is achievable only through the supposition of another prosopopeia. These are, indeed, the pitfalls of the discourse on forgetfulness, in that the latter concept can be thematized by an omniscient narrator alone, that is, by an instance that can remember what is to be forgotten (Benjamin once called such an instance *Gedenken Gottes*, God's remembrance or perhaps even God's memory, e.g., 1923, p. 70). The natural silence of the animal, which corresponds to the depicted amnesia, is hence a silence *sub specie narratoris*, which is to say, a represented silence (precisely in the same way nature is the great and perhaps the only subject for representation). Analogously, the irony in the passage is built by the possibility of attributing forgetfulness (contrast with, "After the question, the animal said nothing and the human being was left wondering").

The development of the whole essay has perhaps the form of an investigation of the consequences of the paradox mentioned earlier or, rather, on the possibility of an alternative formulation of the question. Such would be the possibility of a nonrepresentational approach of forgetfulness that would not suppose a priori its empire, so to speak. Indeed, Nietzsche's essay is further polarized around the question of the possibility of engendering forgetfulness from within, that is, around the possibility of its being a consequence of language (as a suprahistorical viewpoint would be a consequence of history)—and not a consequence of what Lyotard calls the *metrum*, which is nothing but the beating of what *stands against*. This is, after all, the well-known image of a turning against itself, which has been working for a long time as the rather ambiguous emblem of both reflexivity and criticism: "The origin of historical culture—its quite radical conflict with the spirit of any 'new age', any 'modern awareness'—this origin *must* itself be known historically, history *must* itself resolve the problem of history, knowledge *must* turn its sting against itself" (1874, pp. 102-103). Nietzsche's somewhat cryptic notion of a historical knowledge of an origin does point indeed to a peculiar vision of history, in that it supposes by necessity a moment of constitution of history itself (engendered perhaps by its own story). But, on the other hand, the story of "historical culture" cannot (despite Rorty) be faced as the naturalized origin of history: the beginning of the story would have been made possible by the same kind of forgetfulness that the history of a beginning would exorcise. This is what Nietzsche describes as a "zeitweilige Vernichtung...[der] Vergessenheit": "Sometimes...this same life that requires forgetting demands a temporary suspension [I would rather use the less Coleridgean 'annihilation' for Nietzsche's "Vernichtung" here] of this forgetfulness" (ibid., p. 76). And this latter remark is only the converse of the remark that "he who acts...forgets most things so as to do one thing" (ibid., p. 64).

VIII

This latter point can be connected with a highly significant appropriation that contemporary theory of narrative made of the metaphor of decision, not so much in the sense of Propp's (via Bremond) suggestion that there is a logic to narrative possibilities, but rather in the sense of Barthes's suggestion that narrative can be compared to action in that it can be described as a deliberative process. However, if one disregards the first suggestion, one has to understand deliberation here in a very peculiar sense: the sense of a deliberation outside possibility and hence *post factum* (I shall return briefly to this point toward the end of the chapter).

In the *Nicomachean Ethics* Aristotle remarks that "the name [decision, *prohairesis*]...would seem to indicate that [what is decided, *prohaireton*] is chosen [*haireton*] before [*pro*] other things" (*Eth. Nic.*, 1112a). Such a point has, for Aristotle two different but interrelated meanings: "there is no deliberation about some things" (ibid.) and "each of us stops inquiring how to act as soon as he traces the origin to himself, and within himself to the dominant part" (ibid., 1113a). In both cases deliberation is made possible through a procedure of exclusion: the course of deliberation is neither the only possible course nor a "permanent" course (there is, so to speak, no *moral law* where one can find a priori a whole typology of exclusion). But exclusion is also, and most important, a function of the discursive substance of deliberation: the assertion of reasons for action is commited to deliberative discourse, and the moment of *prohairesis* is the moment of the rhetorical configuration of a synthesis of theory and practice within discourse—the moment of judgment. that the course of deliberation is not the only possible course means that the deliberative discourse is somewhat made necessary. As Wittgenstein grimly remarked, "It may be possible that *all enquiry on our part* is set so as to exempt certain propositions from doubt, if they are ever formulated. They lie apart from the route travelled by enquiry" (1969, Section 88). That the course of deliberation is not "permanent" means that the necessity of deliberative discourse entails the prefiguration of its own interruption. Wittgenstein again wrote that "Giving grounds...comes to an end...it is our *acting*" (ibid., Section 204).

Barthes's opinions on narrative in the *S/Z* stage appear to deal closely not so much with modalities of exclusion as with the general idea that there has to be some (unspecified but probably metapsychological) kind of exclusion for narrative to work. But then, of course, his notion of a prohairetic code (to which we shall turn in a moment) is above all the extension of certain metatheoretical properties of his doctrine of reading: "forgetting meanings is not a matter for excurses, an unfortunate defect in performance; it is an affirmative value, a way of asserting the irresponsibility of the text, the pluralism of systems...it is precisely because I forget that I read" (1970, p. 11).

I am not particularly interested here in this latter point, however, which has found more convincing argument perhaps in Gadamer's fight for "the recognition of the fact that there are legitimate prejudices" (1960, p. 246). What interests me here, rather, is the articulation, within Barthes's arguments, between a metatheory of reading and a theory of narrative, as well as the surprising differences vis-à-vis Aristotle (who is, nevertheless, explicitly invoked) in what concerns a typology (and a phenomenology) of exclusion. In fact, after defining prohairesis as "the ability rationally to determine the result of an action" (1970, p. 18), Barthes writes:

> The prohairetic sequence is never more than the result of an artifice of reading: whoever reads the text amasses certain data under some generic titles for actions...and this title embodies the sequence; the sequence exists when and because it can be given a name, it unfolds as this process of naming takes place, as a title is sought or confirmed; its basis is therefore more empirical than rational...(Ibid., p. 19)

The constitution of a sequence is seen as an empirical process of selection in the same sense that reading is one (prohairesis has meanwhile ceased to be a matter of rationality). Indeed, the outcome of such a process is "an artifice of reading," an effect (in the Barthesian sense) of reading itself. And, in spite of the crucial role that the naming of a sequence plays in his theory, Barthes seems to acknowledge that such decisions are ultimately groundless: there is no finite lexicon of names of actions any more than there is a finite lexicon of names of possible actions, and moreover, there is no ultimate justification for the choice of action as a dominant synechdoche here.

But, for Barthes, the moment of selection takes place only through a mediation between the particular and the generic; that is, with a mediation between "data" and "titles." A title can be said to be the real figure ("a title embodies...") of the shapelessness of perception ("an account of appearances," as Barthes calls it, e.g., ibid., p. 83); it is, properly speaking, a configuration of a system of necessity, the moment where data are endowed with a purpose. In this respect, a title indicates a refusal of deliberation (it excludes, so to speak, any "discursification" of exclusion): the moment of transition between the theoretical and the practical is, in a title, the topic of a whole rhetoric of omission (and this, of course, is a venerable problem that can be traced back to Kant). Exclusion is achieved by a denial of judgment, which is to say, by the belief in an automatic subsumption of certain actions by the (moral) law.

The becoming purposeful of data is here the very teleological movement of what is currently known as narrative process. Selection thus signifies both the possibility and the reverse of a purpose, for what is excluded is excluded by the act of attributing a title. We now see how the sense of decision in Barthes's notion of prohairetic code is certainly not the sense it had in the 'will-Bond-answer-the-phone?' running gag of the eighth issue of the journal *Communications*; that is, it is not a matter of selection in *represented* actions. Rather, selection is here the decision to privilege one language, one preexisting law, of attributing some reliability to the paraphrasic virtues of a title (which Barthes calls confidently "an act of lexical transcendence," ibid.) and thus of reducing the alleged plurality of narrative to the form of an observational language—in this sense it can be said, with Barthes, that 'prohairetism comparatively depreciated language ('action', it is said, speaks louder than 'words'): once restored to its prohairetic essence, the operative mock the symbolic, *dismisses* it" (ibid., p. 104). Telling a story, in Barthes's conception, consists, then, in being able to bestow a particular dispensation on narrative discourse, which is the kind of dispensation conveyed by the possibility of ascribing a metalinguistic function to names, to titles—a dispensation analogous to the necessary privilege of the nucleus one can detect in his earlier quadripartition of narrative functions (for example, in Barthes, 1966). Unlike Aristotle, the turning of the discourse of decision into a necessary condition for decision itself is never the issue, here.

Although Barthes offers a doctrine of selection that eventually leads him into a somewhat florid apology for forgetfulness, he does not commit himself to any doctrine of the consequences of forgetfulness: although ascribing prohaireticisms to a "patrimonial hoard of human experiences" (1970, p. 204), he suggests that their typology "seems uncertain or...at least they can be assigned no logic other than that of the probable, of empirics, of the 'already-done' or 'already'written'" (ibid.). The underlying notion, of course, is the notion that there is an equivalence between forgetfulness and consensus and thus that the strategic function of the former, as far as reading is concerned, is indeed to keep the way unhampered for the production of the New and of the More that pertain to the "plural." In this sense, the function of the pastness of the already done (not unlike the teleology of the repressed in Freud's theories) is the eminently handy function of allowing itself to be wiped out by the performativity of the present, which is to say that, in Nietzschean terms, Barthes does not believe that history can ever be the core of a permanent pathology: come what may, the only scenario that reading knows is the scenario of the triumph of life.

Forgetfulness, then, is always treated by the metatheoretical assumption (in Barthes's famous formula) according to which "tout ce qui est noté est notable" (and thus that there is a binding relationship between significance and presence in the sense that the criteria of pertinence for anamnesis are criteria for the manifestation of the general under the form of a symptom). Moreover, such a formula shows that it is really only in a very special sense that one can speak of narrative structures, because, and given the exemplary role of the latter, narrative has become the very proof of structure itself: "The notion of structure does not support the separation of foundation and design, insignificant and significant; structure is not a design, a schema, a diagram: everything signifies something. For proof, we have only to examine the basic (and thus seemingly unimportant) prohairetisms" (1970, p. 51). The distinction I have been intermittently suggesting between what I mean by 'forgotten' and the general apologetic and teleological use of terms such as 'forgetfulness' emphasizes then, in the end, what the "everything" in Barthes's passage *cannot* signify. And thus the forgotten, if *returning* at all, would return not as the manifestation of a presence, alienated or otherwise, but as the necessary absence of a thought of the missing link that causes representation to operate. The postulating of a connection between narrative and its nature, its "title," implies indeed the impossibility to *read* such a connection, as if by that one would show that, to borrow a well-known expression from Quine, there are no roots of reference, or, even better, in de Man's words, that "such is language: it always thrusts but never scores. It always refers but never to the right referent" (1984b, p. 285).

Such is the only cause of Aristotle's concern with the notion of decision, for in this notion are conveyed both the gap between deliberation and action and the possibility of believing that the latter represents the former. And, as Aristotle has seen, the only possible way of keeping a mechanism of perfect equivalences working (and thus of assuring the possibility of correctness, of an adequate selection for action) consists in supposing that the prefix in 'prohairesis' denotes the end of deliberation and thus a judgment. This is to say that, at the same time, the perfection of representation (the consonance between deliberation and action, metalanguage and language, production and effect) is achieved if and only if representation embodies the irreducible difference between its terms.

IX

Once again we are driven back to the articulation between narrative and forgetfulness and indeed to the forgetfulness of the link between story and history. But the difference between a socially shared version of forgetfulness (with the help of notions such as norm or consensus) and the status of the missing link that causes representation to operate in a narrative, in interpretation, is perhaps clearer now. For such a link is not so much the common denominator of all present explanations (or some of them) as what has been forsaken as a positive trait of identity by interpretation. There is, then, no such thing as a socially shared version of forgetfulness, only what can be defined by each narrative as its own memory, a genealogy that can be stated in the very language of the narrative, which inevitably tends also to be an account of how the relationship between story and history was invested with a special normative power. Such accounts are the matter of several often competing techniques of deciphering; but what is deciphered is always the positivity of an expected consensus, and its results are invariably those of the amazement of rediscovery and of the strengthening of reflection.

A nonconsensual dimension of forgetfulness has, perhaps, more to do with what Benjamin called "the allegorical way of seeing":

> in the allegory the observer is confronted with the *facies hippocratica* of history as a petrified, primordial landscape. Everything about history that, from the very beginning, has been untimely, sorrowful, unsuccessful, is expressed in a face—or rather in a death's head [*Die Geschichte in allem was sie Unzeitiges, Leidvolles, Verfehltes von Beginn an hat, prägt sich in einem Antlitz—nein in einem Totenkopfe aus*]. (1928, p. 166)

However, in this sense the infelicities in a story cannot be thematizable as pole of interest (such as decisive events of repression or redemption). The "primordial landscape" of history is indeed what cannot be made the term or the origin of a correspondence, in other words, the "primordial landscape" of history is the refusal to see it as a story and, at the same time, the death of the possibility of not seeing it as such.

It is, perhaps, not surprising that the return of the forgotten in the sense I have been discussing, like the dimensions of the unthinkable, of the inconceivable, is not the return of a concurrent version with the power to refute our present narratives (and thus of a new narrative that would redeem the available explanations from a necessary lack) but rather the intermittent glimpse at a world of nonnaturalized replacements, a world whose elements are, so to speak, deprived of consequence, the world from which nothing *follows*. In this sense, one is always compelled to become the critic of Oscar Wilde's "critics who...will gravely censure the teller of fairy tales for his defective knowledge of natural history" (1889, p. 306), just as one, as Wittgenstein puts it, "might simply say 'O, rubbish! [*Ach Unsinn!*]' to someone who wanted to make objections to the propositions that are beyond doubt. That is, not reply to him but admonish him" (1969, Section 495). What these objections are remote from are the very rules of the conversation, but what those uses refer to is the *forgotten* nature of such rules: links such as the link between history and story, the possibility, which Wittgenstein registers also, of employing words as if they were "like 'Good morning' said to someone in the middle of a conversation" (ibid, Section 464).

In a story, one could say, the unthinkable is the absolutely trivial. Karl Popper remarks that "if we say that the cause of death of Giordano Bruno was being burnt at the stake, we do not need mention the universal law that all living things die when exposed to intense heat. But such a law was tacitly assumed in our causal explanation" (1945, p. 145). Popper, of course, states that "these laws may be so trivial, so much part of our common knowledge, that we need not mention them and rarely notice them" (ibid.). And indeed, from the two preceding passages one can infer a curious mode of interference, the interference of what makes presence possible. From the first passage one can easily infer the ironic (indeed comical) situation of a historian claiming that Bruno died because "all living things die when exposed to intense heat." But one cannot think of such a claim as "a piece of information directed at you" (Wittgenstein, 1969, Section 468). However, one cannot think of the "serious" claim without implying at some level the seriousness of the former piece of information, either. In this sense there is something etymologically, if not literally, obscene in Benjamin's allegorical vision, which is the rather somber silliness of all *facies hippocraticae*; a memento mori conveys a curious disrespect for history, which is to say a curious disrespect for what we are accustomed to consider the versions and indeed the faithfulness to "the facts." For the economy of a historical narrative, as for the economy of all processes of redemption (and thus for the economy of interpretation), there is no *need* to brandish the specter of their own decomposition. Nevertheless, the specter is always somewhat implied in the very act of the formulation of a narrative, which is probably what Nietzsche meant when he referred to the history's turning of its sting against itself. Words like "tacit" in Popper's passage mean also, indeed, the opposite of words like "tacit" in authors like Polanyi; for whereas in the latter sense the tacit dimension is presupposed by the process of the formation of class concepts (e.g., 1962, p. 67), in the former sense it denotes precisely what upsets such a process *and* what renders the process it upsets possible in the first place (one could very well say that the so-called tacit dimension is nothing more than the sum of the prospective and ahistorical necessary infelicities of a given process; and this just means that the tacit dimension is a structural configuration of silliness).

Contrary to what might appear to be the case, it is possible to use the term silliness here with a considerable degree of accuracy. For here, too, silliness denotes a reluctance toward reflection, not just in the sense that Nietzsche's cattle do not think (but look, or so Wittgenstein would say), but also in the sense that prospective infelicity is the mode where the denial of both redemption and revelation is achieved. But this is just another way of saying that forgetfulness is a mode of disbelief in authorized replacements, that is, a mode of disbelief in literality. Here we touch, of course, on another important conflict, in that the *authorization* of a replacement is what forgetfulness denies. An authorized replacement is the procedure of memory or, better perhaps, the procedure of anamnesis; but the lack of the memory anamesis presupposes is, rather, comparable to the interval engendered by discourse as a condition for its speculative working, that is, as the cause of the re- of representation. Such a lack of memory, one would like to say, is the possibility of one's using expressions such as 'more than a simple coincidence', the possibility of what Rorty calls solidarity, narrative or otherwise.

Hermeneutics is never silly in that it invariably conveys the belief that there are no coincidences. Such a belief is, of course, the belief that one can trace a relation between two presences (and not, as it is sometimes said, between a presence and its meaning); and the few figures of such a relation (such as revelation or redemption) are what constitutes meaning. The act of deciphering, which for a long time (including our own) was used as the very emblem of hermeneutics, is not so much in this sense the act of a search for meaning as the very moment of the constitution of meaning or, in other words, the act that performs the mediation between language and the memory of what language has invariably to represent. But meaning, that is, the very seriousness of hermeneutics, its very *thoughtfulness*, one could say, lies in the possibility of establishing anamnesical connections and thus in the particular order such connections display. To see a story as a sign of history can convey either the Jameson-like belief in a revelation of history in narrative or the Rorty-like belief in the redemption of the heterogeneity of narratives by history. But both beliefs are beliefs in the priority of a temporally distinct state—and, indeed, one could very well say that Jameson's and Rorty's memories are located differently. But in no way are the two conceptions distinct as far as the specific temporality of reflection goes. For what the very temporality of reflection precludes is the idea of what Derrida called "a memory...without a past" (1988, p. 644) or, in other words, the infelicities of forgetfulness.

There is the important sense in which the anamnesic circulation that defines the working of a narrative as an explanation ascribes the very boundaries of the changing of narratives and thus what one *can* do in a controversy, for instance. As we have seen, and for the domain of refutational procedures as well as other domains, "narrative philosophy," as Rorty remarks, "should not be expected to fill gaps left vacant by argumentative philosophy" (1985a, p. 136). And indeed, in relation to Derrida, Rorty points out that "whatever a 'graphematics of iterability' might be good for, it would be of no use in polemic. The metaphysics of presence was designed precisely to facilitate argument, to make questions like 'How do you know?' seem natural, and to make a search for first principles and natural resting-places seem obligatory" (ibid., p. 135). But, then again, "narrative philosophy" has to dissolve the problem that the constitution of the communities (of philosophers, scientists, critics) tends to raise; namely, the problem of whether an extracontroversial contact of theories is possible at all. I mentioned earlier in this chapter the particular model of commensurability that narrative explanations presuppose, which is neither formal nor semantic. According to such a model, commensurable theories or vocabularies are those that, in Rorty's terms, do not look bad with each other. The question of controversy, again in Rorty's own terms, is finally the question of how a vocabulary gets discarded. And he answers: "Vocabularies get discarded after looking bad in comparison with other vocabularies, not as a result of an appeal to overarching metavocabularies in which criteria for vocabulary choice can be formulated" (ibid., p. 136). But the notion of "discarding a vocabulary" is hardly compatible with the notion of "forgetting a vocabulary," which Rorty, as we have also seen, considers the narrative homologue of "refuting a proposition" (see note 7). In fact, the former notion presupposes an intentional moment of choice, even if such a choice is deliberately made inconspicuous and conspicuously made casual. Discarding a vocabulary, as it turns out, introduces a possibility that is most disturbing for Rorty's theory: the possibility of proscribing intentionally certain narratives and thus the possibility of superposing narratives to one another. "Looking bad" (and "looking good") are then precisely terms of an "overarching [metavocabulary]...in which criteria for vocabulary choice can be formulated" (ibid.). Which is to say that there seems to be a moment of argumentativity in every "narrative philosophy"; that is, a moment when a narrative explanation has to engage in polemics and, most important, see its vocabulary as a system of propositions and thus to introduce a notion of correspondence between the latter and the metainstance of choice. The process is strikingly similar to Rorty's more or less contrived admission, which we have discussed before, of an inherent a hardness of the facts, independent from any stories one tells about them.

In the shape of these procedures one finds the temporal structure of representation that allows for a form of all stories to be found in every accepted story. In its terms, the relation between narratives cannot help but thematize its very possibility, that is, the possibility of a metafitness that Rorty designates (according to the circumstances) either as solidarity or as "looking good." Indeed, both solidarity and objectivity partake from a similar representational stance that eventually collapses the distinction between *Erklärung* and *Verstehen* in a somewhat circuitous way. Rorty writes:

> There are two principal ways in which reflexive human beings try, by placing their lives in a larger context, to give a sense to

> those lives. The first is by telling a story of their contribution to a community....The second way is to describe themselves as standing in immediate relation to a nonhuman reality....stories of the former kind exemplify the desire for solidarity, and...stories of the latter kind exemplify the desire for objectivity. (1984, p. 3)

Toward the end of the passage Rorty dissolves the opposition between "telling a story" and "to describe" into the notion of "stories" (possibly of several kinds; a genre would be here a *kind* of reflection, a kind of writing, as Rorty's famous epithet goes). But all "stories" exemplify a mediation between "lives" and "a larger context." To be able to tell a story (of any kind) is to be a "reflexive human being," and by being able to tell stories, human beings "give a sense" to their lives. Reflection is, then, here the quality of sense giving and thus an ability of placement.

It is clear that the result of the placement is the elaboration of a connection between a particular and a context. And this means to be able to see the context revealed in the individual (and the individual redeemed in the context). The context, so to speak, becomes the memory of the particular, its presentable past. But Rorty's theory, precisely because it unfolds here under such the empire of reflection, cannot help but take for granted such an ability of placement. Curiously enough, to take for granted means at this juncture to eliminate conceptually the operation of placement, to dismiss as infelicitous or simply silly the question of why only "reflexive human beings" can be, according to the theory, granted the power of telling stories, of putting things into place; that is, the question of the memory of memory (contrary to what it might seem, the equivalent silly question for Lukács is rather the question of whether there should be any implication between recognizing oneself as an object and being able to tell "object stories"). The replacement figured in the narrative moment is, then, perhaps a special kind of replacement: one whose nature is forgotten through its very making sene, through its posterity. It is in a very etymological sense, then, that it can be said that "the community of the liberal intellectuals of the secular modern West...wants to be able to give a *post factum* account of any change of view" (ibid., p. 12). For, by definition, and no matter how prophetic, every account is what represents what it defines as "the facts" (perhaps only events are *ante factum*), just as every account has to misrepresent its representational nature, as if for sense to be made the footsteps of placement (that is, the sign that there was a rhetorical operation to start with) have had to disappear.

One could conclude here with a merry apology for the reinstatement of a pastless memory, even if not necessarily in the naive sense of doing justice to a metaphysical underdog. But such an apology would imply at least two disturbing things: although being an apology for nonrepresentationalism it would remain an apology against a misrepresentation of nonrepresentationalism (in this sense there is something terribly ironic about one's wanting, in a true Benjaminian spirit, to do justice to the German *Trauerspiel*). And, last but by no means the least, it would imply the possibility of a choice between, to put it bluntly, allegory and representation (and such would be always a representational choice, for the reasons extensively indicated earlier). What I call manners of interpretation is perhaps the refusal of certain choices or, even better, the refusal of a general proposition that every situation can be evaluated in terms of the exemplarity of teachable decisional procedures. And, if I am not wrong, the import of the long list of ultimate hermeneutic arguments discussed in this book seems to me to lie not so much in its use or in its function, that is, in their providing ultimate grounds or untranscendable horizons for justification, as in their ever oblique admission or hope that arguments must stop at a certain point, that the anamnesical circulation must be detained, that a certain past must be lost for interpretation to work at all.

Such an admission, however, is not free, in the sense that it cannot be derived from a choice: it appears to be engendered by the very way in which language and explanations work or, perhaps, it appears to be the *result* of rationality in institutions—namely, within philosophy of science and literary criticism—at a certain moment (there is here, of course, the meager consolation for the preceding merry apologist that if all varieties of explanation alike seem to be invariably exemplary and thus to be representations, then all explanations have got to engender their own mimetic demotion somehow).

Moreover, it is not free in a second, and decisive sense: the sense of the burden of disagreement I mentioned earlier on. It is very ironic that the dealing with procedures of erasure be (necessarily, one would want to write here) contaminated by a logic of discovery and thus that such a dealing would take, in its turn, the shape of a narrative of discovery: the more percipient readers would have noticed perhaps the awkward way in which the form of this chapter mimics the opposite of its rhetoric. But then again, such is the sense of the mirror of nature's forgetting of its mirror nature. And such is the sense of a narrative of the mirror of nature's forgetting of its mirror nature forgetting of its narrative condition. So it is only too predictable that such be the sense of my writing 'such is the sense'.

Notes

1. From here on, in this quote, brackets were added by the translator.

2. Discussing the sense of the word 'hypothesis', Peirce remarked that there are at least two different uses of the term:

> the sense in which Newton used the word when he said, *Hypotheses non fingo*. He meant that he was merely giving a general formula for the motions of heavenly bodies, but was not undertaking to mount to the causes of acceleration they exhibit. The inferences of Kepler, on the other hand, were hypotheses in this sense; for he traced out the miscellaneous consequences of the supposition that Mars moved in an ellipse, with the sun at the focus, and showed that both the longitudes and the latitudes resulting from this theory were such as agreed with observation. These two components of the motion were observed; the third, that of approach to or regression from the earth, was supposed. (1978a, p. 707)

In a very good sense, Kepler (Dilthey's example, as we shall see) could have very well said *Hypotheses fingo*. Indeed, what is at stake is precisely what Peirce called "a certain element of guess-work in such an induction" (1978b, p. 526). As is well known, and after his customary terminological hesitations, Peirce termed this third kind of inference *abduction*. The word had perhaps the additional advantage of suggesting to the speakers of English the somewhat marginal (if not the outright illegal) nature of such a procedure. As Peirce put it, "I call all such inference by the peculiar name, *abduction*, because its legitimacy depends upon altogether different principles from those of other kinds of inference" (ibid., p. 525). And the point to which it is marginal to what one could call a certain attitude toward truth is in its being satisfied with explanations that are avowedly "approximately true" (Peirce used the expression in reference to Kepler, again). See K. T. Fann (1970) and Eco and Sebeok (1983).

3. Harold Bloom opposes this passage, in which, according to him, "the 'official' Eliot...idealizes the process of literary transmission" (1982:18) to a never reprinted review of Eliot, "Reflections on Contemporary Poetry," published in 1919, where, according to Bloom again, the "language of metamorphoses and awakening is the language of the family romance, and not of a

simultaneous order defying temporality" (ibid., p. 20). Be that as it may, Eliot's expression "his relation to the dead poets and artists," in the passage from "Tradition and the Individual Talent," is perhaps less "Eliotic" than Bloom would concede.

4. Here I follow closely the exposition of Couturat (1901, pp. 81ff).

5. There is a story to be told here of the "Chinese" inheritance (via Leibniz) of Frege's notion of "a formalized language of pure Thought modelled upon the Language of the Arithmetic," better known as Frege's *Begriffsschrift*, insofar as such a writing (tendentially ideographic) is a writing of non-Chinese (in Jakobson's sense) boundaries. See Frege (1879).

6. Such is perhaps the crucial difference between de Man and critics like Harold Bloom. In a 1981 lecture Bloom described his disagreement with "the best mind I know, Don Paolo as the lively Lentricchia calls him" (1982, p. 30) in the following way: "When Paul de Man tells me that an epistemological stance in regard to a literary text is necessarily more privileged than any aesthetic or moral stance, all I can do is grin cheerfully and rejoin that such a stance is no more or less literary, no more or less a trope, than the most self-abasing belly-prone reverence of Professor Moldy Fig or the self-aggrandizing Bloomian wildness" (ibid.). Such is also, I think, the reason of Richard Rorty's sympathy for Bloom. (e.g., Rorty, 1989, pp. 28-30).

7. Rorty wrote:

> One can also think of philosophy as a matter of telling stories: stories about why we talk as we do and how we might avoid continuing to talk that way. When you find yourself at an argumentative impasse, baffled by your opponent's refusal to stop asking questions which you think you really should not have to answer, you can always shift the ground by raising questions about the vocabulary he or she is using. You can point out that the issue is biased in one opponent's favour by the unfortunate jargon which has developed, a jargon which gives one's opponent an unfair advantage. You can use historical narratives to show why the issue previously discussed is moot and why it needs to be reformulated in terms which are, alas, not yet available. (1985a, pp. 134-135)

In this fragment one finds a whole ethical program of a theory of controversies based upon a commensurability of usages. It is certainly not by chance that the program is of an ethical nature. But, seen in this light, the central issue for such a theory consists in tackling the problem of the modification of use itself. The solution propounded by Rorty is no longer a "syntactic" solution (arguing that certain or all of the sentences employed by the opponent are not well formed) nor is it a "semantic" one (arguing that the "you" and the opponent are not talking about the same thing); it is, of course a "pragmatic" solution, which consists basically in confronting the opponent with the syntactic and semantic consequences of the opponent's own statements (showing thus that norms are in a sense created by discussion itself) and finally appealing to the only norm that is not created by discourse; that is, sense of fairness. Sense of fairness however, is not a mere consequence of the maxim "it is good to imagine all possible points of view" but rather the solution made natural from the impossibility of imagining all possible points of view: a pragmatic justice, so to speak, is imposed by syntactic and semantic aporias and indeed defines a eu-poretics.

All of the procedures suggested by Rorty in the preceding passage are, even if in a different respect, "a matter of telling stories." In the use of "historical narratives" one finds, of course, an exemplary use of narrative that has been invoked from time immemorial. As Rorty writes, "you can use...narratives to show." But this exemplary use in a controversy is different from the mere fablelike use of narrative in that it presupposes necessarily an opponent and, moreover, an opponent endowed, at least for the sake of argument, with the power of producing equally powerful narratives. The equivalent of the demonstration (that is, the exemplarity) is not achieved, then, by the superposition of one narrative on the other, but rather by the suggestion, implicit in the very controversial situation, that more than one narrative is possible in every situation and that *that* is the source of both debatability and of the yearning for an agreement. On the other hand, in what Rorty calls raising questions about the opponent's vocabulary, there is also an important, albeit less obvious, narrative element. Such an element is twofold: it is located both in the showing that the opponent's positions rather represent the final stage of a process originated, for instance, in a choice of vocabulary (and thus that they represent the predictable outcome of a series of determined modifications) and in the showing that the opponent's positions involve a process of "undesirable restriction," a bias (that is, that the opponent's positions are not the only possible outcome of a series of determined steps).

The consequences of one's thinking of philosophy as "a matter of telling stories" determine a series of oppositions vis-à-vis the idea of philosophy as "a matter of deductive argument." The first is a stylistic opposition, indeed the opposition between two modes of connecting sentences; narration is thus opposed to deduction as two stylistic modes for contiguity (my use of the word 'stylistics' here is perhaps a correlative for Rorty's trivialization of the sublimity of logic). The criteria for organizing contiguities are consequently different: the purely formal criterion of deduction can in this respect be contrasted with the positional requisites of vicinity, once it is assumed that all vicinity of propositions partakes of the deepest reasons of use. Such a point implies a second type of opposition; namely, the opposition between the reasons of use and the causes of deduction (again, I am using both terms in Wittgenstein's *Blue Book*'s sense: "giving a reason is like giving a calculation by which you have arrived at a certain result [1958, p. 15] whereas "of the cause one can say that one can't *know* it but can only *conjecture* it" [ibid.]. Taken in this way, a conjecture presupposes always the assumption of what

Rorty calls *rational grounds* (1985a, p. 135); that is, of a principle (no matter how provisional) from which deductions are processed. Giving reasons, however, is an activity linked to the contingency of a *given* justification and then, it is always, in Rorty's terms, the telling of stories "about why we talk as we do" (ibid.)—even if one refuses the next inferential step (which Rorty has to take for validatory motives) that consists in claiming that such stories are also stories about "how we might avoid continuing to talk that way" (ibid.). But the third, and most important, opposition derives precisely from the collapse of causes into reasons (in the sense that Rorty could suggest that what is usually called a *proposition* is a slice of a certain vocabulary and thus part of a story that is necessarily someone's story). As the second opposition was tied mainly to principles of demonstration (and implied not just that "narrative demonstrations" are always reason-giving activities but indeed that all demonstrations are essentially of a narrative kind), so the third opposition is tied to the mechanism of refutation. And once again the distinction between dialectics and rhetoric is condensed into a universal rhetoric (that, in *Contingency, Irony and Solidarity*, Rorty has come to see, curiously enough, as a universal dialectics, see. 1989, p. 78) for which the "right way to construe [the] question [of knowledge] is...'What am I going to have to do to convince you?'" (1985, p. 136). However, Rorty does not seem to rely too much on the virtues of universal persuasion; that is, on the matter-of-factly convincing aura of properly told stories. For him, a story does not have the automatic power to refute incompatible stories, in the strong sense that there is something one *cannot* do to convince someone else. Discussing the absence of "rational grounds for rejecting realism...if we can overcome the metaphysics of presence" (ibid., p. 135), Rorty remarks that "The notion of 'rational grounds' is not in place once one adopts a narrative strategy....For if we ever did get rid of all the jargon of the tradition, we should not even be able to state the realist's position, much less argue against it. The enemy would have been forgotten rather than refuted....You can only argue against a proposition, not against a vocabulary" (ibid., pp. 135-136). One has in the end, thus, an opposition between refuting and forgetting, the latter term being associated with a "narrative strategy." And even if the intentional moment of rhetorical refutation is still endowed with a considerable power ("Vocabularies get discarded after looking bad in comparison with other vocabularies, not as a result of an appeal to overarching metavocabularies in which criteria for vocabulary choice can be formulated," ibid., p. 136)—which is to say that there is a sense in which it is possible to refute, albeit not dialectically, a vocabulary—there comes a time when the only way to conceive of the desire to wipe out the opponent, of the "elenchic" moment, is to be in terms of a nonintentional act: the act of forgetting. And if narratives do not have causes they can have, in Rorty's formulation, a curious effect: they erase reasons.

Works Cited

Attributed translations have not been modified, except when noted. Terms, expressions or sentences in brackets within a quote refer in most cases to the original text and are inserted whenever the sense of either the original or the translation raises doubts, or when a point to be made draws on the original text rather than on the translation. Nonattributed translations are my own.

Aristotle. *Eth. Nic. Nicomachean Ethics*, trans. T. Irwin, Indianapolis: Hackett, 1985.

— *Rhet. Art of Rhetoric*, trans. J. H. Freese, Loeb Classical Library, Cambridge, Mass, and London: Harvard University Press and W. Heinemann, 1967.

— *Poet. Poetics*, trans. W. H. Fyfe, Loeb Classical Library, Cambridge, Mass, and London: Harvard University Press and W. Heinemann, 1982.

Augustine. *Doc. Christ. De doctrina christiana*, ed. J. Martin, In *Aurelii Augustini Opera* (4:1) in *Corpus Christianorum—Series latina*, Brepols, Turnhout, 1962, vol. 32, 1-167; ,and trans. D. W. Robertson, Jr., *On Christian Doctrine*, Indianapolis: Boobs-Merrill, 1984.

Austin, J. L. 1950. "Truth." In *Philosophical Papers*, ed. J. O. Urmson and G. J. Warnock. London: Oxford University Press, 1970.

— 1962. *How to Do Things with Words*, ed. J. O. Urmson and M. Sbisà, Cambridge, Mass: Harvard University Press, 1975.

Ayer, A. J., ed. 1959. *Logical Positivism*. Westport, Conn.: Greenwood Press, 1978.

Barthes, R. 1966. "Introduction à l'analyse structurale des récits." *Communications* 8: 1-27

—— 1970. *S/Z*, trans. R. Miller, New York: Hill and Wang, 1974.

Benjamin, W. 1923. "Die Aufgabe des Übersetzers." In *Gesammelte Schriften*, ed. T. Rexroth, Frankfurt: Suhrkamp, 1980, vol. 10, pp. 9-21. H. Zohn, trans. "The Task of the Translator." In *Illuminations. Essays and Reflections*, ed. H. Arendt, New York: Schocken Books, 1985, pp. 69-82.

—— 1928. *Ursprung des deutschen Trauerspiels*. In *Gesammelte Schriften*, ed. R. Tiedemann and H. Schweppenhäuser, Frankfurt: Suhrkamp,1980, vol. 1, pp. 203-430. J. Osborne, trans. *The Origin of German Tragic Drama*, London: Verso, 1985.

—— 1936. "Der Erzähler." In *Gesammelte Schriften*, ed. T. Rexroth, Frankfurt: Suhrkamp, 1980, vol. 5, pp. 438-465. H. Zohn, trans. "The Storyteller." In *Illuminations. Essays, and Reflections*, ed. H. Arendt, New York: Schocken Books, 1985, pp. 83-109.

Bloom, H. 1982. *The Breaking of the Vessels*, Chicago: University of Chicago Press.

Carnap, R. 1931. "Überwindung der Metaphysik durch Logische Analyse der Sprache." A. Pap, trans. "The Elimination of Metaphysics Through Logical Analysis of Language." In Ayer, 1959, pp. 60-81.

Cohen, R., ed. 1989. *The Future of Literary Theory*, New York: Routledge.

Couturat, L. 1901. *La Logique de Leibniz d'après des documents inédits*, Hildesheim: Georg Olms, 1961.

Culler, J. 1982. *On Deconstruction. Theory and Criticism After Structuralism*, New York: Cornell University Press, 1989.

Curtius, E. R. 1948. *Europäische Literatur und lateinisches Mittelalter*,W. R. Trask, trans. *European Literature and the Latin Middle Ages*, New York: Pantheon Books, 1953.

Danto, A. C. 1989. "Beautiful Science and the Future of Criticism." In Cohen, 1989, pp. 370-385.

Dascal, M. 1987. *Leibniz. Language, Signs, and Thought*, Amsterdam: Benjamins.

De Man, P. 1966. "Form and Intent in the American New Criticism." In *Blindness and Insight*, 1983, pp. 20-35.

— 1970. "Literary History and Literary Modernity." In *Blindness and Insight*, pp. 142-165.

— 1971. "The Rhetoric of Blindness: Jacques Derrida's Reading of Rousseau." In *Blindness and Insight*, 1983, pp. 102-141.

— 1972. "Literature and Language: A Commentary." In *Blindness and Insight*, 1983, pp. 277-289.

— 1979. *Allegories of Reading. Figural Language in Rousseau, Nietzsche, Rilke, and Proust*, New Haven, Conn.: Yale University Press.

— 1982a. "The Resistance to Theory." In *The Resistance to Theory*, Minneapolis: University of Minnesota Press, 1986, pp. 3-20.

— 1982b. "The Return to Philology." In *The Resistance to Theory*, pp. 21-26

— 1983. *Blindness and Insight. Essays in the Rhetoric of Contemporary Criticism*, Minneapolis: University of Minnesota Press.

— 1984a. "Phenomenality and Materiality in Kant." In Shapiro and Sica, 1984, pp. 121-144.

— 1984b. "Aesthetic Formalization: Kleist's *Über das Marionettentheater*". In *The Rhetoric of Romanticism*, New York: Columbia University Press, pp. 263-290.

— 1985. "Conclusions: Walter Benjamin's *The Task of the Translator*." In *The Resistance to Theory*, Minneapolis: University of Minnesota Press, 1986, pp. 73-105.

Dennett, D. C. 1981. "Reflections [on D. R. Hofstadter's "A Conversation with Einstein's Brain"]." In Hofstadter and Dennett, 1981, pp. 457-460.

Derrida, J. 1972. "Signature évènement contexte," trans. S. Weber and J. Mehlman, "Signature Event Context." *Glyph* 1977, pp. 172-197.

— 1988. "Like the Sound of the Sea Deep within a Shell: Paul de Man's War," trans. P. Kamuf. *Critical Inquiry*, 14, no. 3: pp. 590-653.

Dilthey, W. 1927. "Das Verstehen anderer Personen und ihren

Lebenäusserungen," In *Gesammelte Schriften*, ed. B. Groethuysen, Leipzig: Teubner, vol. 7, pp. 205-220. J. J. Kuehl, trans. "The Understanding of other Persons and Their Life-Expressions." In Gardiner, 1959, pp. 211-225.

Eco, U. and Sebeok, T. A. eds. 1983 *The Sign of Three. Dupin, Holmes, Peirce.* Bloomington: Indiana University Press, 1988.

Eliot, T. S. 1917. "Tradition and the Individual Talent." In *Selected Essays*, New York: Harcourt and Brace, 1950, pp. 3-11.

Fann, K. T. 1970. *Peirce's Theory of Abduction*, The Hague: Martinus Nijhoff.

Fenollosa, E. 1920. *The Chinese Written Character as a Medium for Poetry [An Ars Poetica]*, New York: Arrow, 1936.

Fish, S. 1982. "Working on the Chain Gang: Interpretation in Law and Literature." *Texas Law Review* 60, no. 3: pp. 551-567.

Frege, G. 1879. *Begriffschrift*, partially translated by P. T. Geach in *Translations from the Philosophical Writings of Gottlob Frege*, ed. P. Geach and M. Black, Oxford: Basil Blackwell, 1966, pp. 1-20.

Freud, S. 1908. "Der Dichter und das Phantasieren," In *Studienausgabe*, ed. A. Mitscherlich, A. Richards, and J. Strachey, Frankfurt: Fischer, 1982, vol. 10, pp. 169-179. I.F. Grant Duff, trans., "Creative Writers and Day-dreaming," In *Standard Edition*, London: Hogarth Press, 1978, vol. 9, pp. 142-153.

— 1912. "Nachtrag zur 2. Auflage." In *Studienausgabe*, 1982, vol. 10, pp. 84-85. J. Strachey et. al., trans., "Postscript to the Second Edition" [of *Gradiva*]." In *Standard Edition*, 1978, vol. 9, pp. 94-95.

Gadamer, H. -G. 1960. *Wahrheit und Methode. Grundzüge einer philosophischen Hermeneutik*. Tübingen: J. C. G. Mohr, 1965. G. Barden- J. Cumming, trans., *Truth and Method*, New York: Crossroad, 1986.

Gardiner, P., ed. 1959. *Theories of History*, Glencoe, Ill.: The Free Press and George Allen & Unwin.

Hegel, G. W. F. 1833. *Einleitung in die Geschichte der Philosophie*, In *Werke in zwanzig Bänden*, ed. E. Moldenhauer and K. M. Michel, Frankfurt: Suhrkamp, 1980, vol. 18, pp. 11-170. T. M. Knox and A. V. Miller, trans., *Introduction to the Lectures on the History of Philosophy*, Oxford: Clarendon Press, 1985.

— 1837. *Vorlesungen über die Philosophie der Geschicte*, In *Werke in zwanzig Bäuden*, 1980, vol. 12. J. Sibree trans., *The Philosophy of History*, New York: Dover Books, 1956.

— 1842: *Vorlesungen über Asthetik, Werke in zwanzig Bänden*, 1980, vols. 13-15. T. M. Knox, trans., *Aesthetics. Lectures on Fine Art*, Oxford: Clarendon Press, 1975, 2 vols.

Heidegger, M. 1929. "Was ist Metaphysik?" In *Wegmarken*, Frankfurt: Klostermann, 1967, pp. 1-19. Hull-Crick, trans. "What is Metaphysics?" In *Existence and Being*, ed. W. Brock, London: Vision, 1949, pp. 353-380.

— 1943. "Nachwort zu Was ist Metaphysik?" In *Wegmarken*, Frankfurt: Klostermann, 1929, pp. 99-108; and trans. Hull-Crick, "Postscript." In *Existence and Being*, 1949, pp. 380-392.

— 1947. *Platons Lehre von der Wahrheit. Mit einem Brief über den "Humanismus,"*, Bern: A. Francke.

— 1949. "Einleitung zu Was ist Metaphysik? Der Rückgang in den Grund der Metaphysik." In *Wegmarken*, Frankfurt: Klostermann, 1967, pp. 195-211. W. Kaufmann, trans., "The Way Back into the Ground of Metaphysics." In *Existentialism from Dostoevsky to Sartre*, ed. W. Kaufmann, Cleveland: World, 1962, pp. 206-221.

— 1962. *Die Frage nach dem Ding. Zu Kants Lehre von den transzendentalen Grundsätzen*, in *Gesamtausgabe. II.Abteilung: Vorlesungen 1923-1944*, Frankfurt: Klostermann, 1984, vol. 41. W. Barton, Jr., and V. Deutsch, trans., *What Is a Thing?*, Chicago: Henry Regnery, 1967.

Hempel, C. G. 1950. "The Empiricist Criterion of Meaning." In Ayer, 1959, pp. 108-129.

Hirsch, Jr., E. D. 1960. "Objective Interpretation." In Hirsch, 1967, pp. 209-242.

— 1967. *Validity in Interpretation*, New Haven, Conn.: Yale University Press

— 1987. *Cultural Literacy. What Every American Needs to Know*, Boston: Houghton

Hofstadter, D. R., and Dennett, D. C. eds. 1981. *The Mind's I. Fantasies and Reflections on Self and Soul*, New York: Bantam Books, 1982.

Jakobson, R. 1934. "Co je poezie?" M. Helm, trans., "What is Poetry?" In *Selected Writings*, The Hague: Mouton, 1975, vol. 3, pp. 740-750.

— 1960. "Linguistics and Poetics." In *Selected Writings*, vol. 3, pp. 18-51.

— 1966. "Grammatical Parallelism and Its Russian Facet." In *Selected Writings*, vol. 3, pp. 98-135.

— 1968. "Poetry of Grammar and Grammar of Poetry." In *Selected Writings*, vol. 3, pp. 87-97.

Jameson, F. 1971. *Marxism and Form. Twentieth-Century Dialectical Theories of Literature*, Princeton, N.J.: Princeton University Press, 1974.

— 1981. *The Political Unconscious. Narrative as a Socially Symbolic Act*, Cornell, N.Y.: Ithaca University Press, 1985.

— 1984. "Foreword." In Lyotard, 1979, pp. vii-xxi.

Johnson, S. 1750a. "*The Rambler*, 14 [The Difference Between an Author's Writings and His Conversation]." In *The Yale Edition of the Works of Samuel Johnson*, ed. W. J. Bate and A. B. Strauss, New Haven, Conn.: Yale University Press, 1969, vol. 3, pp. 74-80.

— 1750b. "*The Rambler*, 23 [The Contrariety of Criticism, The Vanity of Objection. An Author Obliged to Depend upon his Judgement]." In *The Yale Edition of the Works of Samuel Johnson*, vol. 3, pp. 125-130.

— 1750c. "*The Rambler*, 60 [The Dignity and Usefulness of Biography]." In *The Yale Edition of the Works of Samuel Johnson*, vol. 3, pp. 318-323.

Juhl, P. D. 1980. *Interpretation, An Essay in the Philosophy of Literary Criticism*, Princeton, N.J.: Princeton University Press.

Kant, I. 1798. *Der Streit der Fakultäten*, trans. M. J. Gregor, In *The Conflict of the Faculties-Der Streit der Fakultäten*, New York: Abaris Books, 1979.

Kavanagh, T. M. 1989a. (ed.), *The Limits of Theory*, Stanford, Calif.: Stanford University Press.

— 1989b. "Introduction." In Kavanagh, 1989a, pp. 1-22.

Keats, J. 1817. "[Letter to George and Tom Keats, 21, 27(?) December 1817]." In *The Letters of John Keats*, ed. H. E. Rollins, Cambridge, Mass.: Harvard University Press, 1958, vol. 1, pp. 191-194.

Kermode, F. 1981. "The Single Correct Interpretation." In *Essays on Fiction 1971-82*, London: Routledge and Kegan Paul, 1983, pp. 201-220.

Kimmerle, H. 1962. "Hermeneutische Theorie oder ontologische Hermeneutik," trans. F. Seifert, "Hermeneutical Theory of Ontological Hermeneutics." In *History and Hermeneutics. Journal for Theology and the Church,* 4, ed. R. W. Funk, New York: Harper & Row, 1967, pp. 107-121.

Kircher, A. 1667. *China Monumentis qua Sacris qua Profanis. Nec non variis Naturae et Artis Spectaculis. Aliarumque rerum memorabilium Argumentis Illustrata,* ed. H. K. Kulöy. Kathmandu: Ratna Pustak Bhandar, 1979.

Knapp, S. and Michaels, W. Benn. 1982. "Against Theory." In Mitchell, 1985, pp. 11-30.

— 1983. "A Reply to our Critics." In Mitchell, 1985, pp. 95-105.

— 1987. "Against Theory 2: Hermeneutics and Deconstruction." In *Critical Inquiry*, 14, no. 1: pp. 49-68.

Lach, D. F. 1940. "The Chinese Studies of Andreas Müller." In *Journal of the American Oriental Society* 60. pp. 564-575.

— 1945. "Leibniz and China." *Journal of the History of Ideas*, 4: pp. 436-455.

— 1957. *The Preface to Leibniz' Novissima Sinica. Commentary. Translation. Text.*, Honolulu: University of Hawaii Press.

Leibniz, G. W. 1697. "Praefatium [to *Novissima Sinica*]." D. F. Lach, trans., "[Translation of Leibniz's Preface]." In Lach, 1957, pp. 87-97 and 68-86.

— C. "[Sur la Charactéristique et la langue universelle]." In *Opuscules et fragments inédits de Leibniz*, ed. L. Couturat, Hildesheim: Georg Olms, 1961, pp. 284-285.

— E. *Nouveaux essais sur l'entendement humain* in *Sämtliche Schriften und Briefe*, ed. Preussische (jetzt Deutsche), Akademie der Wissenschaften zu Berlin, Berlin: Akademie Verlag, 1962, pp. 39-527.

— M. "[Leibniz an Joh. Sigismund Elsholz 24 Iunii 1969]." In *Sämtliche*

Schriften und Briefe Darmstadt: Otto Michel, 1927, vol. 2, pp. 491-492. D. F. Lach, trans., in Lach, 1940, pp. 568-569.

— O. "[Leibnitius de connexione inter res et verba, seu potius de linguarum origine]." In *Opuscules et fragments inédits de Leibniz*, ed. L. Couturat. Hildesheim: Georg Olms, 1961, pp. 151-152. M. Dascal, trans., "On the Connection Between Things and Words or Rather on the Origin of Languages." In Dascal, 1987, pp. 189-190.

— S. "[Fundamenta Calculi Ratiocinatori]." In *Die philosophischen Schriften von G. W. Leibniz*, ed. C. I. Gerhardt, Hildesheim: Georg Olms, 1965. M. Dascal, trans., "Thought, Signs and the Foundations of Logic." In Dascal, 1987, pp. 181-188.

— T. "[Table de definitions]." In *Opuscules et fragments inédits de Leibniz*, ed. L. Couturat. Hildesheim: Georg Olms, 1961, pp. 437-510.

Lyotard, J. -F. 1979. *La condition postmoderne: rapport sur le savoir*, G. Bennington and B. Massumi, trans., *The Postmodern Condition: A Report on Knowledge*, Minneapolis: University of Minnesota Press, 1985.

— 1983. *Le différend*, Paris: Minuit.

Lukács, G. 1923. *Geschichte und Klassbewusstsein*, R. Livingstone, trans. *History and Class Consciousness. Studies in Marxist Dialectics*, Cambridge, Mass.: MIT Press, 1988.

Macaulay, T. B. 1828. "Hallam's History." In *Essays*, ed. A. J. Grieve, London: Dent-Hutton, 1907, vol. 1, pp. 1-76.

— 1831. "Samuel Johnson." In *Essays*, vol. 2, pp. 523-562.

Miller, J. Hillis 1987. *The Ethics of Reading: Kant, de Man, Eliot, Trollope, James, and Benjamin*, New York: Columbia University Press.

Mink, L. O. 1981. "Everyman His or Her Own Analyst." *Critical Inquiry*, 7 no. 4: pp. 777-783.

Mitchell, W. J. T., ed. 1985. *Against Theory. Literary Studies and the New Pragmatism.*, Chicago: University of Chicago Press.

Montaigne, M. de. Av. "[Avis] Au lecteur." In *Les Essais de Montaigne*, ed. P. Villey. Paris: PUF, 1978, vol. 1, p. 3. D. M. Frame, trans., "To the Reader."

In *The Complete Works of Montaigne*, London: Hamish Hamilton, p. 2.

— II, 1. "De l'inconstance de nos actions." In *Les Essais de Montaigne*, 1978, vol. 1, pp. 331-338. D. M. Frame, trans., "Of the Inconsistency of our Actions." In *The Complete Works of Montaigne*, 1978, pp. 239-249.

— III, 2. "Du repentir." In *Les Essais de Montaigne*, 1978, vol. 2, pp. 804-817. D. M. Frame, trans., "Of Repentance." In *The Complete Works of Montaigne*, 1978, pp. 610-621.

— III, 13. "De l'experience." In *Les Essais de Montaigne*, 1978, vol. 2, pp. 1064-1116. D. M. Frame, trans., "Of Experience." In *The Complete Works of Montaigne*, 1978, pp. 815-857.

Nagel, T. 1974. "What Is It Like to Be a Bat?" In Hofstadter and Dennett, 1981, pp. 391-402.

Nietzsche, F. W. 1873. "Ueber Wahrheit und Lüge im aussermoralischen Sinne." In *Sämtliche Werke, Kritische Studienausgabe*, ed. G. Colli and M. Montinari, Munich and Berlin: D. J. Parent-de Gruyter, 1980, vol. 1, pp. 873-890. D. J. Parent, trans., "On Truth and Lying in an Extra-Moral Sense." In *Friedrich Nietzsche on Rhetoric and Language*, ed. S. L. Gilman. New York: Oxford University Press, 1989, pp. 246-257.

— 1874. "Vom Nutzen und Nachteil der Historie für das Leben." In *Sämtliche Werke*, vol. 1, pp. 243-334. R. J. Hollingdale, trans., "On the Uses and Disadvantages of History for Life." In *Untimely Meditations*, Cambridge: Cambridge University Press, 1987, pp. 57-123.

Norris, C. 1988. *Paul de Man, Deconstruction and the Critique of Ideology*, New York: Routledge.

Novalis, (F. von, Hardenberg). 1798a. "Dialogen." In *Novalis Werke*, ed. G. Schulz. Munich: Beck, 1981, pp. 415-425. J. Crick ,trans., "Dialogues." In Wheeler, 1984, pp. 93-102.

— 1798b. "Monolog." In *Novalis Werke*, pp. 426-427. J. Crick, trans., "Monologue." In Wheeler, 1984, pp. 92-93.

— 1799.[*Aus dem* Allgemeinen Brouillon 1798-1799]. In Wheeler, 1984, pp. 445-498.

Nozick, R. 1980. "Fiction." In Hofstadter and Dennett, 1981, pp. 461-464.

Peirce, C. S. 1978a. "A Theory of Probable Inference." In *Collected Papers of C. S. Peirce*, ed. C. Hartshorne and P. Weiss. Cambridge, Mass.: Belknap Press of Harvard University, vol. 2, pp. 694-754.

— 1978b. "Hume on Miracles." In *Collected Papers of C. S. Peirce*, vol. 6, pp. 522-547.

Polanyi, M. 1962. "Tacit Knowing: Its Bearing on Some Problems of Philosophy." In *Knowing and Being*, ed. M. Greene. London: Routledge and Kegan Paul, 1969, pp. 159-180.

Popper, K. 1945. *The Poverty of Historicism*, London: Routledge and Kegan Paul, 1960.

Pound, E. 1913. "The Serious Artist." In *Literary Essays of Ezra Pound*, ed. T. S. Eliot. Norfolk: New Directions, 1954, pp. 41-57.

— 1936. "Foreword." In Fenollosa, 1920, pp. 5-6.

— 1937. "Immediate Need of Confucius." In *Impact. Essays on Ignorance and the Decline of American Civilization*, ed. N. Stock. Chicago: Henry Regnery, 1960, pp. 197-205.

— 1938. *Guide to Kulchur*. Norfolk: New Directions, 1951.

— 1942. *Carta da Visita* J. Drummond, trans., "A Visiting Card," In *Impact. Essays on Ignorance and the Decline of American Civilization*, ed. N. Stock. Chicago: Henry Regnery, 1960, pp. 44-74.MM

— 1944. *Oro e lavoro*, J. Drummond, trans., "The Enemy Is Ignorance" In *Impact*, pp. 98-117.

Putnam, H. 1978. *Meaning and the Moral Sciences*. London: Routledge and Kegan Paul.

— 1984. "The Craving for Objectivity." *New Literary History*, 15 no. 2: pp. 229-239.

— 1985. "A Comparison of Something with something Else." *New Literary History*, 17 no. 1, pp. 61-79.

Rajchman, J. and West, C. eds. 1985. *Post-Analytic Philosophy*, New York: Columbia University Press.

Ricoeur, P. 1979. "La fonction narrative." J. B. Thompson, trans., "The Narrative Function." In *Hermeneutics and the Human Sciences*, ed. J. B. Thompson. Cambridge and Paris: Cambridge University Press and Maison des Sciences de l'Homme, 1987, pp. 274-296.

Rorty, R. 1979. *Philosophy and the Mirror of Nature*, Princeton, N.J.: Princeton University Press.

— 1984. "Solidarity and Objectivity." In Rajchman and West, 1985, pp. 3-19.

— 1985a. "Philosophy Without Principles." In Mitchell, 1985, pp.132-138.

— 1985b. "Texts and Lumps." *New Literary History*, 17 no. 1: pp. 1-16.

— 1989. *Contingency, Irony, and Solidarity*. Cambridge: Cambridge University Press.

Rousseau, J. -J. 1755. *Discours sur l'origine et les fondements de l'inégalité parmi les hommes*, ed. J. Starobinski. In *Oeuvres complètes*, Paris: Pléiade, Gallimard, 1966, vol. 3, pp. 109-223.

Sainte-Beuve, C. A. 1862. "Chateaubriand." In A. Schinz, ed. *Nineteenth Century French Readings*, New York: Holt, 1955, vol. 2, pp. 16-22.

Schlegel, F. von. 1797a, *Zur Philologie*, ed. E. Behler. In *Kritische Ausgabe*, Munich: F. Schöningh-Thomas, 1981, vol. 16, pp. 33-81.

— 1797b. "[Kritische Fragmente in] *Lyceum der schönen Künste*," ed. H. Eichner. In *Kritische Ausgabe*, Munich: F. Schöningh-Thomas, vol. 2, pp. 147-163. Partial translation, E. Behler-R. Struc, "Selected Aphorisms from the *Lyceum*." In *Dialogue on Poetry and Literary Aphorisms*, ed. E. Behler-R. Struc. University Park: Pennsylvania State University Press, 1968, pp. 121-132.

— 1800a. *Gespräch über die Poesie*, ed. H. Eichner. In *Kritische Ausgabe*, Munich: F. Schöningh-Thomas, 1967, vol. 2, pp. 284-362. E. Behler-R. Struc, trans., "Dialogue on Poetry." In *Dialogue on Poetry and Literary Aphorisms*. ed. E. Behler-R. Struc, University Park: Pennsylvania State University Press, 1968, pp. 51-117.

— 1800b. "Über die Unverständlichkeit," ed. H. Eichner. In *Kritische Ausgabe*. F. Schöningh-Thomas, 1967, vol. 2, pp. 363-372. P. Firchow, trans., "On Incomprehensibility." In K. M. Wheeler, ed., 1984, pp. 32-40.

Schleiermacher, F. D. E. 1. "[Die Aphorismen von 1805 und 1809]." In

Hermeneutik, ed. H. Kimmerle. Heidelberg: Carl Winter and Universitätsverlag, 1959, pp. 27-50. J. Duke- J. Forstman, trans. "[The Aphorisms of 1805 and 1809-10]." In *Hermeneutics: The Handwritten Manuscripts*, Atlanta: Scholars Press, 1986, pp. 41-64.

—— 2a. "[Der erste Entwurf aus der Zeit zwischen 1810 und 1819]." in *Hermeneutik*, 1959, pp. 51-76. J. Duke-J. Forstman, trans., "The First Draft of 1809-1810." In *Hermeneutics*, 1986, pp. 67-90.

—— 2b. "[A Loose Page, From 1810-1811]." In *Hermeneutics*, 1986, pp. 91-94.

—— 3. *"[Die kompendienartige Darstellung von 1819 (mit Randbemerkungen von 1828)]."* In *Hermeneutik*, 1959, pp. 77-109. J. Duke-J. Forstman, trans., "[The Compendium of 1819 and the Marginal Notes of 1828]." In *Hermeneutics*, 1986, pp. 95-152.

—— 4. "[Die gesonderte Darstellung des Zweiten Teils aus der Zeit zwischen 1820 und 1829]." In *Hermeneutik*, 1959, pp. 111-120. J. Duke-J. Forstman, trans., "[The Separate Exposition of the Second Part, from 1826-1827]," In *Hermeneutics*, 1986, pp. 161-174.

—— 5. "[Die Akademiereden von 1829]." In *Hermeneutik*, 1959, pp. 121-156. J. Duke-J. Forstman, trans., "[The Two Academy Addresses of 1829]." In *Hermeneutics*, 1986, pp. 175-214.

Shapiro, G., and Sica, A., eds. 1984. *Hermeneutics. Questions and Prospects*, Amherst: University of Massachusetts Press.

Szondi, P. 1970. "L'herméneutique de Schleiermacher," trans. H. Mendelsohn, "Schleiermacher's Hermeneutics Today." In *On Textual Understanding and Other Essays*, Minneapolis: University of Minnesota Press, 1986, p. 95-113.

—— 1975. "Einfürhrung in die literarische Hermeneutik", trans. T. Bahti, "Introduction to Literary Hermeneutics." In *New Literary History*, 10, no. 1, pp. 17-29.

Wheeler, K. M., ed. 1984. *German Aesthetic and Literary Criticism: The Romantic Ironists and Goethe*. Cambridge: Cambridge University Press.

White, H. 1980. "The Value of Narrativity in the Representation of Reality." *Critical Inquiry*, 7, no. 1: pp. 5-27.

Wilde, O. 1889. "The Decay of Lying." In *The Artist as Critic, Critical Essays of*

Oscar Wilde, ed. R. Ellmann. New York: Random House, 1969, pp. 290-320.

Wimsatt, W. K. and Beardsley, M. C. 1946. "The Intentional Fallacy," In *The Verbal Icon, Studies in the Meaning of Poetry*, Lexington: University of Kentucky Press, 1954, pp. 2-18.

Wittgenstein, L. 1953. *Philosophische Untersuchungen*, ed. G. E. M. Anscombe, R. Rhees, and G. H. von Wright. G. E. M. Anscombe, trans., *Philosophical Investigations*, Oxford: Basil Blackwell, 1967.

— 1958. *Preliminary Studies for the 'Philosophical Investigations' Generally Known as The Blue and Brown Books*, ed. R. Rhees. Oxford: Basil Blackwell.

— 1966. *Lectures and Conversations on Aesthetics, Psychology, and Religious Belief*, ed. C. Barrett. Berkeley: University of California Press.

— 1969. *Über Gewissheit*, ed. G. E. M. Anscombe and G. H. von Wright. D. Paul and G. E. M. Anscombe, trans., *On Certainty*, New York: Harper and Row, 1972.

Index